JOURNAL FOR THE STUDY OF THE NEW TESTAMENT
SUPPLEMENT SERIES
150

Executive Editor
Stanley E. Porter

Editorial Board
David Catchpole, R. Alan Culpepper, Margaret Davies,
James D.G. Dunn, Craig A. Evans, Stephen Fowl, Robert Fowler,
Robert Jewett, Elizabeth Struthers Malbon, Robert W. Wall

Sheffield Academic Press

Virtue amidst Vice

The Catalog of Virtues
in 2 Peter 1

J. Daryl Charles

Journal for the Study of the New Testament
Supplement Series 150

Copyright © 1997 Sheffield Academic Press

Published by Sheffield Academic Press Ltd
Mansion House
19 Kingfield Road
Sheffield S11 9AS
England

Printed on acid-free paper in Great Britain
by Bookcraft Ltd
Midsomer Norton, Bath

British Library Cataloguing in Publication Data

A catalogue record for this book is available
from the British Library

ISBN 1-85075-686-4

Contents

Preface   7
Abbreviations   9

Chapter 1
2 PETER COMMENTARY: AN APPRAISAL   11
    'Early Catholicism': A Reassessment   11
    Paraenesis and 2 Peter   37

Chapter 2
LITERARY STRATEGY IN 2 PETER   44
    2 Peter and Social Location   44
    2 Peter and Testamental Genre   49
    2 Peter and Jude: A Contrast in Social Location   76

Chapter 3
ETHICS AND VIRTUE IN 2 PETER   84
    The Virtuous Life: Tracing a Petrine Theme   84
    The Virtuous Life: Setting the Context   95

Chapter 4
THE MORAL WORLD OF GRECO-ROMAN PAGANISM   99
    Virtue and the Stoic Worldview   99
    The Interaction of Stoic and Christian Worldviews   105

Chapter 5
THE ETHICAL CATALOG AS A PEDAGOGICAL DEVICE   112
    The Language and Logic of Virtue   112
    Ethical Catalogs in Jewish Literature
    and the New Testament   119

Chapter 6
THE CATALOG OF VIRTUES IN 2 PETER 1.5-7   128
        The Basis for Virtue (1.1-4)   129
        The Catalog of Virtues (1.5-7)   138
        The Necessity of Virtue (1.8-11)   148

Chapter 7
CONCLUSION: THE FUNCTION OF THE CATALOG
OF VIRTUES IN 2 PETER 1.5-7   153

Appendix
PREDESTINATION, PERSEVERANCE
AND THE PROBLEM OF APOSTASY   159

Bibliography   175
Index of References   184
Index of Authors   192

This monograph represents the confluence of several exegetical and theological concerns. Issuing out of prior work in Jude is an intrigue with subtleties of nuance and differences of perspective that distinguish literary strategy in 2 Peter from Jude. Critical scholarship's attention to the obvious literary relationship between the two epistles raises important questions about how they diverge. Wherein lie the peculiarities? To what might these differences be attributable?

A further motivation for this study is a relative dissatisfaction with standard interpretive approaches to 2 Peter. Traditional commentary on 2 Peter tends to be highly derivative in character, given the predominance of 'early Catholic' assumptions that have governed the letter's exegesis over the last century. What undergirds these exegetical assumptions? How might they determine the trajectory of 2 Peter interpretation? What bearing might these assumptions have on the epistle as a literary unit? To what extent might they impinge upon or inhibit the discovery of a literary rhetorical strategy at work in the letter?

Finally, 2 Peter lacks a significant place in discussions of New Testament ethics. This state of affairs—while owing in part to the aforementioned exegetical history of the epistle—is striking, inasmuch as 2 Peter is couched in the language of paraenesis. Curiously, the letter is all but absent in standard textbooks treating ethics in the New Testament. Why is this the case? What are the consequences of such oversight, and what might be gained as a result of recovering the ethical burden of 2 Peter?

Standard approaches to 2 Peter, with good reason, entail treating the epistle together with Jude. Methodologically, this is inevitable, given the amount of material they hold in common.

The association between 2 Peter and Jude that draws on the result of literary criticism has yet another side. Significantly, it is this side that tends to receive short shrift and thus provides the basis for the present study. The consensual view of New Testament scholarship is that doctrine—specifically, false doctrine—constitutes the burden of 2 Peter, presupposing a gnostic or protognostic rationale. As Jonathan Knight observes, 2 Peter is 'addressed to a situation... dominated by what the author held to be inappropriate teaching', containing 'evidence for an eschatological disillusionment on the part of those whom he criticized...'.[1]

The explanation for this purported 'eschatological disillusionment' invariably is doctrinal, predicated on an 'early Catholic' reading of 2 Peter. *Inter alia* an unintended consequence of the 'early Catholic' thesis (see Chapter 1) has been insufficient attention given to the paraenetic character of the letter. It is to the task of reexamining this paraenetic component that the chapters that follow are devoted.

In light of the conspicuous literary relationship between Jude and 2 Peter, literary markers that differentiate the two works reveal an important contrast in the social milieu of the two audiences. Compared to a Jewish matrix to which Jude's readers would appear linked, corresponding markers in 2 Peter reflect strongly Gentile (pagan) cultural influences (see Chapter 2). 2 Peter offers a window into the moral world and philosophical discourse of Greco-Roman paganism—a world in which moral relativism and moral scepticism, consummating in a denial of moral accountability, are on display. In 2 Peter 1, the writer reminds his audience of the imperative to cultivate virtue in a way that will 'supply confirming evidence' of their calling and election (1.10). Similarly, in concluding the epistle the writer poses the inescapable rhetorical question: What sort of lives, morally speaking, should be lived, given the exigencies of the present situation (3.11)?

A key element in 2 Peter's hortatory strategy is the application of Christian paraenesis by borrowing contemporary Hellenistic moral ideals and categories. At the heart of this attempt at moral persuasion is the writer's adaptation of a catalog of virtues (1.5-7), which is intended to counter moral lapse in the community. That believers have been recipients of divinely-imputed righteousness (1.1) and a full knowledge of God (1.2)—indeed, of 'everything needed for life and godliness' (1.3)—constitutes no guarantee of a moral life. The challenge set before the community is to validate its profession with virtuous living—this amidst a cultural climate that can only encourage vice.

1. Jonathan Knight, *2 Peter and Jude* (NTG; Sheffield: Sheffield Academic Press, 1995), p. 10.

ABBREVIATIONS

AB	Anchor Bible
APOT	R.H. Charles (ed.), *Apocrypha and Pseudepigrapha of the Old Testament in English* (2 vols.; Oxford: Clarendon Press, 1913)
ASNU	Acta seminarii neotestamentici upsaliensis
BAGD	Walter Bauer, William F. Arndt, F. William Gingrich and Frederick W. Danker, *A Greek–English Lexicon of the New Testament and Other Early Christian Literature* (Chicago: University of Chicago Press, 2nd edn, 1958)
BBR	*Bulletin of Biblical Research*
BCBC	Believers Church Bible Commentary
BibS	Biblische Studien
BuL	*Bibel und Leben*
BNTC	Black's New Testament Commentaries
BZNW	Beihefte zur *ZNW*
CBQ	*Catholic Biblical Quarterly*
CIG	*Corpus inscriptionum graecarum*
ConBNT	Coniectanea biblica, New Testament
EBib	Etudes bibliques
EvQ	*Evangelical Quarterly*
Expos	*Expositor*
ExpTim	*Expository Times*
GRBS	*Greek, Roman, and Byzantine Studies*
HAW	Handbuch zur Altertumswissenschaft
HNT	Handbuch zum Neuen Testament
HTKNT	Herders theologischer Kommentar zum Neuen Testament
HUCA	*Hebrew Union College Annual*
IBC	Interpreters Bible Commentary
ICC	International Critical Commentary
JAC	*Jahrbuch für Antike und Christentum*
JBL	*Journal of Biblical Literature*
JETS	*Journal of the Evangelical Theological Society*
JSJ	*Journal for the Study of Judaism in the Persian, Hellenistic and Roman Period*
JSNT	*Journal for the Study of the New Testament*
JSNTSup	*Journal for the Study of the New Testament*, Supplement Series
JTS	*Journal of Theological Studies*
NIBC	New International Bible Commentary
NovT	*Novum Testamentum*

NovTSup	*Novum Testamentum*, Supplements
NTAbh	Neutestamentliche Abhandlungen
NTD	Das Neue Testament Deutsch
NTG	New Testament Guides
NTS	*New Testament Studies*
RAC	*Reallexikon für Antike und Christentum*
RB	*Revue biblique*
RestQ	*Restoration Quarterly*
SB	Sources bibliques
SBB	Stuttgarter biblische Beiträge
SBLDS	SBL Dissertation Series
SBLSCS	SBL Septuagint and Cognate Studies
SBS	Stuttgarter Bibelstudien
Scr	*Scripture*
SHC	Studies in Hellenistic Culture
SPB	Studia postbiblica
SVF	*Stoicorum Veterum Fragmenta*
SVTQ	*St Vladimirs Theological Quarterly*
TDNT	Theological Dictionary of the New Testament
THKNT	Theologischer Handkommentar zum Neuen Testament
ThQ	*Theologische Quartalschrift*
TJ	Trinity Journal
TLZ	*Theologische Literaturzeitung*
TNTC	Tyndale New Testament Commentaries
TQ	*Theologische Quartalschrift*
TS	*Theological Studies*
TTZ	*Trierer theologische Zeitschrift*
TU	Texte und Untersuchungen
TZ	*Theologische Zeitschrift*
VC	*Vigiliae christianae*
WBC	Word Biblical Commentary
WUNT	Wissenschaftliche Untersuchungen zum Neuen Testament
ZKT	*Zeitschrift für katholische Theologie*
ZNW	*Zeitschrift für die neutestamentliche Wissenschaft*
ZTK	*Zeitschrift für Theologie und Kirche*

Chapter 1

2 PETER COMMENTARY: AN APPRAISAL

'Early Catholicism': A Reassessment

We must observe first the historical fact that no Christian church or group has in the event treated the New Testament writings as uniformly canonical. . . Perhaps most arresting of all, we must remind ourselves that. . . *orthodoxy itself is based on a canon within a canon.* . . Certainly, if the New Testament serves *any* continuing usefulness for Christians today, *nothing less than that canon within the canon will do.* . . Nor. . . would I want to say, that the New Testament writings are canonical because they were more inspired than other later Christian writings. Almost every Christian who wrote in an authoritative way during the first two centuries of Christianity claimed the same sort of inspiration for their writing as Paul had for his. And I would want to insist that in not a few compositions Martin Luther and John Wesley, for example, were as, if not more inspired, than the author of II Peter. Nor certainly would I attempt to define New Testament canonicity in terms of some kind of orthodoxy, for our findings are clearly that no real concept of orthodoxy as yet existed in the first century and that in terms of later orthodoxy the New Testament writings themselves can hardly be called wholly 'orthodox'.[1]

The principle criterion of New Testament canonicity imposed in the early church was not prophetic inspiration but apostolic authorship—or, if not authorship, then authority. In an environment where apostolic tradition counted for so much, the source and norm of that tradition were naturally found in the writings of apostles or of men closely associated with apostles. . . Authority precedes canonicity: that is to say, the various writings do not derive their authority from their inclusion in the canon: they were included in the canon because their authenticity was recognized. . . With our longer perspective we can say that the early church, in recognizing the books which make up the New Testament canon as uniquely worthy to stand alongside the sacred scriptures of the old covenant, was guided by

---

1. J.D.G. Dunn, *Unity and Diversity in the New Testament: An Inquiry into the Character of Earliest Christianity* (Philadelphia: Westminster Press, 1977), pp. 374-86 (emphasis his).

a wisdom higher than its own. . . The question has been raised whether it
is legitimate for us to defend the early church's decision about admission
and exclusion with arguments quite different from those which were used at
the time. . . But we have no option if we accept the canon: we must defend
our acceptance of it with arguments which *we* hold to be valid. . . [W]e
have received the twenty-seven books of the New Testament, and while
individual readers or teachers may make distinctions between those among
them which are 'capital' and those which are of lower grade, our church
tradition has made no such distinction. . . [W]e know how depreciatory
is the judgement passed today by many scholars in this tradition on those
parts of the New Testament which smack of 'primitive catholicism' . . . No
doubt. . . diverse strands of traditions—indeed diverse traditions—may
be detected, but although critical scholars may emphasize their diversity,
the church, both ancient and modern, has been more conscious of their
overall unity.[2]

Contrasted above are two views of the New Testament, two approaches to canonicity, two views of Christian 'orthodoxy'. By the first
it is understood that there is little or no difference in the writings of
the first two Christian centuries in terms of their inspiration, claims to
apostolic authority and right to canonicity. Any authority the New Testament writings might have is primarily material authority from within
(such as a 'canon within a canon'). According to the second, the writings of the New Testament are authoritative not because they were
ultimately included in the canon; rather, they were recognized as part
of the canon precisely because of their authority and apostolic imprint.[3]

2.   F.F. Bruce, 'Tradition and the Canon of Scripture', in D.K. McKim (ed.),
The Authoritative Word: Essays on the Nature of Scripture (Grand Rapids: Eerdmans,
1983), pp. 74-83 (emphasis his).

3.   The sharp distinction between the theology and history of the New Testament
writings normally adduced by critical scholarship needs some qualification. That the
biblical books were written with a foremost theological purpose is not in question,
nor is the ultimate question confronting us the particular process by which the Scriptures came into being. Rather, the larger issue is the nature of a God-directed history
in which and through which revelation comes to Israel and the church, thus forming
the theological contours of its canon. To posit the distinction, as P. Achtemeier does
('How the Scriptures Were Formed', in D.K. McKim [ed.], *The Authoritative
Word: Essays on the Nature of Scripture* [Grand Rapids: Eerdmans, 1983], pp. 12-
13), of continuity and discontinuity between the Old Testament and New Testament
is, to be sure, a fundamental hermeneutical consideration. Less satisfying (and objective), however, is Achtemeier's observation that critical scholarship, which 'arose in
an effort to free interpretation of the Bible from prior understandings of what it could
or could not say', has been more aware of its biases and preunderstandings in its

That is, the formal authority of the New Testament rests upon something outside of its individual writers—an assumption that does not confuse the origin of the New Testament canon with the canon's reception by the church.

Two approaches to the New Testament text. Two different starting points. Whichever starting-point one chooses will determine one's theological trajectory and exegetical conclusions. Before charting a trajectory, however, let us consider the matter of starting-point.

Assumptions. No one is without them, no one is neutral. Basic assumptions about reality—about the 'permanent things', as Chesterton was fond of calling them—come to light as a reflection of one's worldview. In biblical theology, these operating assumptions manifest themselves in an endless variety of ways. They may express themselves in the form of an historical positivism that scrutinizes faith and truth-claims under the rubric of a 'history of religions'. They may appear in the form of a modernizing enterprise that seeks to strip religious content of its 'mythical' shell and make the Scriptures relevant for the contemporary mind. Or they may be couched in the distinction between 'unity and diversity', so as to leave us with the question: Is it legitimate to speak of a single orthodoxy within primitive Christianity? Or, more fundamentally, is it at all proper to use the concept 'orthodoxy'?[4]

In no book of the New Testament is this dilemma regarding assumptions more pronounced, with the exegetical results more divergent, than 2 Peter. And yet, based on a survey of literature for 2 Peter, one would scarcely know that there are competing interpretive paradigms. For roughly the last 150 years, the governing presupposition of New Testament scholarship has been that in 2 Peter (and Jude) a second-century church at war with the forces of gnosticism is on display. This view, while admittedly not conclusive, nevertheless is seen to be highly corroborative and nearly unanimous in its consensus. Curiously,

> the idea dies hard that no heresy showing the slightest parallels with Gnosticism could possibly have appeared before the end of the first century. The facts are that all the data that can be collected from 2 Peter (and Jude) are

scholarly handling of the biblical text than religious conservatives have. Achtemeier writes: 'In this area, it is the conservative, not the critical scholar, who is open to the charge of imposing a prior category onto the understanding of Scripture' ('Scriptures', p. 13 n. 11).

4.   By implication, 'orthodox' views require the existence of 'heterodox' views, and thus, the need for theological parameters.

insufficient to identify the movement with any known second-century system. Rather do they suggest a general mental and moral atmosphere which
would have been conducive for the development of systematic Gnosticism.[5]

A perusal of most standard introductions to the New Testament quickly
identifies prevailing assumptions regarding the New Testament documents. Willi Marxsen, in his *Introduction to the New Testament*, reso-
lutely states what is a *sine qua non* for critical scholarship:

> If it is possible to allot the separate writings [of the New Testament] their
> place in the various lines of tradition and to understand them in their his-
> torical context, then a problem which has often been hotly disputed becomes
> considerably less important—that of pseudonymity. So long as we assume
> the traditional idea of canonicity and accept as permanently normative only
> what derives from the apostles or the disciples of the apostles, as did the
> early Church, 'not genuine' is a serious charge to make. . . But if we admit
> its pseudonymity we are far more likely to place the letter in its particular
> historical context and to be able to understand it. We can therefore state quite
> simply that it was when the Pauline authorship was seen to be untenable
> and no longer formed any obstacle to exegesis that we were able for the
> first time to 'grasp' the full meaning of the letter. . . Whether we draw the
> line at the beginning of the second century or earlier is simply a matter of
> choice. If we make the cut at the beginning of the second century, we are
> faced with a relatively compact body of literature. We could perhaps ex-
> change 2 Peter for the Didache and Jude for 1 Clement, but this is of no
> significance as far as basic principles are concerned, and we should there-
> fore not make it a problem.[6]

Consider what for Marxsen—who speaks for the wider mainstream of
critical scholarship—is merely assumed. The 'historical' placing of certain New Testament documents renders the question of authorship and
pseudonymity 'considerably less important'. For example, by finally
viewing Pauline authorship in certain cases as 'untenable', it 'no longer
forms any obstacle to exegesis', thereby allowing us 'for the first time
to "grasp" the full meaning of the letter'. And whether we make the
canonical cut-off point for New Testament documents the late first or
early second century, drawing the line is merely a matter of taste, since
the exchange of '2 Peter for the Didache and Jude for 1 Clement' is 'of

5. D. Guthrie, *New Testament Introduction* (Leicester/Downers Grove: Inter-
Varsity Press, 4th edn, 1990), p. 828.
6. *Introduction to the New Testament: An Approach to its Problem* (trans.
G. Buswell; Philadelphia: Fortress Press, 1970), pp. 12-13.

no significance'. To distinguish between Jude and 1 Clement or 2 Peter and the Didache is to create in the end an unnecessary 'problem'.

In 1958 Marxsen published his influential *Der 'Frühkatholizismus' im Neuen Testament* roughly concurrent with the period in which Ernst Käsemann was making inroads in biblical scholarship both in Europe and in the U.S. with the 'early Catholic' thesis.[7] In laying out the *Sitz im Leben* of 2 Peter, Marxsen writes:

> This document gives us a glimpse of the situation of the Church at a relatively late period. The eschatology which looks to an imminent End has fallen into the background, and one has to adjust oneself to living in the world (cf. esp. the Pastorals). The Church is in process [sic] of becoming an institution. The Spirit is linked with tradition and with the ministry—and is passed on by the laying on of hands. The point has now been reached where one has to make clear where one differs from those among whom the Spirit is still 'freely' active. In the post-Pauline period—long after Paul, in fact, for he has already become a 'literary entity' belonging to the past—the futurist eschatology of the Church is attacked by the Gnostics. 'Where is the promise of his coming? For from the day that the fathers fell asleep, all things continue as they were from the beginning of the creation' (iii.4). Though far removed from the beginnings of the Church, the author is seeking to remain in continuity with these beginnings and sets out an 'apologia for the primitive Christian eschatology' in its apocalyptic form.[8]

That it is impossible to explore 2 Peter without passing the tollbooth of 'early Catholicism' is evidenced both by (a) the relative neglect of 2 Peter by New Testament scholarship and (b) the highly derivative nature of commentary on 2 Peter over the years. Relatively few, or so it would seem, have questioned the need to pay the toll in the first place. While an 'early Catholic' reading of the New Testament is by no means confined to 2 Peter—or the 'catholic epistles' for that matter—it is here that it is applied in its most concentrated form.[9] Almost universally assumed to be the latest of the New Testament writings,[10] 2 Peter is also widely held to be the most dubious, and hence, problematic.

7. See n. 23 on the evolution of Käsemann's project.

8. W. Marxsen, *Der 'Frühkatholizismus' im Neuen Testament* (BibS, 21; Neukirchen: Neukirchener Verlag, 1958), p. 244.

9. The remark by K.H. Neufeld ('Frühkatholizismus—Idee und Begriff', *ZKT* 94 [1972], p. 1) that 'early Catholicism' has played 'eine beachtliche Rolle' ('a notable role') in New Testament studies, stated mildly, qualifies as a theological understatement.

10. Critical scholarship, in the main, tends to favor a dating of the epistle that ranges

In relative terms, 'early Catholicism' is a recent phenomenon in the technical language of theological and biblical studies, even when its undergirding presuppositions are manifest in biblical scholarship from the time of F.C. Baur onward. Nineteenth- and early twentieth-century German scholars have employed a variety of terms to communicate the 'early Catholic' idea, speaking of a 'werdende katholische Kirche', 'katholischer Christentum', 'ältester Katholizismus', 'Entwicklung zum Katholizismus', 'Anfänge der katholischen Kirche', 'Grundzüge des alten Katholizismus', or 'katholisch werdender Heidenchristentum'.

Use of the term 'Catholic' in connection with a New Testament document is to suggest that for biblical scholars the writing is to be viewed as a post-apostolic development in the life of the church—a period removed by several generations from the apostles and eyewitnesses of the Lord. In his massive *Die Mitte der Schrift*, Siegfried Schulz states:

> The early Catholicism of the New Testament cuts off the foregoing temporary period of early Christianity, with its characteristic apocalyptic approach to the Parousia and accompanying lifestyle. Strictly speaking, early Catholicism no more belongs to the early church, which conceived of itself in apocalyptic terms.[11]

Indeed, for Ernst Käsemann, perhaps the most influential proponent of 'early Catholicism', it becomes 'apparent that nascent catholicism was the historically necessary outcome of an original Christianity whose apocalyptic expectation had not been fulfilled'.[12]

Representative of most commentators on the catholic epistles, Hans Windisch denominates 2 Peter and Jude as 'catholic' insofar as the opponents being denounced are threatening the *whole* of the church—a decidedly second-century development.[13] K.H. Schelkle's verdict is

from the late first or early second century (e.g. R.J. Bauckham, *Jude, 2 Peter* [WBC, 50; Waco, TX: Word Books, 1983], pp. 157-62), that is roughly one generation removed from the apostles, to the late second century (e.g. A. Vögtle, 'Die Schriftwerdung der apostolischen Paradosis nach 2. Petr 1,12-15', in *Neuen Testament und Geschichte: O. Cullmann zum 70. Geburtstag* [Zürich: Theologischer Verlag; Tübingen: Mohr-Siebeck, 1972], pp. 297-305), during which time the New Testament canon was taking shape.

11. S. Schulz, *Die Mitte der Zeit: Frühkatholizismus im Neuen Testament als Herausforderung an den Protestantismus* (Stuttgart: Kreuz, 1976), p. 77.

12. E. Käsemann, 'Paul and Early Catholicism', in *New Testament Questions of Today* (Philadelphia: Fortress Press, 1969), p. 242.

13. H. Windisch, *Die katholischen Briefe* (Tübingen: Mohr, 2nd edn, 1930), p. 38.

unequivocal: 'The letters (2 Peter and Jude) say themselves that the generations of the church are past. . . The Apostolic era is closed and lies behind.'[14] Ferdinand Hahn summarizes the underlying assumption of most commentators in approaching the catholic epistles:

> Even though the implications might not yet be clearly seen, there is a practical awareness that the apostolic era is surely closed and that the immediate postapostolic period is soon ending. Hence, now the present tradition-material must be preserved in its basic meaning and form.[15]

'Early Catholicism', then, is purported to reflect the institutionalization of the post-apostolic church, wherein the reader encounters the codification of beliefs into creedal confessions (that is, *fides qua creditur*) and the notion of a canon for the purposes of defending the faith against Gnostic heresy. Evidences of the need for a teaching office—which replaces the charismatic work of the Spirit—and the church's growing institutionalization—evidenced by a growing dichotomy of priests and laity (due to the administration of the sacraments and discipline)—characterize this generally pervasive post-apostolic mentality. The term 'early Catholicism' is to be understood as representing the period of transition from earliest Christianity to the so-called ancient Church, which is completed with the disappearance of the imminent expectation of the Parousia and the emergence of a legalistic endurance ethic and 'natural' theology.[16]

---

14. K.H. Schelkle, 'Spätapostolische Briefe als frühkatholisches Zeugnis', in J. Blinzer *et al.* (eds.), *Neutestamentliche Aufsätze für J. Schmid* (Regensburg: Pustet, 1963), p. 225 (my translation).

15. 'Randbemerkungen zum Judasbrief', *TZ* 37 (1981), pp. 209-10 (my translation).

16. See, for example Marxsen, *Der 'Frühkatholizismus'*; F. Mussner, 'Frühkatholizismus', *TTZ* 68 (1959), pp. 237-45; *idem*, 'Spätapostolische Briefe', pp. 225-32; *idem*, 'Die Ablösung des Apostolischen durch das nachapostolische Zeitalter und ihre Konsequenzen', in H. Feld and J. Nolte (eds.), *Wort Gottes in der Zeit* (Festschrift K.H. Schelkle; Düsseldorf: Patmos, 1972), pp. 166-77; H. Küng, 'Frühkatholizismus im Neün Testament als kontroverstheologisches Problem', *ThQ* 142 (1962), pp. 385-424; K.H. Schelkle, 'Spätapostolische Briefe', pp. 225-32; idem, *Die Petrusbriefe. Der Judasbrief* (HTKNT, 13.2; Freiburg: Herder, 1961), pp. 241-45; E. Käsemann, 'An Apologia for Primitive Christian Eschatology', in *Essays on New Testament Themes* (trans. W.J. Montague; London: SCM Press, 1964), pp. 135-57; *idem*, 'Paul and Early Catholicism', in *New Testament Questions of Today* (Philadelphia: Fortress Press, 1969), pp. 236-51; J.H. Elliott, 'A Catholic Gospel: Reflections on "Early Catholicism" in the New Testament', *CBQ* 31 (1969),

Although similar assumptions about the date and composition of 2 Peter were held by nineteenth-century scholars, twentieth-century biblical scholarship has been particularly occupied with the notion of the *Parousieverzögerung*, the delay of the Parousia. Viewed from within the confines of modern critical theological investigation, the Parousia hope has encountered considerable opposition. This opposition, rooted in our cultural *Zeitgeist*, has expressed itself theologically in several ways. For some scholars, it has taken the form of the belief that Jesus' eschatological expectation over time proved to be false, that he was mistaken.[17] Others have argued that the church wholly misunderstood Jesus' hope.[18] On yet another level, the eschatology of the New Testament has been thought to require 'demythologization' and reinterpretation.[19]

One notable difficulty for biblical scholars and theologians has been the New Testament's seeming insistence on the nearness of the end.[20] Critical scholarship has maintained that 2 Peter reflects a severe crisis that is provoked by an *unexpected* Parousia delay. It is argued that a 'fixation' on an imminent Parousia expectation forces the early church over time to rearrange its priorities.[21] Justification for this purported post-apostolic development is said to be a de-eschatologizing, de-ethicizing and de-centralizing of primitive Christianity as it interacted increasingly with Gentile culture.[22] For Ernst Käsemann, whose forcefully articulated 'early Catholic' arguments have inspired nearly four

pp. 213-23; A. Vögtle, 'Kirche und Schriftprinzip nach dem Neuen Testament', *BuL* 12 (1971), pp. 153-62, 260-81; U. Luz, 'Erwägungen zur Entstehung des "Frühkatholizismus"', *ZNW* 65 (1974), pp. 88-111; and Schulz, *Die Mitte der Zeit*.

17. For example A. Schweizer, *The Mystery of the Kingdom of God* (London: Macmillan, 1925).

18. For example B.H. Streeter, 'Synoptic Criticism and the Eschatological Problem', in W. Sanday (ed.), *Studies in the Synoptic Problem* (London: Macmillan, 1909), pp. 229-46.

19. For example R. Bultmann, 'New Testment and Mythology', in H.W. Bartsch (ed.), *Kerygma and Myth* (2 vols.; London: Methuen, 1954), pp. 1-12.

20. It is with the hope of putting this theological problem in proper perspective that A.L. Moore, in his important investigation of New Testament eschatology, *The Parousia in the New Testament* (Leiden: Brill, 1966), proceeds. Moore seeks to determine whether the Parousia hope was undelimited or altogether differently oriented.

21. Thus F. Mussner, 'Ablösung', p. 169 n. 12.

22. M. Werner, *The Formation of Christian Dogma* (London: A. & C. Black, 1957), p. 25, and Käsemann, 'An Apologia', pp. 169-95.

decades of New Testament scholarship,[23] the Parousia delay constitutes a major 'stumbling-block' in 2 Peter. Addressing the Berliner
Gemeinschaft für Evangelishe Theologie in 1952, Käsemann concluded
that 'the Second Epistle of Peter is from beginning to end a document
expressing an early Catholic viewpoint and is perhaps the most dubious writing in the canon'.[24] For Käsemann, the letter not infrequently
displays irreconcilable theological contradictions.[25]

An even less enthusiastic assessment of 2 Peter comes from Gunter
Klein, in an essay titled 'Der zweite Petrusbrief und der neutestamentliche Kanon':

> The author does a miserable job of presenting his case. . . He wants to
> restore the fragile doctrine of last things to a new credibility, but he is only
> able to destroy it yet further. In spite of how vigorously he asserts him-
> self, he is basically helpless. . . This defender of Christian hope has had
> his feet pulled out from under him. . . The dubious manner with which
> he treats his subject is a clear reflection of the writer's own lack of self-
> assurance.[26]

Klein concludes:

> It is precisely such a New Testament writer with this sort of mentality—
> the only person [in the New Testament] defending the newly emergent
> canonical awareness—who fits our idea of a unified canon the least. . .

23. Kasemann's investigation of the 'early Catholic' phenomenon, by his account,
began in the early 1940s as he encountered the 'problem of contradictory conceptions
of Spirit, Church, office and tradition. . . within the New Testament' that were 'at
first extremely disturbing' to him ('Paul and Early Catholicism', p. 236 n.1). This
problem, Käsemann observes, was 'immediately radicalized and complicated because
it was very soon apparent that it could not be confined to the two strands of Paulin-
ism and the theology of Luke together with the Pastorals' (p. 236).
24. An English translation of this address (see 'Eine Apologia für die urchristliche
Eschatologie', *ZTK* 49 [1952], pp. 272-96) appeared in 1964: 'An Apologia for Primitive Christian Eschatology', in *Essays on New Testament Themes* (London: SCM
Press, 1964), pp. 135-57.
25. 'Apologia', pp. 156-57. Critical of Käsemann's position—and Käsemann's
overwhelmingly subjective presuppositions that were brought to his 'early Catholic'
reading—is J.W. Drane, who examines several presuppositional flaws in 'Eschatology, Ecclesiology and Catholicity in the New Testament', *ExpTim* 83 (1971–72),
pp. 180-84.
26. G. Klein, 'Der zweite Petrusbrief und der neutestamentliche Kanon', in
Ärgernisse: Konfrontationen mit dem Neuen Testament (Munich: Chr. Kaiser
Verlag, 1970), pp. 111-12 (my translation).

This writer could not have possibly dreamt that his own letter would join—and in fact follow—in the same canonical collection the letters of Paul, whose writings he held to be suspect. . . For this reason, the clearly inescapable question puts our assurance of faith to the test, namely, whether we can ultimately consider the epistle of 2 Peter, with its conceptualization of canon, to be canonical.[27]

The highly uncomplementary view of 2 Peter, however, is not an isolated phenomenon. Wolfgang Schrage, author of a highly acclaimed primer on New Testament ethics, draws a similar conclusion regarding 2 Peter in his commentary on the catholic epistles:

Even when the epistle is lacking in theological depth and spiritual energy . . . it is not simply worthless. Above all, it mediates historical insights into the church's crisis resulting from second-century heresy.[28]

Given this rather negative assessment of 2 Peter, one is left with the general impression that among biblical scholars the supposed presence of 'early Catholicism' in the New Testament has been the theological equivalent of eating spinach or kissing one's sister. While by no means the *real thing*, 'early Catholic' writings—for better or worse—are part of canonical realities nonetheless, and therefore, must be tolerated. So R.H. Fuller:

Not all aspects of early Catholicism are salutary, e.g., its conventional bourgeois morality, its propositional understanding of faith, its relegation of the eschatological hope to the last chapter of dogmatics, the total suppression of the charismata. But these writings are balanced by the presence of earlier apostolic writings in the New Testament, viz., the gospel tradition, the kerygmatic traditions in Acts and the genuine Pauline letters. Without the institutional forms of early Catholicism, these apostolic elements would have evaporated in the speculative mythology, the dualistic asceticism and libertinism, and the false spiritual enthusiasm of gnosticism.[29]

One may question whether both Protestant and Catholic scholars have embraced with equal fervor the 'early Catholic' approach to the writings of the New Testament. Despite the perception that Protestant

27. Klein, 'Der zweite Petrusbrief', p. 112.
28. H. Balz and W. Schrage, *Die katholischen Briefe: Die Briefe des Jakobus, Petrus, Johannes und Judas* (NTD, 10; Göttingen: Vandenhoeck & Ruprecht, 1973), p. 123.
29. R.H. Fuller, *A Critical Introduction to the New Testament* (London: Gerald Duckworth, 1966), p. 167.

exegetes have been far less sparing in their view of 2 Peter than their Catholic counterparts, this distinction, if it ever did exist, is inconsequential. Historical-critical scholarship has broadly appropriated the assumptions of 'early Catholicism' regarding the general epistles—and regarding 2 Peter—almost universally.[30]

Given this 'half embrace' by biblical scholarship, it goes without saying that writings such as 2 Peter and Jude have labored under a heavy load. Not only do they constitute a generally neglected part of the New Testament canon, but by virtue of their reputed sub-apostolic origin they have consistently been thought to lack the authority and theological value that, for example, Pauline literature might possess. Like spinach, they may be a necessary part of the canonical diet, but they certainly don't taste the way they should.

Hence, we are confronted with several obstacles in attempting to probe 2 Peter. On the one level stands its relative neglect—among theologians, biblical scholars and laity. This neglect may have more or less to do with the widespread perception that the epistle does not belong to the 'canon within the canon', that is, the inner circle of purely Pauline or authentically apostolic writings of the New Testament. On another level, the epistle finds itself in the hammerlock of 'early Catholic' preconception. For scholars like Siegfried Schulz, not only is the debate over 2 Peter's place in the canon 'inappropriate' (*'unsachgemäss'*) apart from subordination to the 'early Catholic' scheme, it is in fact 'boring' (*'langweilig'*), and therefore, pointless.[31] Because the epistle is believed to mirror later ecclesiastical developments, the task of exegesis has been subsumed under what seemingly has become an air-tight 'early Catholic' rubric. There is thus room for only one conclusion: 2 Peter

---

30. T. Fornberg's assertion that the Catholic view of the relationship between Scripture and tradition would cause Catholic exegetes not to read 2 Peter 'with similarly hostile eyes' as Protestants needs some modification (*An Early Church in a Pluralistic Society: A Study of 2 Peter* [ConBNT, 9; Lund: Gleerup, 1977], pp. 5-6). The historic differences that were erected through the Reformation divide have been felt most keenly in systematic theology. In the realm of historical-critical exegesis, however, this chasm in relative terms has been negligible. Over the last five decades, Protestant and Catholic scholars have embraced 'early Catholic' assumptions about 2 Peter to an equal degree. In point of fact, one is hard pressed to name one Catholic exegete who considers the epistle to be authentic.

31. Schulz, *Die Mitte der Schrift*, p. 294.

reflects a 'hollow orthodoxy'[32] due not in the least to the fading of the
Parousia hope in a post-apostolic climate.

> In short, in II Peter the original language of apocalyptic fervour has become
> the more dogmatically calculated language of 'the last things'. *If 'early
> Catholicism' is a reaction to the repeated disappointment of apocalyptic
> hopes then II Peter is a prime example of early Catholicism.*[33]

The present study, it should be emphasized at the outset, is not about
'early Catholicism'. Nor is it given to an analysis of current issues in
New Testament studies. Rather, it is a modest attempt to probe a relatively obscure portion of a relatively obscure New Testament document, with the hope of doing some literary and exegetical justice along
the way. Nevertheless, one must start with presuppositions, since it is
presuppositions that govern the interpretive framework with which
scholarship proceeds.

It must be stressed that the problem with the 'early Catholic' thesis
is not in its observation of second-century ecclesiastical phenomena.
That these phenomena emerge in the sub-apostolic era is indisputable.
Nor can it be denied that the New Testament contains foreshadows of
'early Catholic' theological tendencies which come to full bloom in the
second century. Rather, the problem of the thesis lies with its starting-
point. 'Early Catholicism' begins with the assumption that apostolic
authorship presents an 'obstacle' to New Testament exegesis. Being presupposed, as we have seen, is that (1) the writer is far removed from
the beginnings of the church; (2) pseudonymity allows us 'for the first
time to "grasp" the full meaning of the letter'; and (3) the *Didache* or *1
Clement* or *Barnabas*, with no theological consequence, can be 'substi-
tuted' in the canon for Jude and 2 Peter. In the end, what this means for
2 Peter is that we can say with Dunn: Luther's insights are at times
more 'inspired' than those of our epistle.

If we assume under the theological rubric of 'unity and diversity' in
the New Testament that its diversity cancels out or is greater than the
overarching unity, as much of critical scholarship is prepared to do, the
alternatives before us are not many. Indeed, the only option is a speculative reconstruction of the history of the text based on the view that
the canon is a human anthology. If, however, we start with the assumption that our data base is the entire canon (established for eminently

---

32. So Dunn, *Unity and Diversity*, p. 350.
33. Dunn, *Unity and Diversity*, p. 351 (emphasis his).

theological reasons), we are spared the alternative of speculative histor-ical reasoning, and we place our exegetical methodology within—rather than outside—the necessary and guiding constraints of the church's his-torical consensus. Moreover, this normative assumption about the New Testament text facilitates the emergence of a biblical theology. Other-wise, the task of theology is impossible due to the multiple interpreta-tions arising from the extreme skepticism over against the viability of doing theology in the first place.[34]

Because of the influence of his ideas on 2 Peter scholarship, Ernst Käsemann once more engages us at a critical juncture in our discus-sion. The distinction between unity and diversity in the New Testament leads Käsemann to prefer certain documents and theological distinctions in the New Testament over others—what has come to be known as the 'canon within a canon'. He writes:

> Does the canon of the New Testament constitute the foundation of the unity of the Church? In view of the many different versions of the Chris-tian proclamation to be found in the New Testament, the historian must return a negative answer to this question.[35]

Justification for this division, according to Käsemann, is severalfold: (1) the presence of four Gospel narratives rather than one; (2) the purported difficulty in reconstructing both the historical Jesus and the primitive church; (3) the great diversity of early Christian kerygma; and (4) the consequent incompatibility of theological tensions and con-tradictions that result an 'violent collision' elsewhere in the New Tes-tament.[36] These premises confirm Käsemann's thesis. It can only mean that

> the New Testament canon does not, as such, constitute the foundation of the unity of the Church. On the contrary, as such (that is, in its accessibility to the historian) it provides the basis for the multiplicity of the confession. . .

---

34. This dilemma has been succinctly summarized by G.R. Osborne, *The Herme-neutical Spiral: A Comprehensive Introduction to Biblical Interpretation* (Downers Grove: InterVarsity Press, 1991), p. 271.

35. E. Käsemann, 'The Canon of the New Testament and the Unity of the Church', in *Essays on New Testament Themes* (Philadelphia: Fortress Press, 1964), p. 95. A thorough discussion of the canonical issue proceeds in his untranslated work, *Das Neue Testament als Kanon: Dokumentation und kritische Analyse zur gegenwärtigen Diskussion* (Göttingen: Vandenhoeck & Ruprecht, 1970).

36. Käsemann, 'Canon', pp. 95-103.

> In terms of our present problem, this means that we cannot keep God imprisoned even within the canon of the New Testament.[37]

For Käsemann—and proponents of 'early Catholicism'—there can be no confessional claims to finality and authority. But this approach to the documents of the New Testament, in spite of its great appeal, will not suffice. Rather, the canon must be taken as a whole, informing our perspective on the Scriptures that allows neither the community nor historical-critical scholarship to adjudicate over the canonical text itself.[38]

What are the consequences for biblical scholarship if we adopt the view that 'there can be no confessional claims to finality and authority' regarding the documents of the New Testament? Should we in fact not 'imprison God within the canon of the New Testament'? Or should we? What is the evidence that God *himself* has confined Christian revelation to the New Testament corpus?

In his essay 'The New Testament as Canon',[39] R.B. Gaffin, Jr, has anticipated these questions, along with their far-reaching consequences. Gaffin's response—and the issue is by no means tangential to the exegetical enterprise—is based on the observation that the historic Christian confession is subject to scrutiny on two fundamental and inextricable levels—the historical and the theological. First, what accounts for *how* the church adjudicated over and accepted the 27 books as canon? What were the criteria? Secondly, was and is the church warranted in recognizing these 27 as canon? Did the church make the corrrect decision? Was it perhaps mistaken?

Gaffin's conclusion—a conclusion that is consonant with the church's historical and consensual understanding of canon—is that in the study of the Bible historical and theological questions may not be divorced from each other.[40] Rather, they inevitably condition one another:

37. Käsemann, 'Canon', pp. 103-105.
38. Thus Osborne, *Spiral*, p. 273.
39. R.B. Gaffin, Jr, 'The New Testment as Canon', in H.M. Conn (ed.), *Inerrancy and Hermeneutic: A Tradition, A Challenge, A Debate* (Grand Rapids: Baker, 1988), pp. 165-83.
40. Hence, the flawed starting-point of Käsemann *et al.*, who assume that the exegetical enterprise can proceed along 'historical' lines apart from the infusion of theological commitments. To defer to the consensus of the church historically is not to be obscurantist; rather, it is to acknowledge the limitations of both the interpretive community and the exegete.

> When theologial reflection takes place in isolation from historical inves-
> tigation, the former becomes abstract and speculative; in concentrating on
> the theological side of the canon question, we must be careful not to forget
> or distort the historical picture.[41]

An important step in helping correct the distortion of the historical picture surrounding 2 Peter was the publication in 1983 of Richard Bauckham's rich commentary on Jude and 2 Peter. Bauckham was moved to observe that

> The whole concept of 'early Catholicism' as New Testament scholars
> have used it to illuminate the history of first-century Christianity is ripe for
> radical reexamination. It has undoubtedly promoted too simple a picture of
> the development of Christianity.[42]

What is it about the 'early Catholic' reading of 2 Peter that necessitates in Bauckham's thinking a 'radical reexamination'? Is one altogether justified in speaking of 'early Catholicism' within the New Testament? Do the purported 'early Catholic' documents of the New Testament not in fact distinguish themselves from sub-apostolic non-canonical writings? And is it possible that the 'early Catholic' grid to a certain extent may be responsible for the highly derivative nature of commentary on 2 Peter (and Jude) over the last century-and-a-half?

Can the 'early Catholic' reading of 2 Peter indeed be exegetically sustained? What shall we say to scholarship that does not share Käsemann's insistence that 2 Peter 'from beginning to end' is perhaps 'the most dubious writing in the canon' and 'the clearest possible testimony to the onset of early Catholicism'?[43] Is the 'early Catholic' reading quite possibly a reading that begins with certain externally imposed assumptions regarding the nature of second-century Christianity which predetermine the interpretative outcome rather than a reading that is informed by internal exegetical markers and ultimately guided by the church's historical consensus? Is an alternative reading of the epistle at all plausible?[44]

The aforementioned call by Bauckham for reexamination of the 'early Catholic' approach to 2 Peter that has become firmly entrenched

41. Gaffin, 'New Testament', p. 166.
42. Bauckham, *Jude, 2 Peter*, p. 8.
43. Käsemann, 'Apologia', pp. 169, 195.
44. Fornberg describes the 'early Catholic' category as 'artificial' and 'unable to do justice' to this epistle's interpretation (*Early Church*, pp. 5-6).

in biblical scholarship is surely a welcome sign.[45] Addressing the eschatological element in 2 Peter, Bauckham rightly notes that far from aban-
doning the hope of the Parousia, the writer avows with great earnest
that the eschatological day of reckoning is certain. That a pastorally sensitive explanation for the 'delay' is given (3.8-13) cannot legitimately
be construed to mean that the Parousia hope is being allowed to 'fade'.
To the contrary, the text militates against such a reading; rather, the
author attributes this delay to divine longsuffering:

> The Lord does not delay his promise, in the sense that some understand
> 'delay'; rather [ἀλλά], he is longsuffering toward you, not wishing that any
> might perish but rather [ἀλλά] that all might make room for repentance.
> (3.9)

Moreover, to the false teacher, the false prophet, and the moral sceptic,
the Parousia is not a hope but a *threat*.[46] The primary issue, from the
standpoint of the writer, is not the *timing* but the *fact* of a day of
reckoning.

The observations of Leonard Goppelt,[47] John Drane[48] and Michael
Green[49] converge at this point and invite our reconsideration. Those
scholars who follow Käsemann's lead in ascribing to 2 Peter a late date
due to a 'fading Parousia hope' fail to note that the earliest New Testament letters we possess, 1 and 2 Thessalonians, were written precisely
with a view of addressing this issue.[50] Indeed, the reconstruction of the

---

45. As shown by Fornberg's survey of 2 Peter scholarship up through 1976, there
has existed a virtually unanimous consensus that the epistle is post-apostolic (*Early
Church*, p. 7 n.3). Notable exceptions to this are vol. III of Donald Guthrie's *Intro-
duction to the New Testament*, published in 1962 (*Hebrews to Revelation* [London:
Tyndale Press, 1962], pp. 137-85) and subsequently merged into one volume; pub-
lication the year before of Guthrie's University of London dissertation, 'Early Christian
Pseudepigraphy and its Antecedents'; and E.M.B. Green's *2 Peter Reconsidered*
(London: Tyndale Press, 1961).

46. Thus M. Green, *2 Peter and Jude* (TNTC, 18; Leicester: InterVarsity Press;
Grand Rapids: Eerdmans, repr. 1989), p. 27.

47. L. Goppelt, 'The Nature of the Early Church', in W. Klassen and G. Snyder
(eds.), *Current Issues in New Testament Interpretation* (Grand Rapids: Eerdmans,
1962), pp. 193-209.

48. Drane, 'Eschatology', pp. 180-84.

49. Green, *2 Peter and Jude*, pp. 27-28.

50. It is exegetically sustainable to conclude from Pauline teaching in 2 Thess. 1
and 2 that the Parousia can in fact delay. Paul's response is not to be seen as a cor-
rective for a delimited hope that was previously held, rather the exact same message

early church as 'disillusioned' by the delay of the Parousia is deci-
sively refuted by an examination of early Christian literature. First, the
narrower question about the expectation of the end would appear to
have been seldom raised by the church.[51] Secondly, both early and later
New Testament documents have the same eschatological tension. Agreeing with the tension in 1 and 2 Thessalonians are Heb. 10.36-39; Jas.
5.8; 1 Pet. 4.7 and Rev. 22.20.[52] Even in subapostolic writings this is
still the case—for example, *Did.* 10.6; *1 Clem.* 23.5; *2 Clem.* 12.1, 6;
Barn. 4.3; and *Herm. Vis.* 3.8, 9. Consequently, the New Testament
writers cannot legitimately be viewed as influenced by a disappointment in a 'fading Parousia hope', for in a repeated manner they proclaim the nearness of the end, even when wrestling with the tensions
created by non-imminence.

In terms of eschatological perspective, the epistle to the Hebrews
might take a place alongside 2 Peter. The slackening of hope in Hebrews
is not the result of a fading Parousia hope; it issues rather from the tensions inherent in living in the present world. The readers are exhorted
to persevere. Perhaps they encounter cultural challenges not unlike the
readers of 2 Peter. But the church's peculiar temptation in Hebrews is
one of not persisting in the face of trial and persecution. The community is exhorted not to 'fail to obtain the grace of God' (12.15). Both
Hebrews and 2 Peter utilize the language of paraenesis.[53] Both employ
repentance and typology to exhort their respective audiences to faithfulness in the present situation.[54] Yet, while the one has a decidedly
theological texture, that of the other is chiefly moral.

he had already preached at Thessalonica (cf. 2.5, 15). Thus Moore, *Parousia*,
pp. 110-14.

51. Thus Goppelt, 'Nature', pp. 198-99. It does surface in 2 Thess. 2.1-12; Heb.
10.36-37; Jas 5.7-8; 1 Pet. 4.7 and Rev. 22.20. 1 Thess. 4.13-18 chiefly addresses
the *nature* of the Parousia and not its imminence. 2 Pet. 3, thought by most to treat the
question of Parousia delay, concerns the *fact* of the Parousia in light of the theme of
moral responsibility, not its timing.

52. The observation by J. Chaine ('Cosmogonie aquatique et conflagration finale
d'après la Secunde Petri', *RB* 46 [1937], p. 207) is most appropriate and bears repeating: 'Come, Lord Jesus!' expresses the cry of the heart, not the sense of chronological
certitude.

53. Heb. 13.22: παρακαλῶ δὲ ὑμᾶς, ἀδελφοί, ἀνέχεσθε τοῦ λόγου τῆς
παρακλήσεως.

54. Consider Goppelt's useful comparison of the epistle to the Hebrews and

In response to Käsemann (and those who echo his view of a 'fading Parousia hope'), it needs to be emphasized that the eschatological perspective of the New Testament is that of *watchful expectancy* and not assurance that the Parousia would occur during the apostles' and early disciples' lifetime. Jesus' eschatological framework can be expressed in the axiom 'no one knows the hour'.[55] Paul speaks of 'earnest expectation',[56] the earth's 'groaning',[57] and 'the ends of the ages'.[58] Significantly, 2 Peter utilizes the thief metaphor, maintaining continuity with the apocalyptic element in Jesus' and Paul's perspective.[59]

If in fact the New Testament gives evidence of an 'early Catholic' church evacuating an imminent Parousia hope, a more serious issue emerges. There is some merit to the suggestion of Oscar Cullmann that in light of Jesus' confident assertions about a possible imminent Parousia, the church surely would have been tempted to abandon its allegiance to him after the 'cardinal error' had been exposed.[60] In the end, it is supremely hard to overlook the pastoral implications of a 'mistaken' Parousia hope. If Jesus was speaking only apocalyptically with a temporal nearness in view for the purposes of encouraging his flock, his pastoral expedience leads to quite delusory—and pastorally deleterious—results. Yet, this is what Käsemann would have us believe when he asserts:

> We have to state clearly and without evasion that this hope proved to be a delusion and that with it there collapsed at the same time the whole theological framework of apocalyptic.[61]

If, as Käsemann vigorously maintains, Christian disciples of the second generation onward were to become thoroughly disillusioned, the

Hermas, wherein the difference between 'apostolic' and 'post-apostolic' perspectives is appropriately illustrated ('Nature', pp. 198-99).

55. Mt. 24.36-51; Mk 13.32; Lk. 12.35-40.

56. Rom. 8.19; Phil. 1.20.

57. Rom. 8.23; 2 Cor. 5.2.

58. 1 Cor. 10.11.

59. Mt. 24.43; Lk. 12.39; 1 Thess. 5.2; 2 Pet. 3.10; cf. Rev. 3.3. Particularly helpful in this regard is A.L. Moore's treatment of the church's near eschatological expectation in *Parousia*, pp. 160-74.

60. O. Cullmann, 'Das wahre durch die ausgebliebene Parousia gestellte neutestamentliche Problem', *TZ* 3 (1947), pp. 177-78.

61. E. Käsemann, 'The Beginnings of Christian Theology', in *New Testament Questions for Today* (Philadelphia: Fortress Press, 1969), p. 106.

Christian community in time could hardly take seriously—much less authoritatively—Jesus' words ἐγὼ δὲ λέγω or ἀμὴν λέγω ὑμῖν.

Because the imminent Parousia expectation is perceived to be the 'tragender Grund' of Jesus' message, proponents of 'early Catholicism' posit that the church understood itself as 'the last generation before the end' and thus must confront the 'peinliche Illusion' of this mistaken belief.[62] Such an 'illusion', it is reasoned, surely 'disturbed' the church to the point of being 'explosive' in its ramifications.[63]

Responding to the language of 'crisis', 'disturbance', 'illusion' and 'catastrophe' employed by many German theologians, I. Howard Marshall has written that while the imminence of the Parousia was indeed part of Jesus' teaching, it is not what Käsemann and others have made it out to be.[64] Similarly, Jaroslav Pelikan considers it 'a gross exaggeration of the evidence' to describe the eclipse of apocalyptic vision as 'catastrophic' for generations that followed the apostles.[65] According to Pelikan, this view errs on two counts: (1) it is based on too simplistic a caricature of Jesus' and the early church's teaching, and (2) it is not corroborated by second-century texts, as one looks in vain for evidence of this 'distressing illusion', that is, the bitter disappointment over a delay in the Parousia. What the texts do suggest, rather, is a shift within the polarity of the 'already–not yet' tension inherent in the Christian message and a renewed appreciation for ethical imperatives that address the church's relationship to the world.[66]

Along with Marshall and Pelikan, S.E. Johnson is also critical of the 'early Catholic' position. Johnson stresses that a delay in the Parousia was less important to the early church than maintaining the link between Jesus' teaching and developing Christian doctrine.[67]

Ultimately, those who hold that Jesus' view of the future did not include an interval between the resurrection and the Parousia are forced

---

62. So E. Grässer, *Die Naherwartung Jesu* (SB, 61; Stuttgart: KBW, 1973), pp. 13-14.

63. Grässer, *Naherwartung*, p. 36.

64. I.H. Marshall, 'Is Apocalyptic the Mother of Christian Theology', in G.F. Hawthorne and O. Betz (eds.), *Tradition and Interpretation in the New Testament* (Grand Rapids: Eerdmans; Tübingen: Mohr-Siebeck, 1987), pp. 33-42.

65. J. Pelikan, *The Christian Tradition. I. The Emergence of the Catholic Tradition (100-600)* (Chicago: University of Chicago Press, 1971), pp. 123-24.

66. Pelikan, *Christian Tradition*, pp. 124, 130-31.

67. S.E. Johnson, 'Asia Minor and Early Christianity', in J. Neusner (ed.), *Christianity, Judaism and Other Greco-Roman Cults* (Leiden: Brill, 1975), p. 119.

to ignore or deny that Jesus anticipated a new community, the church. This conclusion greatly obscures Jesus' ethical teaching, the bulk of which presupposes endurance, waiting and faithfulness. And it ignores Jesus' anticipation and promise of the Spirit as advocate for and guardian of the new community, thematically developed at great length in the Fourth Gospel.[68]

In short, the 'early Catholic' view exaggerates one aspect of Jesus' teaching (an imminent return) at the expense of New Testament teaching that constitutes the very *foundation* of the church. Käsemann's error is that by delimiting the expectations of the early church, he ends up setting a kind of *terminus ante eventu* for its occurrence. The implication, as Marshall wryly notes, is that this hope, which has dragged on for the last 1900 years, is a mistaken one![69]

There is, however, substantial evidence to believe that Jesus' outlook presupposed an interval between the resurrection and Parousia. One is justified in acknowledging that the 'already–not yet' tension inherent in the kingdom of God was present in the teaching of Jesus (and perpetuated by apostolic teaching). At issue is the self-awareness of the incarnate Son of God. This outlook takes into account future missionary activity, the giving of the Spirit, and the mandate of the church to become the new Israel among the nations.

The connection between the new community and the Spirit merits fuller consideration. Undercut by the 'early Catholic' perspective is the significance of Jesus' commissioning of the disciples, specifically the imperative to disciple '*all* nations' and remember that his presence is promised 'to the end of the age' (Mt. 28.16-20). In Luke, the link between the 'great commission' and the Spirit is much more explicit: 'Behold, I am sending upon you the promise of my Father, so wait. . . until you have been clothed with power' (Lk. 24.49). In the book of Acts, everything that occurs to the church is viewed from and predicated upon the perspective of Pentecost. In fact, this perspective begins with Jesus. With the resurrection and ascension, the new community is prepared to receive the Spirit (Acts 1.1-5). With the coming of the Spirit, the eschaton has arrived. The horizon of the new community, formerly limited by a restricted eschatological framework—'Lord is

68. It is legitimate to argue, with O. Cullmann, that the 'end time' was in fact the experience of the Spirit ('Parousie-verzögerung und Urchristentum', *TLZ* 83 [1958], p. 11).

69. Marshall, 'Apocalyptic', p. 40.

this the time when you will restore the kingdom to Israel?' (1.6)—is now extended: 'You shall receive power after the Holy Spirit has come upon you, and you will be my witnesses in Jerusalem, in all Judea and Samaria, and *to the ends of the earth*' (1.8).

The final inability of scholarship, as A.L. Moore points out, to force Jesus to conform to a pre-cast mold in terms of methodology suggests not only that our methodology is questionable—and perhaps wrong on occasion—but also that Jesus was consistently attentive to human attempts at restricting his perspective.[70] Scholarly attempts at explaining the eschatological element in the New Testament are prone to err on several sides. They may, for example, limit the scope of Jesus' eschatological expectations both temporally and theologically on the one hand, while implying through exegetical solutions that the early church was undiscerning on the other. Not infrequently, critical scholarship's reconstruction of the so-called 'early Catholic' scenario tends to cast the church as spiritually dull or undiscerning. So F. Mussner:

> The detachment [from the apostolic period] represents a vacuum in the church's history that almost gives the impression of a 'fracture'. . . . One must imagine oneself in that situation, with the burning question that confronted them: The apostles are dead. *What now*? Reflecting back on Jesus offers about as much of an answer as what they were to do with the problem of the law.[71]

By attributing short-sightedness or misunderstanding to the writers of the New Testament, exegetes themselves fail to discern the revelatory or theological character of New Testament literature. The fall of Jerusalem may be rightly understood as a signal manifestation of God's sovereignty in judging Israel, yet it is not specifically christocentric.[72] Thus, it does not alter one's theology of the kingdom of God, since the kingdom transcends the events of AD 70. Jesus' prophetic forecast in the Synoptics may have contained allusions to these near events, while at the same time being applicable to multitudes of future generations.

---

70. Moore, *Parousia*, p. 102. A relevant example of how the prophetic view frequently remains obscure to human perception is the telescope effect of prophetic speech, which tends to read events near and far in a way that renders indiscernible the time in between. This telescoping of divine activity would seem to be on display in Mt. 24 = Mk 13 = Lk. 21.

71. Mussner, 'Ablösung', pp. 169-70 (my translation, emphasis his).

72. The implications of this line of thinking are developed by Moore (*Parousia*, pp. 104-107).

There is a difference, even when it remains hidden to the human eye, between revelation that is fulfilled in imminent historical events and revelation that applies to the Parousia.[73]

Our reconsideration of the New Testament's eschatological perspective leads us in the direction of certain conclusions. These conclusions, in turn, require of us a willingness to rethink basic 'early Catholic' assumptions. Is it plausible that the supposed 'delay' in the Parousia hope, said to be on display in 2 Peter, may be rather the result of a wrong exegetical starting-point? Does the use of 'early Catholicism' as a term imply *a priori* a wrong theological judgment?

It is useful at this point to consider the realities confronting the early church—a mixture of Jewish and Gentile converts—that issued out of living in Gentile culture. The influence of pagan Hellenism in which the church was spawned can be seen to create both external and internal dilemmas. These dilemmas illustrate a necessary tension that exists between eschatology and ethics in the New Testament. Externally, the church encounters hostility from surrounding culture. By withdrawing from the heathen pattern of life the Christians invite antagonism toward their very existence. This antagonism is responsible for the fact that 'brethren all around the world are undergoing the same kinds of suffering' (1 Pet. 5.9). Such is reflected by Tacitus's observation concerning Neronian persecution of Christians. Their transgression was not criminal, only that they were *odium aeneris humani*.

The internal dilemma, however, is an equally daunting pastoral challenge. The ever-present danger confronting the Christian community is a lapse of ethical standards and a return—whether in mere initial patterns of forgetfulness or in wholesale apostasy—to the former way of life characterizing the heathen. This debilitating return to life patterned after the world may be clearly seen in the writings of the New Testament *fully apart* from the justification of Gnostic retardation.[74] It is this challenge that is being mirrored in 2 Peter.[75]

73. Thus T.W.B. Richardson, *An Introduction to the Theology of the New Testament* (London: SPCK, 1958), p. 55.

74. Consider, by way of example, Rom. 6 and 7, much of 1 Corinthians, and material from Heb. 6; 10 and 13. Goppelt's observations in this regard are particularly helpful ('Nature', pp. 193-209).

75. The priority in 2 Peter of ethics over eschatology or doctrine per se—a thesis developed more fully in the following pages—is strengthened when 2 Peter is contrasted with 1 and 2 Thessalonians. In the Thessalonian correspondence, the problem

In addition to our assessment of the so-called Parousia delay, additional criticisms that ultimately bear on our reading of 2 Peter might be offered of Käsemann's position—a position conveniently summarized by Dunn.[76] In 2 Peter, as in Jude, no reference to church office-holders appears.[77] To the contrary, the flock is admonished to guard itself. The readers are exhorted to 'make every effort' to strengthen the ethical underpinnings of their faith (1.5). Whereas the assumption of Käsemann and 'early Catholic' proponents is that doctrine is being guarded by an office or institution, a more plausible explanation—based on the text itself—is that the audience, planted amid Gentile culture, is struggling with the ethical requirements that betoken vital Christian faith. 2 Peter is a call for the community to *guard itself.*

It is on the ecclesiastical level that 'early Catholic' assumptions especially invite our interaction. Commenting on the church's 'necessity of new orders' that is 'conclusively demonstrated by the [second-century] struggle against enthusiasm', Käsemann writes:

> In borrowing from Jewish Christianity, the Church was compelled to bind the Spirit to the office. The Church had to be placed under an authority which would no longer allow its right and power to be constantly questioned and which would no longer require that both of these be derived from its proclamation. At this juncture the institution as such receives authority, right, power and Spirit.[78]

The period which Käsemann has in mind—early to mid-second century—is by no means the church's first encounter with 'enthusiasm'. One can legitimately point to a major outbreak of enthusiasm during the mid-first century—in Corinth. And precisely how Paul was compelled to respond to this outbreak is instructive. In the introduction to his first epistle to the Corinthians, the apostle rejoices that

consists in the theological *mysterion* of the Parousia—what realities, clothed in mystery, attend the coming of the Lord.

76. *Unity and Diversity*, p. 344. A discussion by Dunn of the three primary features of early Catholicism—the fading of the Parousia hope, growing institutionalization, and crystallization of the faith into set forms—as they reputedly surface in the New Testament canon follows this summary (pp. 244-62).

77. Bauckham, *Jude, 2 Peter*, pp. 152-53; see also J.D. Charles, *Literary Strategy in the Epistle of Jude* (Scranton: University of Scranton/London Associated University Presses, 1993), pp. 87-88.

78. Käsemann, 'Paul', pp. 247-48.

> every manner you have been enriched in him [Christ Jesus]—in speech
> and knowledge of every kind—in accordance with how the testimony of
> Christ was confirmed in you, so that you do not lack any gift.[79]

That is, despite the varying levels of immaturity characterizing
Corinthian faith, Paul is *not* anti-enthusiast. To the contrary, he praises
the Corinthian believers for their zeal in this regard, even when such
zeal has not been harnessed to a wisdom that is motivated by and rooted
in love.

The 'early Catholic' assumption that the church over time was 'compelled to bind the Spirit to the [episcopal] office'[80] would appear to be
sustained only by measuring second-century ecclesiastical developments
and reading them back into the writings of the New Testament. And it
is precisely to this reading that documents such as 2 Peter and Jude
over the last 150 years have been more or less held captive. Yet it is
specifically the notion of the Spirit *not* being bound to an office that
distinguishes the New Testament from the Old Testament, the New
Covenant from the Old. The Spirit, who operated formally through
the prophetic, priestly and kingly offices in the old scheme of things,
now is given to God's people collectively. This is the underlying thesis
of the book of Acts. The 'early Catholic' reading of the New Testament, by contrast, ignores the New Testament's explicit teaching that
the Spirit is *no longer* confined to an office. Rather, in Christ, a deinstitutionalization has taken place. Indeed, a deinstitutionalization of office
remains a characteristic of the church, a reality to which subsequent
generations, in *repeated fulfillment* of Peter's prophecy at Pentecost,
give witness: 'For this promise [the Spirit] is for you, for your children, and for all who are generationally removed, everyone whom the
Lord will call to himself' (Acts 2.39). In contrast, the 'early Catholic'
rubric leads Ernst Käsemann to interpret 2 Pet. 1.21 in the following
manner:

> But it cannot now be guaranteed that every Christian *ipso facto* possesses
> the Spirit, although Paul could still say in Rom. 8.9: 'Whoever has not the
> Spirit of Christ is none of his'. In early Catholicism the Spirit is bound to
> the official ministry. The community is seen, not only organizationally but

---

79. 1 Cor. 1.5-7a.

80. Representative of this view, which is shared by many, are Käsemann ('Paul',
pp. 248-49; 'Apologia', pp. 190-91) and W. Grundmann, *Der Brief des Judas und
der zweite Brief des Petrus* (THKNT, 15; Berlin: Evangelische Verlaganstalt, 1974),
p. 61.

theologically, as the generality of the laity. Exegesis cannot be given over into its hands. Its proper activity consists in hearing and obeying what the teaching ministry says to it. And so faith is transformed unmistakably into *fides implicita*: I believe what the Church believes.[81]

In looking for verification of the 'early Catholic' hypothesis in 2 Peter, our suspicions are not easily cast aside. The assumed need for ecclesiastical control over doctrine, integral to the 'early Catholic' hypothesis, does not manifest itself in 2 Peter in the way that Käsemann has maintained.[82] Rather, in the letter it is the Spirit who is depicted as enacting control[83]—not an institution, not an office, but the inspiration of the Holy Spirit at work in the people of God (ὑπὸ πνεύματος ἁγίου φερόμενοι ἐλάλησαν ἀπὸ θεοῦ ἄνθρωποι, 1.21). In this regard, Bauckham is correct to observe that 1.20-21 has nothing to do with scriptural interpretation, the church's official teaching office or a 'primitive form of magisterium', as is frequently assumed by commentators.[84] The issue at hand, supported by the epistle's contextual flow, is prophetic and authoritative *inspiration*. The author, who is claiming to be an eyewitness of the Transfiguration (1.16-18), is vigorous in his assertion: 'Thus we have the prophetic message attested' (1.19). It is the inspiration of the Spirit, who 'carries along' (φέρω)[85] those speaking for God, that is said to convey authority (cf. 1 Cor. 2.1-16).

Thus, 2 Peter, as does Jude, appeals to its readers on a *moral rather than authoritarian or institutional* basis. This scenario stands in marked contrast to that envisioned by Käsemann, where the intrusion of Gnosticism calls for an ecclesiastically 'tightened' response. This thesis is

81. Käsemann, 'Apologia', pp. 190-91.

82. In R.A. Falconer's view, it is this silence concerning ecclesiastical organization in 2 Peter, coupled with the letter's conspicuous absence of second-century heretical phenomena, that point to a date for the epistle within the lifetime of the apostle ('Is 2 Peter a Genuine Epistle to the Christians of Samaria?', *Expos* 6.5 [1902], pp. 459-60; 6.6 [1902], p. 127). Similarly, J.A.T. Robinson points out the absence of any trace of Gnosticism in 2 Peter and Jude, conceding that most of the social markers in 2 Peter suggest it to be first century (*Redating the New Testament* [Philadelphia: Westminster Press, 1976], pp. 175-91).

83. Cf. Jude 19-20.

84. *Jude, 2 Peter*, p. 233. Nor does it have to do with the teaching gift, as suggested by J.T. Curran, 'The Teaching of 2 Peter i.20', *TS* 4 (1943), pp. 364-67.

85. The image is one of being 'driven' by the wind of the Spirit (cf. its usage in Acts 27.15). Thus we have to do with *inspiration*, not interpretation.

confirmed when we consider the basic motifs and solutions to the
church's threat mounted by Ignatius, Clement or Hermas: calling for
the bishop, through whom Christ's authority is necessarily channeled;
securing the church's authority by doing 'everything according to the
order'; proclaiming penance and rationed forms of grace.

Moreover, the allusion to Paul in 3.15-16, viewed by some as evidence that tips the scale in favor of the 'early Catholic' view, can be
naturally interpreted to refer to the difficulty of humanly understanding Pauline teaching in general. This reading would seem to find cor-
roborating evidence in the preceding discussion of God's mysterious
longsuffering (3.8-13): all aspects of the economy of God are not transparent to human understanding. 3.15-16 can also be understood in the
sense of a doctrinal-ethical perversion[86]—for example, a distortion of
Paul's emphasis on justification by faith, whereby individuals promote
a faith without ethical fiber, a grace that is divorced from morality.

In addition, text-critical light has been shed on 2 Pet. 3.16 that has
important exegetical implications. Whereas most translations of the
verb 'twist' ($\sigma\tau\rho\epsilon\beta\lambda\acuteo\omega$) have the present tense, p. 72 has the future;
thus, not 'they twist', but 'they will twist'.[87] If, then, this statement is a
forecast, as one exegete has suggested, one is 'free to think that such a
forecast might have been made before the onset of the Jewish revolt in
67'.[88] It is clear from Col. 4.16 that Paul's letter to the Christians at
Colossae was to be forwarded to the church in other regions of Asia
Minor. This would indicate that in all probability Paul's epistles were
known and collected fairly early on.[89] It is not unreasonable, if the destination of 2 Peter is Asia Minor, that the epistle to the Colossians would
have been read by the Christians being addressed in 2 Peter. At bottom, what is suggested by the more recent textual evidence is the removal of an important obstacle to dating 2 Peter within the lifetime of
the apostle.[90] Any reading of 3.16 that construes a 'distortion' or misunderstanding of Paul to mean a chronological distance of several generations between the apostles and the readers tends to diminish both

86. $\delta\upsilon\sigma\nu\acuteo\eta\tau o\varsigma$, 'hard to understand', may connote 'obscure' or 'ambiguous'.

87. Other witnesses also have the future—codices C and P and several minuscules.

88. J. Crehan, 'New Light on 2 Peter from the Bodmer Papyrus', in E.A.
Livingstone (ed.), *Studia Evangelica* (Berlin: Akademie, 1982), VII, pp. 145-49.

89. On the gathering of a Pauline corpus, see D. Trobisch, *Paul's Letter Collection: Tracing the Origins* (Minneapolis: Fortress Press, 1994).

90. So Crehan, 'New Light', p. 145.

the apologetic argument being developed in 2 Peter 3 and the literary connection between chs. 2 and 3.

Text-critical considerations aside, if we are to assume the traditional late dating of the epistle, then it follows that the author and readers would long have had access to all of Paul's letters, in which case the statement in 3.15-16 makes less sense if penned by a pseudepigrapher.[91] Green's observation, at this point, deserves emphasis. The difference between first- and second-century references to Paul is worth noting. To 'Peter', he is a 'beloved brother'; to Polycarp, he is 'the blessed and glorious Paul'. In the second century, one tended to view Paul either as an arch-villain or as the apostle *par excellence*; it is, however, highly dubious that he would have been referred to as a 'dear brother'.[92]

Paraenesis and 2 Peter

Given the sway of 'early Catholic' interpretation over traditional 2 Peter commentary, exegetical developments in recent years are encouraging. Bauckham is among those who have noted the paraenetic and midrashic character of material in the general epistles, which in turn has provided fresh interpretive insights into an admittedly difficult New Testament document such as 2 Peter.[93] The Christian paraenetic tradition is perhaps most richly on display in the general epistles—notably, in James, 1 and 2 Peter and Jude, where ethics and 'pastoral

91. Thus the argument of Guthrie, *Introduction*, pp. 824-27, bears consideration.

92. Green, *2 Peter and Jude*, pp. 158-59. Given the virtual unanimity on the one hand among critical scholars that 2 Peter is a pseudepigraphon yet the reticence on the other hand to stigmatize it as a literary 'forgery', mainstream New Testament scholarship has preferred to take a more moderate position regarding the epistle's authenticity. A necessary distinction between canonicity and authenticity is seen to exist that simultaneously offers tacit acknowledgment of the church's historical consensus regarding the letter yet allows *a priori* the possibility for pseudonymous literature to be a part of the New Testament corpus.

93. See R.J. Bauckham, 'James, 1 and 2 Peter, Jude', in D.A. Carson and H.G.M. Williamson (eds.), *It Is Written: Scripture Citing Scripture. Essays in Honour of B. Lindars* (Cambridge: Cambridge University Press, 1988), pp. 303-17; and E.E. Ellis, *Prophecy and Hermeneutic in Early Christianity* (WUNT, 18; Tübingen: Mohr, 1978). On the paraenetic character of 2 Peter, see I.H. Marshall, *Kept by the Power of God* (Minneapolis: Bethany Fellowship, 1969), pp. 168-71; T. Fornberg, *Early Church*, pp. 94-110; as well as the introduction to J.D. Charles, *Jude and 2 Peter* (BCBC; Scottdale, PA: Herald Press, forthcoming).

theology' rather than theological formulations of doctrine per se are accentuated.[94] R.W. Wall's observation concerning James is on target and applicable to the general epistles as a whole: while James shares a common theological conception with Paul, the former emphasizes the community's *ethic*, whereas the latter emphasizes its *theological convictions*. A reading of the entire New Testament, consequently, which takes into account both ethical and doctrinal emphases, prevents both the formation of faith without validating works as well as a legalism that is void of grace.[95]

The priority of ethics over doctrine,[96] which is not to minimize the importance of the latter in the epistle, has important implications for the study of 2 Peter,[97] since it has been broadly assumed by commentators that doctrine—and specifically, false doctrine in the form of eschatological denial—is the burden of the writer.[98] The lack of attention

94. This particular contribution of the general epistles to the New Testament canon is explored in J.D. Charles, 'The Old Testament in the General Epistles', in R.P. Martin and P.H. Davids (eds.), *Dictionary of the Later New Testament* (Downers Grove: InterVarsity Press, forthcoming).

95. R.W. Wall, 'James as Apocalyptic Paraenesis', *RestQ* 32 (1990), p. 22.

96. The paraenetic distinctive is reflected in Seneca's contrast of teaching (*institutio*) and admonition (*admonitio*) (*Ep. Mor.* 94.45).

97. This has significant bearing on the unit under investigation, 1.5-7. Although A. Vögtle's *Die Tugend- und Lasterkataloge im Neuen Testament* (NTAbh, 16; Münster: Aschendorff, 1936) remains one of four standard texts (all of which are German) for exploring virtue and vice in the New Testament against a Hellenistic backdrop, only four pages of this volume are devoted to the section 'The Virtue Lists in the Petrine Epistles' (pp. 188-91). Similar can be said of the other three: O. Zöckler, *Die Tugendlehre des Christentums* (Gütersloh: C. Bertelsmann, 1904); S. Wibbing, *Die Tugend- und Lasterkataloge im Neuen Testament und ihre Traditionsgeschichte unter besonderer Berücksichtigung der Qumrantexte* (BZNW, 25; Berlin: A. Töpelmann, 1959); and E. Kamlah, *Die Form der katalogischen Paränese im Neuen Testament* (Tübingen: Mohr, 1964). Much remains to be done in measuring 2 Peter's contribution to New Testament ethics.

98. In objecting to our contention that ethics rather than doctrine per se is the thrust of 2 Peter, one might point to the allusion to ψευδοπροφῆται and ψευδοδιδάσκαλοι in 2.1 as confirming evidence that doctrine—and specifically, heresy—is the primary emphasis of the epistle. I have argued elsewhere (see Chapter 3) that the ψευδοπροφῆται, aside from the writer's personal interest in prophets or prophecy (so H.C.C. Cavallin, 'The False Teachers of 2 Peter as Pseudo-prophets', *NovT* 21 [1979], pp. 263-70), relate to Israel of old: 'But false prophets also arose [in the past] among the people [i.e., Israel]'. Of the 'false teachers' mentioned in 2.1, it is stated that they 'will be [in the future] among you'. ψευδοδιδάσκαλοι is to be

that 2 Peter receives—among laity and biblical scholars—is unfortunate precisely because of its considerable contribution to Christian ethics.

On a textbook level, there is a curious absence of 2 Peter in discussions of New Testament ethics. To illustrate, Willi Marxsen's *New Testament Foundations for Christian Ethics*[99] omits any reference to or citation of 2 Peter. In two massive (untranslated) German volumes published within the past decade, *Neues Testament und Ethik*[100] and *Neutestamentliche Ethik*,[101] out of 1251 pages of text *six* are devoted to ethics in 2 Peter—all appearing in the latter volume, none in the former. In Wolfgang Schrage's *The Ethics of the New Testament*,[102] described by Victor Paul Furnish (*Theological Ethics in Paul*) as 'the finest recent treatment of ethics in the New Testament that I have read', seven lines at the conclusion of the section devoted to 1 Peter are given to Jude and 2 Peter in passing. Jack T. Sanders's *Ethics in the New Testament*[103] devotes just over a page to Jude and 2 Peter. Ceslas Spicq's imposing *Théologie morale du Nouveau Testament*,[104] Rudolph

understood as a moral condemnation rather than a technically precise description of the pastoral problem. What are the teachers teaching? Freedom (2.19), not bad doctrine per se. Far too much regarding ψευδοδιδάσκαλοι is insinuated by commentators into the text, much of which is alien to the literary context. The assumption typically follows that the presence of the description 'false teachers' is proof of a second-century scenario, in which protognostic or Gnostic heresy is threatening to knock down the theological door. But this exegetical conclusion is arrived at by ignoring the development of the literary argument, which is paraenetic (that is, moral and hortatory) and not doctrinal in character. Moreover, the argument of 2 Pet. 3 is not that certain 'teachers' are promoting a particular eschatological perspective; rather, it is that some—specifically, the apostate of 2.19-22 who are tauting moral 'freedom'—indeed are denying moral accountability and the fact of eschatological judgment.

99. W. Marxsen, *New Testament Foundations for Christian Ethics* (trans. O.C. Dean, Jr; Minneapolis: Fortress Press, 1993).

100. H. Merklein (ed.), *Neues Testament und Ethik* (Stuttgart: KBW, 1989).

101. S. Schulz (ed.), *Neutestamentliche Ethik* (Zürich: Theologischer Verlag, 1987).

102. W. Schrage, *The Ethics of the New Testament* (trans. D.E. Green; Philadelphia: Fortress Press, 1988).

103. J.T. Sanders, *Ethics in the New Testament* (Philadelphia: Fortress Press, 1975).

104. C. Spicq, *Théologie morale du Nouveau Testament* (2 vols.; Paris: Gabalda, 1970).

Schnackenburg's *The Moral Teaching of the New Testament*,[105] and
R.H. Marshall's *The Challenge of New Testament Ethics*[106] all contain
no discussion of ethics in 2 Peter. Wayne Meeks' probing of the grammar of early Christian morals, *The Moral World of the First Christians*,[107] also omits any reference to 2 Peter as well.

The conspicuous absence of 2 Peter in New Testament ethics, then,
confronts us with the obvious question: Why do primers on New Testament ethics almost uniformly fail to include the epistle in their discussions? Surely the reason is not because of an absence of moral vocabulary. Moral grammar, as it turns out, is *most dense* in the general
epistles. (Only in the Johannine epistles does this feature recede.) Ethics
and virtue, exhortation and moral typology abound in 2 Peter, which
exhibits similarities to James, 1 Peter and Jude in its paraenetic-rhetor-
ical character. As a form of prescriptive and proscriptive exhortation,[108] paraenesis is devised to promote practical rules for behaviour
in common situations and adopts styles that range from censure to con-
solation.[109] Moral categories are assumed and thus are not explicated
in paraenetic exhortation. Because the exhorter proceeds on the basis of
what is already plainly known, he disavows the need for further instruction, merely reminding his audience of knowledge they already possess.
It is helpful to compare two samples of paraenesis, one from the New
Testament (2 Peter) and one from pagan literature, both of which have
the markings of the paraenetic tradition:

> I know you need no telling, but my love for you prompts me to remind
> you to keep in mind and put into practice what you know already, or else it
> would be better for you to remain ignorant. Remember. . . [110]

105. R. Schnackenburg, *The Moral Teaching of the New Testament* (2 vols.;
trans. J. Holland-Smith and W.J. O'Hara; Freiburg: Herder, 1965).

106. R.H. Marshall, *The Challenge of New Testament Ethics* (London: SPCK,
1947).

107. W.A. Meeks, *The Moral World of the First Christians* (Philadelphia:
Westminster Press, 1986).

108. The role of *exhortatio* or the λόγος παραινήτικος in Hellenistic rhetoric is
delineated by Quintilian, for example, in *Inst.* 3.6.47; 9.2.103.

109. A. Malherbe, *Moral Exhortation: A Greco-Roman Sourcebook* (Philadelphia: Westminster Press, 1986), pp. 124-25.

110. Pliny, *Letter to Maximus* 8.24 (the English translation appearing in *Letters
and Panegyricus* [LCL; trans. B. Radice; Cambridge, MA: Harvard University Press,
1969], pp. 72-73).

> Therefore I intend to keep on reminding you of these things, though you
> already know them and are established in the truth that has come to you. . .
> I think it right. . . to refresh your memory. . . so that. . . you may be able
> at any time to recall these things. . . I am trying to arouse your sincere
> intention by reminding you: remember. . .[111]

Where concreteness is necessary for the readers, moral paradigms are
a common feature in the paraenetic tradition and serve the purposes of
illustration.[112] In addition to its characteristic use of paradigms, the
λόγος παραινήτικος typically incorporates the elements of regulatory
rules of conduct, ethical proscriptions, ethical justifications, warnings
and catalogs of vice and/or virtue.[113] The social situation of paraenesis, moreover, dictates a relationship of the author to his readers which
is that of a father-figure to a son or mentor to his disciple, the effect
of which is moral authority that accompanies his exhortations.[114] On
the assumption that 2 Peter is pseudepigraphal, any attempts to reconcile the 'fictive' and the real occasion of the letter are problematic and
purely speculative as to the relationship between the real author and his
readers.

What the 'early Catholic' reading of 2 Peter has obscured *inter alia* is
an appreciation of the writer's literary-rhetorical style as well as evidence of the readers' social location, both of which derive from the text
itself. Thankfully, recent trends in biblical scholarship, which recog-
nize the place of 2 Peter in the Christian paraenetic tradition, are
resulting in fresh attempts at interpreting the epistle. In line with the
reminder terminology that characterizes paraenetic literature, in 2
Peter the readers are exhorted to recall—and validate—what they
already know (1.8-15; 3.1-2, 11, 17). Incomparable divine resources

111. 2 Pet. 1.12-15; 3.1a-2a.

112. Malherbe, *Moral Exhortation*, pp. 124-29.

113. On the paraenetic tradition in general, see K. Berger, 'Hellenistische Gattungen im Neuen Testament', in W. Haase (ed.), *Aufstieg und Niedergang der römischen
Welt: Geschichte und Kultur Roms im Spiegel der neuen Forschung* (Berlin: de
Gruyter, 1984), II.25.2, pp. 1075-77. For examples of the use of paraenesis in the
general epistles, see L.G. Perdue, 'Paraenesis in the Epistle of James', *ZNW* 72
(1981), pp. 241-56; P.H. Davids, 'Tradition and Citation in the Epistle of James',
in W.W. Gasque and W.S. LaSor (eds.), *Scripture, Tradition, and Interpretation*
(Grand Rapids: Eerdmans, 1978), pp. 113-26; and T. Martin, *Metaphor and Composition in 1 Peter* (Atlanta: Scholars Press, 1994), pp. 103-21.

114. Berger, 'Gattungen', p. 1076, and S.K. Stowers, *Letter Writing in Greco-
Roman Antiquity* (Philadelphia: Westminster Press, 1986), p. 95.

have been placed at their disposal for 'life and godliness' (1.3). To concretize the matter, moral examples are served up from the past (2.4-10a). The angels who rebelled were disenfranchized and have been reserved for the day of judgment. Noah's generation was condemned because of hardened moral skepticism, while faithful Noah, with his family, was saved. Lot, as well, was rescued by the Lord from the judgment that beset the cities of the plain, thus serving as an example of one who faced the daunting challenges of living in a pagan society where moral standards were continually subject to assault and compromise.

That we have to do in 2 Peter foremost with ethical lapse—over against false doctrine per se—is conveyed not only by the language of paraenesis but also the descriptions of the underlying pastoral problem. Consider the writer's vocabulary: 'pleasure' (ἡδονή), 'licentiousness' (ἀσέλγεια), 'depravity' (φθορά), 'lusts of the flesh' (ἐπιθυμίαι σαρκός), 'covetousness' (πλεονεξία), 'defilement' (μίασμα), 'lawless' (ἄνομος) 'vanity' (ματαιότης), 'irrational beasts' (ἄλογα ζῷα), 'morally corrupt' (ἄθεσμος), 'adulterous' (μοιχαλίδος), 'returning to one's own vomit' (ἐπιστρέψας ἐπὶ τὸ ἴδιον ἐξέραμα), 'wallowing in mud' (κυλισμὸν). Those being described are not people who need right doctrine.[115] These are individuals who have lost their moral sense—and who are revelling therein.

While the implications of 'early Catholic' assumptions for 2 Pet. 1.5-7 may not be as readily apparent as for the epistle as a whole, the focus on doctrine that inheres in an 'early Catholic' reading of 2 Peter has the consequence of eclipsing the paraenetic character of the epistle, and thus, causing the material in 2 Peter 1 to refract somewhat differently. The stress on ethics in ch. 1, rather than being understood in the light of its paraenetic function—namely, an exhortation to recall what

115. Thus the verdict of Fornberg needs some modification when he writes: 'While Jude focuses his anger on Christians practicing immorality the author of 2 Peter had rather to face doctrinal problems. Time and time again he emphasizes eschatology' (p. 59). First, while Jude is concerned to address moral impurity, the vocabulary of 2 Peter is overwhelmingly aimed at moral depravity. Secondly, in its constitution paraenesis is moral exhortation, not doctrinal adjustment. Nothing in 2 Pet. 1 and 2 hints at doctrine, with the notable exception of the reference in 2.1 to ψευδοδιδάσκαλοι, which, we have argued, is not intended to be a technical description. Consistent with the paraenetic tradition, the moral paradigms of 2.4-10a are meant merely to concretize in practical terms what the readers already know. Thirdly, eschatology only surfaces in ch. 3, where it serves to underscore the *fact* of a moral day of reckoning, not a doctrinal framework of chronology per se.

the audience already knows—is consequently interpreted as a post-apostolic 'performance ethic of Hellenistic athleticism',[116] that is, an ethic of asceticism, whereby obedience is no longer predicated on the resurrection power of Christ. Thus, the 'righteousness of God', mentioned in the epistle's greeting (1.1), is only perfunctory and not intended to convey the theological center of the gospel as understood earlier by the apostolic church. Writes Siegfried Schulz: 'In the place of an obedience that is the fruit of a faith born of God, a *new morality* and dualistically motivated ethic—indeed, a new law—has emerged'.[117]

Fresh exegetical approaches to 2 Peter should be welcomed not for the sake of novelty itself but rather because of what they may offer. From a sociological standpoint, 2 Peter contains elements that bear striking resemblance to the social world of first-century Hellenism. At the same time, the theological perspective of 2 Peter shows affinities with the apocalyptic tradition. And the literary character of the epistle places it within the Christian paraenetic tradition while incorporating Hellenistic categories into the overall argument.[118] Competing for primacy among exegetes would appear to be two distinct exegetical trajectories with two contrasting sets of presuppositions: (a) a post-apostolic, 'early Catholic' approach to 2 Peter that envisages turn-of-the-century protognostic or second-century Gnostic heresy being countered with creedal dogma by an increasingly institutionalized church; and (b) a mid- to late- first-century Gentile setting in which the Christian community receives strong moral exhortation in line with the Christian paraenetic tradition. While the former is largely assumed as the starting-point for exegesis of 2 Peter, textual evidence that takes into account sociological, theological and literary-rhetorical components does not commend this interpretive framework to the degree that has long been supposed by critical scholarship. Whether or not the latter trajectory can be sustained as a plausible exegetical alternative will depend in part on social markers—and thus, literary strategies—that are discernible from the text of 2 Peter itself.

---

116. Thus Käsemann, 'Apologia', p. 144, and Schulz, *Mitte*, p. 303.

117. Schulz, *Mitte*, p. 304 (emphasis mine).

118. These elements form the basis of Wall's insightful study as applied to the epistle of James ('James', pp. 11-22).

Chapter 2

LITERARY STRATEGY IN 2 PETER

2 Peter and Social Location

The publication in 1977 of Tord Fornberg's *An Early Church in a Plu-ralistic Society*[1] was significant, inasmuch as it challenged the exegetical starting-point of traditional commentary on 2 Peter. Fornberg's *modus operandi* is to reconstruct the social location of the epistle's readership by paying attention to the numerous social indicators lodged within the text. For example, drawn together in corroboration are the catalog of virtues in 1.5-7, the opponents' promise of freedom in 2.19, and the observation in 3.15-16 that some were distorting Paul. Fornberg's conclusion is that the readers are immersed in a pervasively pagan social environment—perhaps Asia Minor, though Syria and Rome are also a possibility. Given the formidable obstacles to the faith that this first-century cultural climate produces, the community is in need of a pro-phetic reminder that (a) faith without ethical fiber is no real faith at all, and (b) a return to the moral depravity that characterized the former life in the world is catastrophic. Hence, far from being an anthro-pomorphic eschatology by which ethics are relegated to mere reward and retribution,[2] 2 Peter exhibits a conscious literary strategy empha-sizing the virtuous life that is devised to address the urgency of the pastoral situation. This strategy is prompted by ethical lapse in the community—tragically, to the point of apostasy and hardened moral skepticism on the part of some (2.15-16, 20-22; 3.3-5, 17). The final exhortation in 2 Peter is to 'be on guard so that you are not carried away by the error of lawless individuals and fall from your secure position' (3.17).

1. T. Fornberg, *An Early Church in a Pluralistic Society: A Study of 2 Peter* (ConBNT, 9; Lund: Gleerup, 1977).
2. Thus Käsemann, 'Apologia', pp. 181-85.

Following the publication of Fornberg's study, J.H. Neyrey, in a fascinating essay,[3] also dared to question the operating assumptions of the 'early Catholic' hypothesis. Responding to Käsemann's criticisms that parts of 2 Peter were disconnected and 'embarrassing',[4] Neyrey contended that these criticisms were misplaced because Käsemann's analysis 'did not attempt to understand 2 Peter in its proper historical context'.[5] By presenting fresh comparative materials dating roughly contemporary with emergent Christianity, Neyrey's work also contributes toward furnishing a new starting-point by which to reassess the argument of 2 Peter.

Given the standard depiction of the opponents in 2 Peter,[6] namely that the writer is seeking to counter Gnostic heretics, Neyrey's approach is a welcome change. Neyrey furnishes parallels between 2 Peter and Plutarch's *De Sera Numinis Vindicta*, which is purported to mirror an Epicurean polemic against divine providence with its denial of afterlife, and by extension, divine judgment.[7] The polemic consists of four component parts: cosmology, freedom, unfulfilled prophecy and injustice.[8] The value of this tractate, in Neyrey's view, is that, while Plutarch's apologetic cannot be considered as *exclusively* Epicurean, it does represent a commonly employed polemic against theodicy.

There is much in Neyrey's reconstruction to commend. The four pillars of Plutarchian apologetic fit naturally into the schema of 2 Peter without causing the reader to become overly speculative. For example, 'freedom' is promised by Peter's opponents—a freedom that is nothing short of a new slavery (2.19). Moreover, contained within the

---

3. J.H. Neyrey, 'The Form and Background of the Polemic in 2 Peter', *JBL* 99.3 (1980), pp. 407-31.

4. Käsemann, 'Apologia', pp. 194-95.

5. Neyrey, 'Form', p. 407.

6. K. Berger ('Streit um Gottes Vorsehung. Zur Position der Gegner im 2. Petrusbrief', in J.W. van Henten *et al.* [eds.], *Tradition and Re-Interpretation in Jewish and Early Christian Literature* [Leiden: Brill, 1986], p. 121) rightly notes the often stereotypical and superficial attempts by commentators to characterize the opponents. In the end, however, his own solution diverges little from the position he has painstakingly scrutinized. The adversaries in 2 Peter, Berger concludes, exhibit a strongly Jewish-Christian cast (p. 134).

7. On the Epicurean denial of providence, see also more recently J.H. Neyrey, *2 Peter, Jude: A New Translation with Introduction and Commentary* (AB, 37c; New York: Doubleday, 1993), pp. 230-31, 239.

8. Neyrey, 'Form', p. 409.

apologetic that unfolds in ch. 3 is a caricature of the moral skeptic who denies a universe with moral accountability built into it. If 2 Peter 3, as Plutarch's *De Sera*, contains an apologetic response designed to counter strains of Epicurean worldview that have been adopted by some in the community, it is the assumption of freedom from moral accountability that the writer wishes to depose. The skeptic should *not* be so 'free' from worry, and this ἀταραξία must be disturbed at all costs. Christian theism cuts to the heart of Epicurean detachment from a moral universe:

ἀφοβῶν ὁ θεὸς
    ἀνύποπτων ὁ θάνατος
καὶ ταγαθῶν μὲν εὐκη τῶν
    το δὲ δεινὸν εὐεκκαρτερήτων[9]

The skeptics' trademark is their mocking query, 'Where is the promise of his coming?. . . Everything continues just as it always has from the beginning!' (3.3-4).[10] In response to this, both flood and fire typology are marshalled. In addition, 2 Peter 3 contains the nagging question that lies at the heart of theodicy (what Neyrey refers to as 'unfulfilled prophecy'): Where is God in all this? What of divine justice? (3.8-10).[11]

    Three other more recent essays deserve mention, two of these in particular further moving the discussion of ethics and eschatology in 2 Peter in a helpful direction by calling attention to additional apologetic parallels from pagan literature involving cosmology. R. Riesner[12]

9. Philodemus, *Pap. Herc.* 1005.4.19.
10. In Philo (*De prov.* 126-28) we find parallels—particularly, mockery and denial—being countered with apocalyptic eschatology.
11. Where our reading of 2 Pet. 3 diverges from that of Neyrey's reconstruction is reflected in his (a) exegesis of 3.9 (pp. 414-15, 423-27) and (b) failure to detect and interact with the λόγος-speculation of 3.5, 7 as, for example, J. Klinger ('The Second Epistle of Peter: An Essay in Understanding', *SVTQ* 17 [1973], pp. 152-69) has done. Regarding 3.9, Neyrey interprets βραδύνει κύριος τῆς ἐπαγγελίας, 'The Lord is not slow concerning his promise', to be the language of the opponents, that is, words that are intended to be a slur. In light of what immediately precedes in v. 8, however, these words would appear to be addressed to the 'beloved'. Not the opponents but *the faithful* are in view—that is, those who are wrestling with the problem of God's longsuffering in a fallen world. The pastoral need to address misconceptions about divine forebearance (3.8-9), strictly speaking, concerns theodicy, not eschatology.
12. R. Riesner, 'Der zweite Petrus-Brief und die Eschatologie', in G. Maier (ed.), *Zukünftserwartung in biblischer Sicht: Beiträge zur Eschatologie* (Wuppertal: Brockhaus, 1984), pp. 124-43.

compares the description in 2 Peter 3 of cosmic conflagration with the Stoic doctrine of ἐκπύρωσις (cf. 2 Pet. 3.10-12). A fundamental difference in worldview is apparent: there is a radical discontinuity between Judeo-Christian understanding of the cosmos and its Stoic counterpart, even when the former is depicted in Stoic categories. Strongly suggested by Riesner's comparison is a pervasively Hellenistic environment in which the readership finds itself.[13] Hence the writer is conscious to construct a corresponding literary strategy. Employing a similar trajectory, C.P. Thiede supplies further evidence from both pagan literature and the early fathers to suggest that on display in 2 Peter is argumentation which mirrors contemporary pagan-Christian philosophical debates over cosmology and cosmic conflagration.[14] E. Loevestam[15] also concerns himself with the eschatological question in 2 Peter. Noted by Loevestam is the Jewish model of flood-typology as an apologetic response in ch. 3. Parallels from intertestamental literature, the Synoptics, Jude and rabbinic literature are cited. What is missing from Loevestam's otherwise helpful treatment of eschatology and ethics is a discussion of the literary, social and theological distinctives that set 2 Peter apart from Jude. What is the ethical reason behind the polemic of 2 Peter that can be adduced from the combined weight of the letter's textual evidence? What social-cultural milieu can be discerned about the readership?

A main premise of most commentary on 2 Peter is that doctrine—specifically, false doctrine—represents the chief burden of the writer.[16]

---

13. It is quite significant, as C.P. Thiede ('A Pagan Reader of 2 Peter: Cosmic Conflagration in 2 Peter 3 and the *OCTAVIUS* of Minucius Felix', *JSNT* 26 [1986], p. 91 n. 4) has pointed out, that Riesner, a German, is suggesting a date for 2 Peter which might possibly fall within Peter's lifetime.

14. With Bauckham, Green and Loevestam (see n. 15), we would agree that while the argumentation in 2 Peter is dressed in conspicuously Hellenistic garb, a notable strand of Jewish-Christian apocalyptic runs throughout. This can be observed in the letter's prophetic typology (2.4-10a), description of the apostate (2.10b-18), emphasis on prophets and prophecy (1.19-21; 2.1, 15-16), denunciation of false prophets and false teachers (2.1), angelology (2.4, 10b-11), use of the thief metaphor (3.10), and eschatological perspective regarding the day of judgment (3.5-7, 10, 12).

15. E. Loevestam, 'Eschatologie und Tradition im 2. Petrusbrief', in W.C. Weinrich (ed.), *The New Testament Age: Essays in Honor of B. Reicke* (2 vols.; Macon, GA: Mercer University Press, 1984), II, pp. 287-300.

16. W. Micheälis (*Einleitung in das Neue Testament* [Bern: Buchhandlung der Evangelischen Gesellschaft, 3rd edn, 1961], p. 290) is one of the few to maintain

The material in 2 Peter 3 has been thought especially to support this argument. Accordingly, the opponents are said to have promulgated an eschatological viewpoint that must rationalize the 'embarrassment'[17] of a Parousia that is delayed. While it is true that the writer includes in his closing exhortation a reminder of the certainty of the Parousia, the rhetorical function of this allusion serves an ethical and not doctrinal purpose. The issue at hand is scoffing on the part of those who are patently self-indulgent (3.3-6). On display is an infectious moral skepticism that expresses itself in the form of denial (3.4; cf. 2.1-2). This denial is foremost *ethical*: moral relativists are pursuing licentiousness and openly denying truth (2.2). Astonishingly, some have returned to the moral squalor associated with the former life. The writer's purpose, stated in 1.12-15 and reflected in 2 Peter 3 through the use of reiteration (vv. 1-2), caricature (vv. 2-6) and warning (vv. 11 and 17), is not to proffer a particular eschatological viewpoint, but rather to stereotype the moral skeptic ('scoffers will come, scoffing and indulging..., saying', vv. 3-4) and to remind his readers that the *fact* of the destruction of the godless is certain beyond question ('They deliberately ignore... Now do not be ignorant of this one fact... For the day of the Lord will come'). The language of moral exhortation, so prominent in ch. 1, resurfaces in ch. 3: 'I am arousing you by way of reminder' (v. 1); 'what sort of people should you be?' (v. 11); 'therefore... make every effort' (v. 14); 'therefore, beloved, since you are forewarned, beware' (v. 17).

Thus, the verdict of Fornberg, despite the many important caveats he raises regarding traditional commentary, needs some modification. Fornberg writes: 'While Jude focuses his anger on Christians practicing immorality the author of 2 Peter had rather to face doctrinal problems. Time and time again he emphasizes eschatology'.[18] First, while Jude is concerned to address moral impurity, the vocabulary of 2 Peter is *overwhelmingly* aimed at moral depravity.[19] Secondly, in its constitution paraenesis is moral exhortation, not doctrinal adjustment. Little in 2 Peter 1 and 2 hints at doctrine, with the notable exception of the reference in 2.1 to ψευδοδιδάσκαλοι, which, I have argued, is not

---

that eschatology is not the central theme of the epistle, even when he dates 2 Peter well removed from the apostolic era.

17. Thus Käsemann, 'Apologia', p. 170.
18. Fornberg, *Early Church*, p. 59.
19. See Chapter 3.

intended to be a technical description. The moral paradigms of 2.4-
10a, consistent with the paraenetic tradition, are meant merely to concretize in practical terms what the readers already know.[20] Thirdly,
eschatology only surfaces in ch. 3, where it serves to underscore the
fact of a moral day of reckoning, not a doctrinal framework of chronology per se.[21]

Therefore, based on a unified reading of the material in all three
chapters, it would appear that ethics, not doctrine, is the cause of fomen-
tation within the community. What the aforementioned arguments—
particularly those of Riesner and Neyrey—have in common and what
they contribute to the exegetical enterprise through much needed
emphasis is that on some level moral accountability and divine judgment
are being rejected. That the root of the problem is foremost ethical
rather than doctrinal emerges from the caricatures of the apostate and
the moral sceptic in chs. 2 and 3. The material in 2.4-9 and 3.3-7 is
intended to strengthen the overall ethical argument. The trademark of
moral skepticism is its 'denial'—denial of God as δεσπότης (2.1), the
highest (moral) authority, and denial of any notion of retribution and
moral accountability ('Where is the promise of his coming?... All
things continue as they always have!', 3.4).[22]

2 *Peter and Testamental Genre*

Attempts to consider literary strategy through identifying markers in
the readers' social location requires interaction with the hypothesis put
forward by numerous exegetes[23] but argued perhaps most persuasively

20. See the section 'Paraenesis in 2 Peter' in Chapter 1.
21. See the section 'The Virtuous Life: Tracing a Petrine Theme' in Chapter 3.
22. I am not contending that Stoics are the object of the writer's polemic. Apos-
tates and moral reprobates are in view; however, the writer is using conventional—
that is, frequently Stoic—categories in his polemical response.
23. Among them, J. Chaine, *Les épîtres catholiques* (Paris: Etudes Bibliques,
1939), p. 31; R. Leconte, *Les épîtres catholiques de Saint Jacques, Saint Jude, et
Saint Pierre* (Paris: Cerf, 1953), p. 96; B. Reicke, *The Epistles of James, Peter,
and Jude* (AB; New York: Doubleday, 1964), p. 146; C.H. Talbert, 'II Peter and
the Delay of the Parousia', *VC* 20 (1966), p. 140; J.N.D. Kelly, *A Commentary on
the Epistles of Peter and Jude* (BNTC; London: A. & C. Black, 1969), p. 311;
O. Knoch, 'Das Vermächtnis des Petrus: Der 2. Petrusbrief', in H. Feld and J. Nolte
(eds.), *Wort Gottes in der Zeit: Festschrift K.H. Schelkle* (Düsseldorf: Patmos-
Verlag, 1973), pp. 149-65; W. Grundmann, *Der Brief des Judas und der zweite*

by Richard Bauckham. Bauckham maintains that 2 Peter is 'fictionally represented as written shortly before Peter's death. . . and therefore in Rome' using the literary convention of a last will or testament.[24] While our interest for the purposes of the present investigation lies less with dating and the phenomenon of pseudepigraphy than with literary strategy and the compositional unity of the letter, we nonetheless encounter fundamental assumptions about the text of 2 Peter that have an important bearing on the historical situation behind the letter.

In his commentary on 2 Peter, Michael Green summarizes the issues raised by Bauckham perhaps most clearly and consequently deserves to be cited at length. Bauckham

> believes that the literary genre to which 2 Peter belongs made it perfectly evident to the first readers that it was a pseudegraph. Accordingly, no possible question of morality arises. 2 Peter is both a letter and also an example of the type of work we meet in the *Testaments of the Twelve Patriarchs*. That is to say, it sets out the supposed message of the deceased Peter to meet the exigencies of a late-first-century situation where antinomianism was present, heresy was rife and the parousia was mocked. The author's aim was to defend apostolic Christianity in a subapostolic situation, and this he does, not by having recourse to his own authority, but by faithfully mirroring apostolic teaching which he adapts and interprets for his own day. 'Peter's testament' formed the ideal literary vehicle for his plans. Not only did the Testament genre have a long and honoured history in Judaism both within and outside the Old Testament; not only do the main contents of 2 Peter (ethical admonitions and revelations of the future) precisely correspond to those found in most Testaments; but everyone knew these were pseudepigraphs. It went without saying that the same held good of 2 Peter. Nobody ever imagined it came from Peter himself. The literary convention of the Testament was too well known. Such is the theory.[25]

Several passages in the epistle are for Bauckham proof that 2 Peter is to be read according to the testamental genre: 1.3-11, which is said to follow the pattern of the farewell speech of Ezra in *4 Ezra* 14.28-36;

Brief des Petrus (THKNT, 15; Berlin: Evangelische Verlagsanstalt, 1974), p. 55; D.F. Watson, *Invention, Arrangement, and Style: Rhetorical Criticism of Jude and 2 Peter* (SBLDS, 104; Atlanta: Scholars, 1988), pp. 96-97.

24. Bauckham, *Jude, 2 Peter*, pp. 131-35, 158-62; also *idem*, 'Pseudo-Apostolic Letters', *JBL* 107 (1988), pp. 469-94. On Jewish testamental literature, see A.B. Kolenkow, 'The Genre Testament and Forecasts of the Future in the Hellenistic Jewish Milieu', *JSJ* 6 (1975), pp. 57-71.

25. M. Green, *2 Peter and Jude* (TNTC, 18; Leicester, InterVarsity Press; Grand Rapids: Eerdmans, repr. 1989), pp. 34-35.

1.12-15, which contains the typical language of farewell speeches and explicitly states the occasion of the letter (approaching death); and 2.1-3a and 3.1-4, where it is said that future events are forecast.[26] Bauckham writes:

> Second Peter bears so many marks of the testament genre. . . that readers familiar with the genre must have expected it to be fictional. . . [I]n the case of 2 Peter, the presumption that Petrine authorship is fictional is decisively reinforced for us. . . the Petrine authorship was intended to be an entirely *transparent* fiction.[27]

Because 'the testamental function of the farewell speech in no way proceeds from the [apostolic] witness and guarantor of [apostolic] tradition himself',[28] the genre of the farewell speech is understood to reveal an attempt by later generations to 'guarantee' the apostolic tradition faithfully. The *Sitz im Leben* of the farewell speech is identified by J. Munck:

> We can say that it is heresy which is being mirrored in the testament genre. The absence of the apostles marks the coming of the Antichrist. The abandoned church has encountered afflictions that are much more severe now than when the apostle Paul was present.[29]

What clearly emerges is the broad assumption by critical scholarship that these 'functionaries',[30] that is the authors of pseudepigraphal testaments who are chronologically removed from the apostles, nevertheless take a necessary place alongside the prophets and apostles (Eph. 2.20) in guarding and transmitting the apostolic tradition to the sub-apostolic church.

But such verdicts are open to challenge. How can it be so confidently asserted that 2 Peter was 'intended to be entirely transparent fiction'? That pseudonymous 'functionaries' are 'guaranteeing the faithful tranmission of the apostolic tradition'? While a thorough discussion of pseudepigraphy must proceed in another context, the testamental

26. Bauckham, *Jude, 2 Peter*, pp. 132-34.
27. Bauckham, *Jude, 2 Peter*, p. 134 (emphasis his).
28. Thus O. Knoch, *Die 'Testamente' des Petrus und Paulus: Die Sicherung der apostolischen Überlieferung in der spätapostolischen Zeit* (SBB, 62; Stuttgart: KBW, 1973), p. 28.
29. 'Discours d'adieu dans le Nouveau Testament et dans la littérature biblique', in *Aux sources de la tradition chrétienne* (Festschrift M. Goguel; Paris: Neuchâtel, 1950), p. 164 (my translation).
30. This is Knoch's choice of words (*Die 'Testamente'*, p. 31).

thesis, capably represented by Bauckham, requires some discussion by virtue of the weight of biblical scholarship's commitment to this hypothesis. To state the heart of the matter bluntly, as Michael Green has done, Bauckham adduces evidence for the existence of a phenomenon in Christian literature that, according to Donald Guthrie, never even existed.[31] In the end, the views of Guthrie and Bauckham would appear mutually exclusive; together they confront us with the knotty problem of assumptions.

While the question of the variety of pseudepigrapha and the motives of those who produced them have been amply treated elsewhere,[32] discussions frequently fall short of satisfying answers to the questions posed by Bruce Metzger:

> From an ethical point of view, is a pseudepigraphon compatible with honesty and candor, whether by ancient or modern moral standards? From a psychological point of view, how should one estimate an author who impersonates an ancient worthy. . . ? Should we take him seriously, and,

31. D. Guthrie, 'The Development of the Idea of Canonical Pseudepigrapha in New Testament Criticism', in R.P. Martin (ed.), *Vox Evangelica I* (London: Tyndale, 1962), pp. 43-59.

32. See F. Törm, *Die Psychologie der Pseudonymität im Hinblick auf die Literatur des Urchristentums* (Gütersloh: Bertelsmann, 1932); A. Meyer, 'Religiöse Pseudepigraphie als ethisch-psychologisches Problem', *ZNW* 35 (1936), pp. 262-79; J.A. Sint, *Pseudonymität im Altertum: Ihre Formen und ihre Gründe* (Innsbruck: Universitätsverlag, 1960); W. Speyer, 'Religiöse Pseudonymität und literarische Fälschung im Altertum', *JAC* 8.9 (1965–66), pp. 88-125; *idem, Die literarische Fälschung im heidnischen und christlichen Altertum: Ein Versuch ihrer Deutung* (HAW, 1/2; Munich: Beck, 1971); B.M. Metzger, 'Literary Forgeries and Canonical Pseudepigrapha', *JBL* 91 (1972), pp. 3-23; M. Rist, 'Pseudepigraphy and the Early Christians', in D.E. Aune (ed.), *Studies in New Testament and Early Christian Literature: Essays in Honor of A.P. Wikgren* (NovTSup, 33; Leiden: Brill, 1972), pp. 75-91; M. Smith, 'Pseudepigraphy in Israelite Literary Tradition', in K. von Fritz (ed.), *Pseudepigrapha I* (Geneva: Revedin, 1972), pp. 191-215; N. Brox, *Falsche Verfasserangaben: Zur Erklärung der frühchristlichen Pseudepigraphie* (Stuttgart: KBW, 1975); *idem* (ed.), *Pseudepigraphie in der heidnischen und jüdisch-christlichen Antike* (Darmstadt: Wissenschaftliche Buchgesellschaft, 1977); D.G. Meade, *Pseudonymity and Canon: An Investigation into the Relationship of Authorship and Authority in Jewish and Earliest Christian Tradition* (WUNT, 39: Tübingen: Mohr, 1986), pp. 55-66; and E.E. Ellis, 'Pseudonymity and Canonicity of New Testament Documents', in M.J. Wilkins and T. Paige (eds.), *Worship, Theology and Ministry in the Early Church: Essays in Honor of R.P. Martin* (JSNTSup, 87; Sheffield: JSOT Press, 1992), pp. 212-24.

if we do, how does this bear on the question of his sanity? From a theological point of view, should a work that involves a fraud, whether pious
or not, be regarded as incompatible with the character of a message from
God?[33]

In addition, one of the broader methodological problems associated
with the testamental hypothesis—indeed, with any justification for New
Testament pseudepigraphy—is the open-ended and rather hopeless task
of reconciling the 'fictive' with the real occasion. While more recent
attempts at reconciliation by Knoch, Neyrey[34] and Bauckham—following a long line of New Testament scholars—are impressive, in the
end they remain speculation. In fact, as David Meade has correctly
observed, if indeed pseudonymity exists within the New Testament,
then it is a 'double pseudonymity'; that is, it is a pseudonymity of both
author and audience.[35] The question of authenticity is crucial, insofar
as it bears on (even when it is distinct from) the matter of 2 Peter's
literary unity.[36] The question of literary unity, taken up in the following chapter, in turn raises important questions regarding the plausibility of the testamental hypothesis. The problems associated with
testamental pseudepigraphy are not easily dispelled, since both the identity of the author and the social location of the audience are reflected
in the text of the epistle itself.

What is not clear from Bauckham's reconstruction is (a) how one
may flatly assume (as Bauckham does) that the readers in fact 'expected'
2 Peter to be fictional; (b) why the church historically has not understood 2 Peter to be fictional, and thus, pseudepigraphal; and (c) whether
Bauckham has indeed not made more of 1.12-15 than might be warranted by the text itself. We may agree with Bauckham and others that
these verses allude to the prophecy of Peter's death that was spoken of
by Jesus (Jn 21.18-19). That we may rule out the possibility of these
verses being self-referential[37] and autobiographical, however, does not

33. Metzger, 'Literary Forgeries', p. 4.
34. J.H. Neyrey, 'The Apologetic Use of the Transfiguration in 2 Peter 1.16-21',
CBQ 42 (1980), pp. 504-19.
35. Meade, *Pseudonymity and Canon*, p. 127.
36. For a survey of past attempts to explain (or refute) the unity of material in 2
Peter, see M. McNamara, 'The Unity of 2 Peter: A Reconsideration', *Scr* 12 (1960),
pp. 13-19 (14-16).
37. It is legitimate to note at the very outset a difficulty that mainstream biblical
scholarship has not satisfactorily met head-on. If the epistle is pseudepigraphal, the

automatically proceed from the text; rather, this is a qualification that one must accept in order that 2 Peter comport with 'testamental' literature. That 2 Peter is 'transparent' testamental pseudepigraphy, as Bauckham maintains, is open to serious question.

While the pseudepigraphal testament or 'valedictory' address typically contains notice of one's imminent death, paraenesis, eschatological predictions mediated through dreams or visions, an historical review, a transfer of authority, and blessings or curses, it does not follow (as most assume) that 2 Peter is therefore pseudepigraphal. Alone the examples of the farewell address in the New Testament[38] (for example, Lk. 22.24-30, Jn 13–17) would seem to prohibit this conclusion. Absent from 2 Peter are apocalyptic dreams and visions and the element of blessings/curses, both of which are a salient features of standard testamental genre. The stamp of the epistle, by contrast, is decidedly and explicitly *prophetic*—καὶ ἔχομεν βεβαιότερον[39] τον προφητικὸν λόγον[40] (1.19a)—rather than apocalyptic, given the defining features of Jewish-Christian apocalyptic literature. Also absent from 2 Peter is the transfer of authority, which William Kurz describes as the 'primary function' of the biblical farewell address 'to describe and promote transition from original religious leaders... to their successors'[41] (for example, Lk. 22.28-32, cf. Deut. 34.1-4). 2 Peter, additionally, begins with substantial didactic material, which tends not to be a part of pseudepigraphal farewell speeches. Finally and significantly, the allusion in 2 Peter to the writer's death (1.14) is not immediate, neither is it prominent; rather, it is injected only parenthetically *after* the substantial paraenetic and didactic portions of the letter—and this only in a veiled manner. The special appeal of the farewell address, it should be remembered, is the relationship of the audience to the one standing before death (for example, Jn 13–17).

writer would have been more likely to use the signature in 1 Peter, given the wider acceptance of 1 Peter. Bauckham concedes that no other pseudo-Petrine work uses Συμεών and concludes only by stating: 'It is unlikely that Peter himself wrote the letter' (*Jude, 2 Peter*, p. 167).

38. See W.S. Kurz, *Farewell Addresses in the New Testament* (Collegeville, MN: Liturgical Press, 1990).

39. Cf. the use of βέβαιος in 1.10.

40. Against Fornberg (*Early Church*, p. 82), who sees in the expression ὁ προφητικὸς λόγος an actual saying of Scripture, we would interpret this as an allusion to prophetically inspired speech in general.

41. Kurz, *Farewell Addresses*, p. 50.

Rather than incorporating apocalyptic dreams and visions, which are the stuff of pseudepigraphal testaments, 2 Peter contains a bit of historical reminiscence that, contextually, is strategically placed between the writer's statement of purposes (1.12-15) and explanation of prophetic inspiration (1.19-21). The transfiguration account (1.16-18), which differs from the Synoptic version and consequently is generally viewed as evidence of the epistle being inauthentic, is designed to confirm the writer's apostolic authority: καὶ ἔχομεν βεβαιότερον τὸν προφητικὸν λόγον (1.19a). The reminiscence serves two purposes. First, it establishes a thematic link to the παρουσία in chapter 3.[42] It is a foreshadow not only for the apostles but for all believers of 'the power and coming of our Lord Jesus' (1.16; cf. 3.4, 8-10).

Secondly, and more immediately, it testifies to the writer's own authority, given the urgency of the community's present need. The writer's presence on the holy mountain is not some 'cleverly devised[43] myth' for the purpose of deceiving others; rather, it is the apostolic imprint that is left behind for the sake of the church: 'we were eye-witnesses (ἐπόπται) of his majesty... and this voice *we* heard (ἡμεῖς ἠκούσαμεν)'.[44] The three witnesses on the mountain were allowed to see the manner in which God the Father bestowed on the Son his very own δόξα, 'the majestic glory' (ἡ μεγαλοπρεπὴ δόξα). These three are unique among humans in that they consequently possessed privileged insight into the unique relationship between the Father and the Son. Accordingly, they are in a unique position to understand the significance of apostolicity and prophetic inspiration. From the transfiguration experience, the three would learn of the glory and exaltation of the Son, the reality of which was meant to transform both them and the church which they would shepherd.[45]

The two visitors on the mountain, moreover, who represent the old covenant—Moses and Elijah—were considered the greatest of the prophets. In the transfiguration context, they embody in the fullest sense prophetic inspiration and authority. That the account in 2 Pet. 1.16-18

42. Fornberg, *Early Church*, pp. 80-81.
43. The word used here, σοφίζω, can be used both positively and negatively. In 1.16 it carries the negative sense—'to mislead', 'to deceive' or 'craftily devise' (BAGD, p. 760). N. Hillyer (*1 and 2 Peter, Jude* [NIBC 16; Peabody: Hendrickson, 1992], p. 177) cites its usage as a slur applied to the claims of quack doctors.
44. Cf. Dan. 10.5-12.
45. Cf. 1 Pet. 5.1.

differs from the Synoptic version can be understood in light of the writer's redactive interests. In the Synoptics, Peter's humanity is attested over and over again. For example, on the mountain his initial response is to erect three booths as memorials rather than fall down and worship. The allusion to the transfiguration in 2 Peter, by contrast, is intended to have the *opposite* effect, that is, convey moral author- ity—*unmediated* moral authority—for the purpose of addressing criti- cal problems in the Christian community.[46]

Any discussion of the *theology* of canonical over against non-canoni- cal writings remains outside the scope of the present study. Neverthe- less, fully apart from matters of theology and substance that set the New Testament writings apart from pseudepigrapha, our reticence to group 2 Peter uncritically with apocalyptic testaments is further sustained by a comparison of the epistolary and testamental greeting. Consider the introductions to several exemplary testaments:

> A copy of the testament of Reuben: the things which he commanded to his sons before he died in the one hundred twenty-fifth year of his life. . . And he said to them, 'My children, behold I am dying, and I am going the way of my fathers. . . Raise me up so that I can tell my brothers and my children the things that I have hidden in my heart, for behold I am depart- ing from you now.'[47]

> Now on the day when, having fallen ill, he began to settle his affairs, he called his seven sons and three daughters. . . And when he had called his children he said, 'Gather around, my children. . . so that I may show you the things which the Lord did with me and all the things which have hap- pened to me'.[48]

> Abraham lived the measure of his life, 995 years. All the years of his life he lived in quietness, gentleness, and righteousness. . . But even to him came the common and inexorable bitter cup of death and the unforeseen end of life. Therefore the Master God called his archangel Michael and

---

46. It goes without saying that the two differing sets of assumptions that lead to two diverse exegetical conclusions regarding 1.16-18 mirror differing starting points. If 2 Peter is a pseudepigraphon, these verses are an unprecedented literary move by the author to bridge the generational gap separating him from the apostles. If, on the other hand, 2 Peter is genuine, these verses can be understood as an authoritative response to the cancer of apostasy and moral lapse in the community (in which case the presentation of apostolic 'credentials' is not unseemly).

47. *T. Reub.* 1.1-5 (which is the introduction to the pseudepigraphal *Testaments of the Twelve Patriarchs*).

48. *T. Job* 1.1-4.

said to him, 'Commander-in-Chief Michael, go down to Abraham and tell him about his death, so that he may arrange for the disposition of his possessions'.[49]

In addition to our doubts that 2 Peter can be confined merely to the genre testament, neither can we assume with Fornberg that the epistle was 'written when the church became aware of the distance to the first Christian generation, and therefore wished to hold fast to the leading personalities of the first generation in order to solve problems of her own time'.[50] This is an assumption that originates outside of the text and is not required of the text itself. Even when Fornberg correctly points out that 'early Catholicism' is 'an artificial category which cannot do justice to a document such as 2 Peter',[51] the solution that he proposes is not sufficiently free of the underlying 'early Catholic' assumptions of which he is critical.

At this juncture, Paul's 'valedictory' speech to the elders of the church at Ephesus (Acts 20.17-37) may serve to illustrate that a farewell speech may adopt characteristics of a 'last will' or 'testament' genre without being restricted to pseudepigraphal genre. Paul's farewell contains paraenesis, a brief review of his ministry and a prediction concerning the future. It does not, however, contain a prediction of—nor even the faintest allusion to—his death, the forecast of imprisonment and persecution notwithstanding. And the farewell contains no blessings or curses. There is no warrant for considering Luke's account to be inauthentic.[52] Similarly, Jesus' farewell discourse, whether according to the Lukan[53] or Johannine account,[54] illustrates that the use of the farewell speech or testament was somewhat elastic and not confined merely to the genre of apocalyptic pseudepigrapha.

The alternative to speculative attempts at reconciling the 'fictive' and the real occasion of 2 Peter is to opt for a plain reading of the text in 1.13-14. It is not at all unreasonable to conclude as D. Guthrie:

49. *T. Abr.* 1.1-5.
50. Fornberg, *Early Church*, pp. 10-11.
51. Fornberg, *Early Church*, pp. 4-5.
52. For an analysis of Paul's farewell address in Acts 20, see Kurz, *Farewell Addresses*, pp. 33-51.
53. Lk. 22.14-38.
54. Jn 13–17.

It did not require much foresight for an old man to suggest that his end
was not far away. Moreover, a pseudepigraphist writing this would not
appear to add anything to the information contained in the canonical sources,
in spite of writing after the event.[55]

This reading of the text does not depend on whether ταχινή, appearing in 1.14 and reoccurring in 2.1, carries the inflection of 'soon' or
'swift'. The latter, quite naturally, lends plausibility to the notion that
1.14 refers to the *manner* of the apostle's death, which is the main point
of Jesus prediction recorded in Jn 21.18.

Additional evidence supporting Guthrie's claim that 1.13-14 is authentic is Bigg's contention that there is scarcely one stylistically
exemplary sample from antiquity of qualified testamental writing to
which one might point.[56] One still awaits evidence to the contrary. At
the very least, this absence in the literature, coupled with the aforementioned difficulties associated with reconciling 2 Peter to apocalyp
tic testamental literature, places the testamental hypothesis on shaky
ground. Moreover, it should be emphasized, as Earle Ellis[57] has done,
that early Christian writers knew how to transmit the teachings of an
authority figure without engaging in pseudepigraphy. When the Gospel
of Mark begins 'The beginning of the Gospel of Jesus Christ' and the
book of Acts employs a third person narrative style, no one is being
deceived. The writer of 2 Peter, however, if the epistle is a pseudepigraphon, clearly shows evidence of a deceptive intention:

We did not follow cleverly devised myths. . . but we had been eyewitnesses of his majesty (1.16).

We ourselves heard this voice coming from heaven, while we were with
him on the holy mountain (1.18).

Beloved, this is now the second letter I am writing to you. . . (3.1).

. . . just as our beloved brother Paul also wrote to you. . . (3.15).

Can particular ancient writings that were produced in the name of an
honored figure be compared to the apostolic writings of the New Testament? Is it legitimate to classify both types of documents together?

---

55. D. Guthrie, *New Testament Introduction* (Leicester: Apollos; Downers Grove:
InterVarsity Press, 4th edn, 1990), p. 821.

56. C. Bigg, *A Critical and Exegetical Commentary on the Epistles of St Peter
and St Jude* (ICC; New York: Charles Scribner's Sons, 1922), p. 233.

57. Ellis, 'Pseudonymity and Canonicity', p. 220.

Writes Ellis:

> In Paul's usage the term ἀπόστολοι may be used of persons com-
> missioned and sent out by the churches (e.g. 2 Cor. 8.23). But where it is
> qualified as 'apostle of Jesus Christ', it means a direct commission from
> (the risen) Jesus. In all likelihood the term. . . thereby presupposes their
> personal acquaintance with Jesus.[58]

That the documents of the New Testament resist our attempts to be clas-
sified with non-apostolic pseudepigrapha is by no means an arbitrary
ecclesiastical verdict. Rather, it brings us to the heart of the *a priori*
of Christian faith and the authority upon which this faith rests. The
Christian community from the beginning has recognized that the New
Testament documents are be bound up with revelation that is imparted
within history. In precisely what does this authority initially consist?

One cannot speak of the New Testament as authoritative apart from
the concept of apostolicity and the apostolic tradition (cf. 1 Cor. 15.3-
7). Apostles are authoritative inasmuch as they (a) stand in direct relation to Jesus, and thus, are his deputized representatives, and (b) constitute the foundation of the church. Both elements appear to be wed in
the apostolic affirmation: 'You are Peter, and on this rock I will build
my church' (Mt. 16.18).[59] This promise is not made to Peter in the
abstract but in view of his confession (vv. 16-17) and as he, with that
confession, represents the other apostles (the apostolate). The rock
foundation of the church is to be confessing Peter as *primus inter
pares*, first among apostolic equals.[60] In light of Christ's once-for-all
redemptive act, there can be 'no other foundation' (1 Cor. 3.11), as
Paul seeks to enunciate in a discussion of apostolic qualifications.[61]

How aware of this authoritative foundation were the writers of the
New Testament? The apostolic fathers? Modern critical consensus
suggests that this awareness of the church's apostolic foundation had
limited bearing on the church's literary canon. Yet the function of the

58. E.E. Ellis, *Prophecy and Hermeneutic in Early Christianity* (WUNT, 18;
Tübingen: Mohr-Siebeck, 1978), pp. 105-106.
59. On the authenticity of the declaration in Mt. 16.13-20, see S.E. Porter, 'Did
Jesus Ever Teach in Greek?', *TynBul* 44.2 (1993), pp. 229-35.
60. So R.B. Gaffin, Jr, 'The New Testament as Canon', in H.M. Conn (ed.),
Inerrancy and Hermeneutic: A Tradition, A Challenge, A Debate (Grand Rapids:
Baker, 1988), p. 174.
61. Hence a defense of apostolicity such as one finds in 1 Cor. 3–4 and 2 Cor. 11.

apostolate was in fact a *dynamic* model of authority—one that secured
the church *in every era.*

> Apostolic witness, then, is not merely personal testimony. Instead, it is
> infallibly authoritative, legally binding deposition, the kind that stands up
> in a law court. Accordingly, that witness embodies a canonical principle; it
> provides the matrix for a new canon, the emergence of a new body of rev-
> elation to stand alongside the covenantal revelation of the Old Testament.[62]

The implications of the apostolic office are weighty. In their application to the possibility of pseudonymity in the New Testament, they
suggest that, strictly speaking, 'apostolic pseudepigrapha' is a contra-
diction in terms, since not even well-intended literary motives, expressed under the name of an apostle, warrant apostolic authority.
Given the role of the apostle in the early church,

> scholars cannot have it both ways. They cannot identify apostolic letters
> as pseudepigrapha and at the same time declare them to be innocent prod-
> ucts with a right to a place in the canon.[63]

However, that an epistle such as 2 Peter might come from the apostle
in the historical setting illuminated from within is not to say *how* it
might come from him. At some point the question must be addressed
as to whether 2 Peter suggests (or even allows for the remote possibility of) some sort of scribal help via an amanuensis. As applied to historical-critical arguments concerning the New Testament writers' style,
E.I. Robson's admonition deserves repeating: 'We must come to allow
a good deal more to the amanuensis than we have done hitherto'.[64]

---

62. Gaffin, 'The New Testament', p. 176. Thus, H. von Campenhausen's suggestion that apostolicity was not a central issue in determining the canonicity of a
document is predicated on several statements by the fathers that could be interpeted in
different ways, while it simultaneously fails to interact with the witness of the New
Testament itself (*The Formation of the Christian Bible* [Philadelphia: Fortress Press,
1972], pp. 254-61). A similar approach to assessing pseudepigraphy in the New
Testament is found in M. Kiley, *Colossians as Pseudepigraphy* (Sheffield: JSOT
Press, 1986), pp. 17-23. Rist's sweeping conclusion—'There is little evidence that
the early Christians were sensitive to the ethical implications of pseudepigraphy, a
literary deception'—casts the early church in a rather undiscerning light: 'The early
Christians, whether "orthodox" or "heretical", used pseudepigraphy frequently and for
the most part unashamedly in order to promote their special views and doctrines'
('Pseudepigraphy', pp. 90-91).

63. Ellis, 'Pseudonymity and Canonicity', p. 224.

64. E.I. Robson, 'Composition and Dictation in New Testament Books', *JTS* 18
(1917), p. 296.

Cicero, frequently at the end but occasionally in the middle of his letters, offers explanations for writing with his own hand or dictating.[65] He might dictate, for example, when walking[66] or when dining.[67] Similarly, the apostle Paul shows evidence of both practices in his letter-writing: his epistles are stated to have been written with his own hand as well as dictated. Based on the evidence in the New Testament, there would appear to exist (on occasion) a need—and thus, a precedent—for an amanuensis. Writes G.J. Bahr:

> The influence of the secretary would be even greater if he were left to compose the letter himself along general lines laid down by the author. The result would be that the letter might represent the basic thought of the author, but not necessarily his terminology or style. . . It may be that the discrepancy between what Paul wrote and what he spoke was due to the abilities of a secretary who was expert in the composition of letters.[68]

It is, thus, not at all unreasonable to attempt to account for purported 'inconsistencies' between 2 Peter and the 'authentic Petrine tradition' when evidence for such a precedent in the New Testament is present:

> I, Tertius, the one writing this letter, greet you in the Lord (Rom. 16.22).

> I, Paul, write this greeting with my own hand (1 Cor. 16.21).

> See what large letters I make when I am writing in my own hand (Gal. 6.11).

> I, Paul, write this greeting with my own hand (Col. 4.18a).

---

65. E.g., *Fam.* 3.6; *Ad Quint. frat.* 3.3; *Ad Att.* 7.13; 8.12; 13.9,25; 14.21; 16.15. Exploring the possible uses for dictation both by New Testament writers and their literary contemporaries are F.R.M. Hitchcock, 'The Use of *graphein*', *JTS* 31 (1930), pp. 271-75, and G.J. Bahr, 'Paul and Letter Writing in the First Century', *CBQ* 28 (1966), pp. 465-77.

66. *Att.* 2.23.

67. *Att.* 14.21.

68. Bahr, 'Paul and Letter Writing', pp. 475-76. In a similar vein, Robson writes: 'when an ancient writer wanted to write, his one anxiety seems to have been how he could best avoid writing; and the convenience of the slave-amanuensis enabled him so to avoid it, by allowing him to declaim, talk, even babble garrulously, at will, hardly feeling that he was making any special literary effort.' Given the secretary's freedom to insert a salutation or postscript, do his own revising of material or add stylistic and literary artifice, Robson cautions that we must allow a good deal more room for the work of an amanuensis in the New Testament epistles than we have been accustomed to allow ('Composition and Dictation', p. 296).

I, Paul, write this greeting with my own hand. This is the mark in every letter of mine; it is the way I write (2 Thess. 3.17).

Luke alone is with me. Get Mark and bring him with you, for he is useful to me in ministry (2 Tim. 4.11).

I, Paul, am writing this with my own hand (Phlm. 19a).

Through Silvanus, whom I consider a faithful brother, I have written this short letter. . . (1 Pet. 5.12a).

For Jerome, the difference in style and expression between 1 and 2 Peter could be accounted for on the basis of different amanuenses.[69] In Bauckham's view, the language alone 'makes it improbable that the apostle could have written 2 Peter'.[70] Taken together, testamental language and presuppositions about dating 'must be regarded as *entirely conclusive* against Petrine authorship'.[71] Bauckham does allow for the possibility of a secretary, but only in a qualified sense: 'the secretary is not Peter's amanuensis but his agent'.[72] The notion of a Petrine 'agent' over against an amanuensis per se put forward by Bauckham is most tantalizing. Unhappily, this distinction is not developed, nor is the rationale for why the possibility of an amanuensis writing during Peter's lifetime might be categorically ruled out.[73]

69. *Ep. Hed.* 120.9: *duae epistolae quae feruntur Petri stilo inter se et charactere discrepant structuraque uerborum. Ex quo intelligimus pro necessitate rerum diuersis eum usum interpretibus.*

70. Bauckham, *Jude, 2 Peter*, p. 159. But gathering proofs against authenticity based on a statistical analysis of vocabulary is of limited value, since the brevity of the document in the end restricts our use of the data.

71. Bauckham, *Jude, 2 Peter*, p. 159 (emphasis mine). Elsewhere Bauckham asserts that 'there is little material in 2 Peter which could plausibly be regarded as specifically Petrine tradition deriving from the historical Peter' (p. 160), notwithstanding the evidence adduced by Guthrie (*Introduction*, pp. 820-42) and M. Green (*2 Peter Reconsidered* [London: Tyndale, 1961]; *2 Peter and Jude*, pp. 13-39).

72. Bauckham, *Jude, 2 Peter*, p. 159.

73. Bauckham, *Jude, 2 Peter*, p. 159. The protracted treatment by Guthrie (*Introduction*, pp. 805-38) of external evidence in support of 2 Peter's authenticity has not been satisfactorily challenged by proponents of pseudonymity theory. That not only pseudo-Petrine literature but also works of Hermas, Clement and Barnabas were ultimately rejected while 2 Peter was accepted as canonical speaks highly in favor of its authenticity and not against it. Indeed, a satisfactory challenge to both Guthrie (*Introduction*) and Green (presented initially in *2 Peter Reconsidered* and later in *2 Peter and Jude*) as to the full weight of external and internal evidence regarding authenticity has not been forthcoming.

Can this Petrine 'agent' possibly have been a disciple of the apostle? Bauckham is equally convinced of its improbability:

> In view of the lack of specifically Petrine material, he can hardly have been a disciple of Peter who had learned his theology from Peter (and this is even less possible if 1 Peter, from which 2 Peter differs so completely, be thought to embody Peter's teaching to any degree)... But if such a group [a 'Petrine circle' of Christian leaders in Rome] does account for 1 Peter, it could hardly have included the author of 2 Peter, who *in no sense* belongs to the same theological 'school' as the author of 1 Peter.[74]

There is, then, purportedly little material in 2 Peter which could 'plausibly be regarded as specifically Petrine tradition deriving from the historical Peter'.[75]

> Insofar as the summary of Peter's message in 1.3-11 is a summary of common primitive Christian teaching, it is attributable to Peter as much as to any apostle, but insofar as there is anything distinctive about it, notably the Hellenistic terminology, it *must* be regarded as our author's interpretation of the apostolic message in terms of (post-Petrine) Roman theology.[76]

It is difficult to ignore the certitude—indeed, the incontestability—of mainstream critical assumptions, expressed eloquently by Bauckham, that 'Petrine authorship was intended to be an entirely *transparent* fiction'. Indeed, anyone challenging this reigning view of authorship in 2 Peter is held to be something of an obscurantist.[77] That elements regarding 2 Peter's authenticity unduly tax modern sensibilities, resulting in categorical foreclosure of the debate, can be seen in our responses—for example, 'must be regarded as entirely conclusive', 'must be regarded as post-Petrine', 'is in no sense theologically Petrine'. D.G. Meade's monograph, *Pseudonymity and Canon*, which takes up a review of scholarship on the subject, is less a discussion of differing views of canon and pseudonymity than a restating and reaffirming of what historical-critical scholarship has required of the guild. That there

74. Bauckham, *Jude, 2 Peter*, pp. 160-61 (emphasis mine).
75. Bauckham, *Jude, 2 Peter*, p. 160. Although we are left to speculate at this point, the possibility that Peter used different amanuenses cannot be ruled out and may account for the stylistic and lexical differences between 1 and 2 Peter. Bahr ('Paul and Letter Writing', pp. 465-77) observes that Cicero employed different amanuenses, depending on his purpose for writing.
76. Bauckham, *Jude, 2 Peter*, p. 160 (emphasis mine).
77. Foreclosure of the debate, it should be said candidly, has less to do with 'scholarship' per se than with fundamental assumptions about divine revelation.

is negligible room for debate is made clear in his assessment of 2 Peter as well:

> The arguments against authenticity are *overwhelming* . . . 2 Peter demon-
> strates an *unquestionably post-Petrine Sitz im Leben* . . . In face of the
> *preponderance* of arguments against authenticity, it is only with *heroic*
> (*and ingenious*) *tenacity* that a few retain their defence of the Petrine
> tradition.[78]

Meade's chief criticism of (the 'tenacious' and 'ingenuous') Donald Guthrie and Michael Green in their assessment of 2 Peter is that their 'presuppositions are based more on a theological *a priori* than on historical facts'.[79] But is it not legitimate to suggest that (a) the 'historical facts' have been inalterably established by 'early Catholic' theological commitments and (b) the 'early Catholic' view of 2 Peter has made the very *a priori* theological commitments that Meade criticizes?

The general lack of discussion and healthy debate regarding 2 Peter, however, does not constitute the only enigma. Equally puzzling are our attempts to justify noble motives for the presence of pseudepigraphy in 2 Peter:

> The pseudepigraphal device is therefore not a fraudulent means of claim-
> ing apostolic authority, but embodies a claim to be a faithful mediator of
> the apostolic message. Recognizing the canonicity of 2 Peter means rec-
> ognizing the validity of that claim, and it is not clear that this is so alien to
> the early church's criteria of canonicity as it is sometimes alleged.[80]

But the dilemma of why the church would sanction the use of pseudepigraphy in the service of advancing Christian orthodoxy does not evaporate quite as readily as critical scholarship might contend. Its difficulties—and they are many—must be addressed head-on. Our dilemma is particularly vexing, even if we confine ourselves to Pauline paraenesis alone:

> Therefore, let us celebrate. . . with the unleavened bread of sincerity and
> truth (1 Cor. 5.8).

> In every matter you have proved yourselves to be guileless (2 Cor.
> 7.11c).

78. Meade, *Pseudonymity and Canon*, pp. 179-80 (emphasis mine).
79. Meade, *Pseudonymity and Canon*, p. 180.
80. Bauckham, *Jude, 2 Peter*, pp. 161-62. This is Bauckham's response to Green's objection that pseudepigraphy, regardless of the motives behind its practice in antiquity, does not square ethically with the ethical norms laid down by New Testament teaching itself (*Reconsidered*, pp. 34-36; *2 Peter and Jude*, pp. 31-39).

For we cannot do anything against the truth, but only for the truth (2 Cor. 13.8).

Speak the truth in love (Eph. 4.15).

Therefore, put away falsehood and speak the truth to one another (Eph. 4.25).

For the fruit of the light is found in all that is good and right and true (Eph. 5.9).

Do not deceive [ψεύδομαι] one another (Col. 3.9).

We beg of you, brethren,. . . not to be quickly shaken or alarmed, whether by spirit or by word or by letter, as if it were sent from us (2 Thess. 2.1-2).

For this I was appointed a herald and an apostle—I am speaking the truth and do not deceive [ψεύδομαι]—a teacher of the Gentiles in faith and truth (1 Tim. 2.7).

. . . in order that you may know what conduct befits the church of the living God, which is the pillar and bulwark of the truth (1 Tim. 3.15).[81]

The ethical texture of the New Testament, even when confined to Pauline literature, strongly suggests against pseudonymous practice. Orthodoxy, which is to say, right belief, verifies itself in orthopraxy; the two are not divisible. Orthopraxy, moreover, will manifest itself in every domain of life, and for the Christian disciple there is reason to believe that this may even affect the use of literary conventions. Authenticity[82] for the Christian, however, is not so much a philological concern of literary form as it is an issue of faith and life, whereby the truth of Christian revelation is preserved. There is a distinction between imitating literary convention for the sake of rhetorical effect and appropriating apostolic pedigree and eye-witness experience for the sake of authority that is missing.[83] Within the designation 'Christian

---

81. Paul's remark in Phil. 1.18 ('What does it matter but that Christ is preached in every way, whether out of false or true motives') cannot be legitimately adduced to sanction pseudonymity. The context, which has to do with preaching done out of rivalry and envy over against goodwill (1.15), militates against such a conclusion.

82. That apostles and prophets constitute the foundation of the household of faith (Eph. 2.20; 3.5) suggests historical proximity and continuity with the cornerstone himself, Jesus Christ. Out of this unique, once-for-all historical relationship issues authenticity, which is revelatory in nature.

83. On this ethical distinction, see J.S. Candlish, 'On the Moral Character of Pseudonymous Books', *Expos* 4.4 (1891), pp. 91-107, 262-79, and R.D. Shaw,

fiction' that 2 Peter is said to contain lodges something of a contra-diction in terms.[84] Thus, authenticity appears to lie at the very heart of the Christian's calling.[85]

Authenticity, moreover, is important in accordance with the need to preserve Christian orthodox teaching. Christian 'orthodoxy' does not inhere merely in assuming the *name* of a man of authority,[86] as the corpus of pseudo-Petrine literature makes quite clear.[87] Historical proximity, the essence of apostolicity, lies at the heart of the issue. For this reason the 'household of God' is 'built upon the foundation of the apostles and prophets' (Eph. 2.20)—a foundation that no one else can lay (1 Cor. 3.10-15).

Truthfulness, in the view of the New Testament writer, is in accor-dance with godliness (Tit. 1.1); it is the distinctly Christian ethical 'way' (2 Pet. 2.2). The writer in 1 John, whose burden is to charac-terize what is 'true', writes categorically that 'no falsehood can come from the truth' (1 Jn 2.21), regardless of how well intentioned it may be. Significantly, 1 Timothy concludes with a final exhortation to pro-tect the apostolic message: 'Avoid... contradictions of what is pseu-donymously called knowledge' (1 Tim. 6.20).

While a survey of historical-critical views on 2 Peter has been pro-vided by Donald Guthrie[88] and need not be recounted, one pattern can be seen to stand out. The underlying presupposition of pseudonymity theory—whether formulated by nineteenth- or twentieth-century pro-ponents and whatever its justification—would appear to be the principle

---

'Pseudonymity and Interpretation', in *The Pauline Epistles: Introduction and Expos-itory Outlines* (Edinburgh: T. & T. Clark, 1903), pp. 477-86.

84. Notwithstanding Moffatt's explanation of the use of pseudonymity, said to issue out of modesty of a follower toward the master's name (J. Moffatt, *Intro-duction to the Literature of the New Testament* [New York: Charles Scribner's Sons, 1911], p. 41-43). The view of Moffatt assumes a literary outlook of Hellenistic writers apart from the revelatory—and thus, distinctly Christian—component.

85. Rev. 22.18-19 reflects, at the very least, a concern for literary falsification or modification of the revelatory text.

86. Contra H.R. Balz, 'Anonymität und Pseudonymität im Urchristentum', *ZTK* 66 (1969), p. 436, and others.

87. That someone in the sub-apostolic era 'stands in the apostolic tradition' does not convey apostolic authority, contra A. Meyer ('Religiöse Pseudepigraphie als ethisch-psychologisches Problem', *ZNW* 35 [1935], p. 278). Following the apostolic era, which is a unique historical moment, the Holy Spirit collectivizes inspiration.

88. Guthrie, 'Development', pp. 43-59.

that the end justifies the means. Thus understood, because a work was ultimately accepted as canonical by the church, pseudonymity may be accepted without justification. Accordingly, the 'authority' that the writer possesses—whether he is a member of a 'Petrine school', a Petrine 'agent' or an individual several generations removed from the apostle—inheres in the fact that he is 'faithfully interpreting' or 'actualizing anew' the apostolic tradition. Yet the notion that orthodox Christians would have resorted to practices used by Gnostic or protognostic writers and the church would have sanctioned this practice strains credibility. Difficulties with this view are not minor, especially given the fact that none of the purported pseudonymous writings in the New Testament bear close resemblance to Jewish or pseudo-Christian pseudepigrapha.

Adding to the complexity of the genre question is the matter of Jewish and Hellenistic attitudes toward literary pseudepigraphy.[89] Those who view pseudonymity as part of the nature of the New Testament customarily point to the variety of its usage in ancient literature. Whereas the classical period of Greek literature was for the most part free from literary fraud and borrowing, the post-Aristotelian era, in the words of Alfred Gudeman, 'may be said to have made ample amends for this deficiency'.[90] Notably, it was in the area of *epistolary pseudepigraphy* that literary imitation reached its apex.[91] In Hellenistic Jewish circles, however, the only categeory of pseudonymity that does seem to have been acknowledged was that which involved no pretense or deception, that is, where no secrecy was made of a work's pseudepigraphal character, an example being the book of Wisdom, 'written by the friends of Solomon in his honor'. Roger Beckwith gently chides biblical scholarship because of the 'desperate hypotheses' that have been propounded by some writers to avoid drawing the conclusion that Jews and Christians did not reckon pseudepigraphy as an acceptable literary device.[92] It is precisely the concern for pseudonymity that would appear to

89. For contrast and interplay of ancient attitudes toward pseudonymity, see R. Beckwith, *The Old Testament Canon of the New Testament Church* (Grand Rapids: Eerdmans, 1985), pp. 345-54.

90. A. Gudeman, 'Literary Frauds among the Greeks', *Transactions and Proceedings of the American Philological Association* 25 (1894), p. 145.

91. Supplying commentary on the variety and the extent of the phenomenon is Gudeman, 'Literary Frauds', pp. 64-69.

92. Beckwith, *Old Testament Canon*, pp. 354, 414 n. 14.

underlie Paul's exhortation to the Thessalonians not to be shaken 'by a word or by a letter purporting to be from us' (2 Thess. 2.2). The implication is that others were not averse to using his pedigree. The resiliency of pseudonymity theory has prompted J.A.T. Robinson to remark that among biblical scholars 'there is an appetite for pseudonymity that grows by what it feeds on'.[93] In point of fact, some critical scholars, like K.M. Fischer,[94] end up attributing virtually the whole of the New Testament to pseudepigraphal practice.

In the end, it remains a mystery why critical scholarship, which almost universally rejects the authenticity of 2 Peter, considers it necessary to accept—and justify—the morality and authority of an unknown turn-of-the-century or second-century literary imitator, whether one accepts the testamental hypothesis or not. The pseudepigraphy label is all the more striking when a work makes a claim to prophetic authorship and prophetic authority (cf. 2 Pet. 1.16-18, 19-21). If 2 Peter is a pseudepigraphon, the morality of its writer stands all the more in question with his overly strained attempts at appropriating apostolic experience.[95] At the very least, the virtual complete absence of pseudepigraphal epistles in Jewish and Christian apocryphal literature is highly significant for discussions of New Testament pseudepigraphal hypotheses.[96]

93. J.A.T. Robinson, *Redating the New Testament* (London: SCM Press, 1976), p. 186.

94. K.M. Fischer, 'Anmerkungen zur Pseudepigraphie im Neuen Testament', *NTS* 23 (1976), pp. 76-81.

95. Similar points of identification are contained in the pseudepigraphal *Acts of Peter*; among these are witnessing the Transfiguration on the mountain along with the sons of Zebedee, a reference to Peter's denial, and lack of faith while walking on the water. M.R. James (*The Apocryphal New Testament* [Oxford: Clarendon Press, 1924], p. 476) holds the transparency of pseudepigraphy in the epistolary genre to be all too apparent:

> It does appear that the epistle was on the whole too serious an effort for the forger, more liable to detection, perhaps, as a fraud, and not so likely to gain the desired popularity as a narrative or an Apocalypse. Certain it is that our apocryphal epistles are few and not impressive.

Calvin, while alert to the stylistic questions raised by 2 Peter, views pseudepigraphy as inconsistent with the Christian calling and 'fiction unworthy of a minister of Christ' (J. Calvin, *Commentaries on the Catholic Epistles* [trans. J. Owen; Grand Rapids: Eerdmans, 1959], p. 363).

96. This question is taken up by Guthrie in 'Acts and Epistles in Apocryphal

The early fathers, by contrast, exhibit a more critical attitude toward assessing what constituted 'the apostolic tradition'. It is most clear from their writings that if a document were known to be of pseudepigraphal authorship, it would have been excluded from the list of accepted canonical books.[97] Although 2 Peter is the least well attested book in the New Testament,[98] its attestation far exceeds that of any of the non-canonical books.[99] Clement of Alexandria is said by Eusebius[100] to have offered commentary on all the 'Catholic' epistles. Origen[101] accepts it and quotes extensively from it, even when acknowledging that others have doubts.[102] He does so while simultaneously rejecting the pseudepigraphal *Doctrine of Peter*.[103] Eusebius classifies it with James, 2 and 3 John and Jude as ἀντιλεγόμενον, noting that most churches accept it as authentic.[104] He numbers the 'Catholic' epistles as seven.[105] By contrast, the *Apocalypse of Peter* and the *Gospel of Peter*, the history of the latter having been traced by Serapion, Bishop of Antioch (c. 180 CE), are deemed νόθος, and this *precisely on account of the fact that they falsely bear the name of an apostle*.[106]

Eusebius describes something of Serapion's attempts to bring to light what he considered to be heretical statements in the *Gospel of Peter*

Writings', in W.W. Gasque and R.P. Martin (eds.), *Apostolic History and the Gospel: Biblical and Historical Essays in Honour of F.F. Bruce* (Grand Rapids: Eerdmans, 1970), pp. 328-45.

97. Thus L.R. Donelson's remark: 'No one ever seems to have accepted a document as religiously and philosophically prescriptive which was known to be forged' (*Pseudepigraphy and Ethical Argument in the Pastoral Epistles* [HUT, 22; Tübingen: Mohr-Siebeck, 1986], p. 11).

98. The findings of R.E. Picirelli ('Allusions to 2 Peter in the Apostolic Fathers', *JSNT* 33 [1988], pp. 57-83), while not conclusive, would suggest knowledge of 2 Peter by the early fathers.

99. For the external evidence, see Mayor, *Jude and Second Peter*, pp. cxv-cxxiii; for a comparison of 2 Peter and the Apocalypse of Peter, pp. cxxx-cxxxiv.

100. *Hist. eccl.* 6.14.

101. *Hom. in Josh.* 7.1.

102. That others have doubts strengthens the case for authenticity. The early church was not uncritical, neither was it indifferent, toward literary imitation and forgery.

103. *De prin.* 8.

104. *Hist. eccl.* 3.3 (ἀντιλεγόμενον); also 6.25 (ἀμφιβαλλόμενον). In his evaluation of the external evidence, Kelly (*Commentary*, p. 224) does not note the acknowledgment of 2 Peter by others.

105. *Hist. eccl.* 2.23.

106. *Hist. eccl.* 6.12. This is in addition to doctrinal deviation.

for the benefit of some members of the church at Rhossus. Some of
these individuals, according to Eusebius, had 'succumbed to unorthodox
teaching', requiring the Bishop's intervention. Thus Serapion:

> For we, brethren, accept Peter and the other apostles as we would Christ,
> but, as experienced men, we repudiate what is falsely written under their
> name, knowing that we have not had any such things delivered to us. For
> I, when I was with you, supposed that all of you adhered to the right
> faith, and, not having gone through the Gospel which they produced
> under the name of Peter, I said: If this is all that seems to cause you scru-
> ples, let it be read. But now that I have learned from what has been told
> me, that somewhat of heresy was nesting in their mind [literally, 'their
> mind had its lair in a certain heresy'], I will take care to come to you again:
> so, brethren, expect me soon.[107]

Regarding the difference between 'spurious' and 'questioned' works,
Eusebius notes that the *Gospel of Peter*, *Acts of Peter*, *Apocalypse of
Peter* and *Doctrine of Peter* were not handed down among the 'Catholic' Scriptures.[108] Given the pseudo-Petrine literature in circulation in
the second century, this would reasonably explain why early patristic
evidence concerning 2 Peter is scant.

In addition to Cyril, Gregory Nazianzus and Athanasius, the councils
that rejected *Barnabas* and *1 Clement* accepted 2 Peter. Mayor's conclusion regarding the letter is this:

> I think that, if we had nothing else to go upon in deciding the question of
> the authenticity of 2 Peter except external evidence, we should be inclined to
> think that we had in these [patristic] quotations ground for considering that
> Eusebius was justified in his statement that our epistle πολλοῖς χρήσιμος
> φανεῖσα μετὰ τῶν ἄλλων ἐσπουδάσθη γραφῶν.[109]

With the growth of Christianity during the first century, pseudepigraphal apocalypses and prophecies were being produced both in Jewish
and pseudo-Christian circles. In the words of Beckwith:

> The penumbre of the Christian prophetic movement, therefore, would be
> almost bound to include certain people (whether originally Essenes,
> Pharisees, or of some other more mixed or obscure allegiance) who were in
> the secret about the way Jewish apocalyptic was produced, and who could
> think of no better service to the new faith than to adapt existing apocalypses

107. *Hist. eccl.* 6.12 (an English translation of which appears in James, *Apocryphal New Testament*, pp. 13-14).
108. *Hist. eccl.* 3.3.2.
109. Mayor, *Jude and Second Peter*, p. cxxiv.

to make them support Christianity. . . Moreover, Christians in general, belonging as they did to an apocalyptic movement, would have felt a natural interest in such Jewish apocalypses as had become public property. . . and if these seemed to contain passages favourable to Christianity, one might easily have found such passages being used as testimonies in Christian apologetics.[110]

Nevertheless, as far as we can tell, even the Apocrypha did not fulfill in Hellenistic Judaism an *authoritative* function in the strictest sense,[111] just as the fathers of the second and third centuries exercised extreme caution with works that gave the appearance of being pseudepigraphal.[112] It is simply insufficient, as Stanley Porter has cautioned, merely to cite the existence of non-canonical Jewish or Christian documents as proof of its existence in the New Testament.[113] With regard to the Pastoral Epistles, Porter writes:

The fact that these documents are non-canonical is apparently confirmation of the fact that documents that were found to be pseudonymous did not make it into the canon. If anything it might constitute a prima facie argument that the Pastoral Epistles should be considered authentic, since they are in the canon.[114]

110. Beckwith, *Old Testament Canon*, pp. 399-400.

111. Based on an awareness of the cessation of prophecy (cf. Lk. 11.49-51).

112. The disclaimer of K. Aland ('The Problem of Anonymity and Pseudonymity in Christian Literature of the First Two Centuries', in *idem* [ed.], *The Authorship and Integrity of the New Testament* [London: SPCK, 1965], p. 2) that ethical arguments are inappropriate to the debate over pseudepigraphy ('ethics is no proper category for our problem') is open to challenge. Metzger ('Literary Forgeries', pp. 13-14) has cautioned that pseudepigraphy even practiced with the best of motives is suspect. He asks: How can it be so confidently known that such writings would deceive no one? And if nobody was taken in by the pseudepigraphal device, why the need to adopt it in the first place? Indeed, that Christians, whose practice of honesty and truthfulness had to be above reproach, would have uncritically adopted a literary practice of questionable virtue is in fact highly doubtful. Pseudepigraphy in the service of orthodoxy encounters stiff resistance from the texture of Jesus' ethical teaching, not to mention that of Paul (cf. esp. 2 Thess. 2.2) and the rest of the New Testament. Demonstrating greater sensitivity to the ethical argument is T.D. Lea, 'Pseudonymity and the New Testament', in D.A. Black and D.S. Dockery (eds.), *New Testament Criticism and Interpretation* (Grand Rapids: Zondervan, 1991), pp. 535-59.

113. S.E. Porter, 'Pauline Authorship and the Pastoral Epistles: Implications for Canon', *BBR* 5 (1995), p. 115.

114. Porter, 'Pauline Authorship', pp. 115-16.

Though by no means articulated, the unspoken assumption frequently conveyed by modern critical scholarship is that the ancients were less critical and (necessarily) less discriminating as to the normative criteria by which 'inspired', 'sacred', and thus, 'canonical' status should be adjudicated. This assumption, however, would appear to lack substantiation.

In surveying the character of New Testament apocryphal writings such as the *Gospel of Thomas*, the *Acts of Paul* or the *Apocalypse of Peter*, one is led to conclude with Eusebius that they are 'far removed from apostolic usage', their content and thought-world being 'wholly discordant with true orthodoxy'.[115] For the church,

> the warning of Jesus against attributing too great authority to tradition (Mark 7.1-13) did much to preserve the unique position to the Scriptures over against other teaching, oral or written, although uncertainty in time developed over the question whether some of the Apocrypha and Pseudepigrapha were not Scriptures themselves. The Church was, of course, given its own authoritative interpretation of the Old Testament Scriptures by Jesus and the apostles, but since Christianity was a thorough-going prophetic movement, claiming a new outpouring of the Holy Spirit, withdrawn when prophecy ceased, the writings in which this interpretation was incorporated formed. . . a new body of Scriptures, which took its place alongside the old one.[116]

It is both the privilege and the responsibility of Christian exegetes and theologians, when treating matters of Christian tradition, to defer to that very tradition. The reason, obvious enough though ever in need of being restated, is that the exegete and the theologian represent a small part of that tradition and are not above it. Exegetical theology is not done in a cultural vacuum; rather, it mirrors particular assumptions of that era. Therefore, it is important that exegesis and theology be done within the context of and in subordination to the church's broader historical tradition.

The question of pseudonymity and testamental genre associated with the documents of the New Testament affords us a valuable test-case for this interaction with the classical Christian tradition. How has the

---

115. *Hist. eccl.* 3.3.25. The pseudepigraphal *Acts of Paul*, for example, constitutes an important witness to the church's attitude toward pseudepigraphy at a time when the New Testament canon was gaining increasing fixation (thus Guthrie, 'Acts and Epistles', pp. 328-45).

116. Beckwith, *Old Testament Canon*, p. 408.

church historically evaluated this issue?[117] The Holy Spirit, whose role is to guide the church in interpretive matters, has a history. This history, in spite of modern (and 'postmodern') hubris, is not confined to insights of the nineteenth and twentieth centuries, nor is it restricted to historicist or historical-critical contributions, useful and necessary as they may be. Insofar as the tendency of modern biblical scholarship has been to embrace the at times reductionist character of historicist models of interpretation, the exegete is challenged continually to glean from the fruits of other ages, particularly that of the apostolic fathers. For the modern scholar, whose approach to the biblical text presumes that it cannot contain the revealed word of God, literary justifications such as pseudonymity in the New Testament require little rationale. Thus, modern exegesis is needful of the counter-balance of patristic exegesis. This, of course, will entail a return to careful study of the classical Christian tradition, which itself has been undermined by cultural forces at war with the creedal tradition. This will furthermore require of us a willingness to listen to what the church has always believed. And what has the church historically believed concerning 2 Peter? It became the

117. While it is true, as A. Chester and R. Martin write, that the status of 2 Peter 'as part of the New Testament canon with normative value is both an ancient and a modern challenge' (*The Theology of the Letters of James, Peter, and Jude* [Cambridge; Cambridge University Press, 1994], p. 147), this challenge should not be overstated, which has been the tendency of critical scholarship. That the letter 'struggled to gain acceptance among the early canon-makers' (p. 147) needs a twofold qualification. First, it was precisely because of spurious Petrine documents in the second century that the early fathers entertained doubts. This critical discernment is to be expected and, in the end, weighs in favor of 2 Peter—if it is genuine—rather than raising doubts. It is simultaneously because of 2 Peter's theological orthodoxy—over against pseudo-Petrine writings—that patristic doubts were indeed overcome. Secondly, one's view of 2 Peter's 'normative value' is inextricably related to one's understanding of canon. If it is assumed that it was the responsibility of the church over time to 'make canon', then one is forced to accept the possibility that the church may have made a wrong decision—by excluding a document that belonged to canon or including a document that was not apostolic. But to acknowledge the difference between 'canon-making' and canon-recognizing is to acknowledge two differing views of canon. The one assumes that the church (more or less) arbitrarily adjudicated over a plurality of writings that could have remained included or excluded. The other view of canon is that, like the sacred Scriptures of the old covenant, a higher wisdom was guiding the whole processs—a wisdom that was manifest, humanly speaking, through apostolic authority and sub-apostolic consensus, and, divinely speaking, through the guidance of the Holy Spirit.

consensus of the church—a consensus that was abiding for roughly seventeen centuries to follow—that the epistle is authentically Petrine[118] and thus (a) stands in the prophetic tradition of the Old Testament, (b) was part of the Christian apostolic-prophetic tradition inspired by the Holy Spirit, and (c) was incorporated into the New Testament canon not as a mere appendix but as sacred Scripture on the basis of its apostolic-prophetic imprint.[119]

Ultimately, the only *a priori* argument against an apparently reasonable and—to the modern mind—inoffensive hypothesis such as testamental pseudepigraphy is the moral argument, as Guthrie, Green and Lea have suggested. Not only does the writer claim to be Peter (1.1), this claim is constantly and *overtly* implied (1.13-14, 16-18, 20-21; 2.1[?]; 3.15)—indeed, to a notable excess, if the work is in fact a pseudepigraphon. Perhaps in the practice of pseudepigraphy we only have to do, as Bauckham and others suggest, with a harmless bit of literary manipulation honorably undertaken and set in the service of Christian orthodoxy.[120] But in the final analysis it must be conceded that the evidence suggests otherwise—evidence that brings together the collective weight of Jewish attitudes toward prophetic inspiration and Old Testament canonicity, patristic attitudes toward pseudonymity and the apostolic tradition, and not least, the New Testament itself. As already

---

118. To maintain that 2 Peter ultimately comes from the apostle Peter is not to say *how* it comes from him. The answer to this question remains speculation and, therefore, beyond our accessibility. Calvin's assessment—and the Reformer was not uncritical regarding the matter of Petrine authorship—was that 'If 2 Peter be received as canonical, we must allow Peter to be the author', based on (a) the name attached and (b) the testimony of experience with Christ. Calvin did allow for a disciple of Peter to do the writing, though not one removed from the apostle himself (*Commentaries*, p. 363).

119. For a comprehensive bibliography of literature up to 1965 on ancient pseudepigraphy, see W. Speyer, 'Fälschung, literarische', *RAC*, VII, pp. 271-78. A more recent survey of the literature is found in Charles, *Literary Strategy*, pp. 81-90. For a recent attempt to justify the use of pseudepigraphy in the New Testament, see Meade's *Pseudonymity and Canon*.

120. It would seem that from the ethical contours of the Scriptures themselves, noble intentions are not sufficient warrant in and of themselves; this is to say, the end does not justify the means. Abraham sought to manipulate the fulfillment of God's promise; the fruits of his well-intended actions are ever with us yet today. Jacob was no stranger to deceit in the service of procuring familial blessing. The episode of Nadab and Abihu (Lev. 10.1-5) is perhaps the most graphic illustration of the insufficiency of good intentions: the sons of Aaron were consumed by the fire of the Lord.

observed, Paul's attitude toward its practice—and its possibility (2 Thess. 2.2; 3.17)—was less than bemusement. Indeed, the evidence *strongly* suggests, both among the New Testament writers and their literary contemporaries, that the practice was not condoned. Green summarizes this dilemma:

> It was into a church exercising this sort of discrimination that we are asked to believe 2 Peter was surreptitiously inserted. I find it very hard to believe. It is not as though we were plentifully supplied with examples of orthodox pseudepigrapha which were cheerfully accepted by the second-century church and later generations. After carefully examining the problem Guthrie feels obliged to say, 'There is no evidence in Christian literature for the idea of a conventional literary device, by which an author as a matter of literary custom, and with the full approbation of his circle of readers, publishes his own productions in another's name. There was always an ulterior motive.'[121]

A proper method of exegetical inquiry requires, before a writing is judged to be pseudepigraphal, that it must be examined within the context from which it professes to originate.[122] Historical-critical investigation of 2 Peter, with notable exceptions, has been reticent to undertake a study of the epistle based on this starting-point. The writer of 2 Peter makes conspicuously bold and authoritative claims—claims to apostleship and privileged apostolic eyewitness experience that cannot be so easily dismissed or attributed to 'transparent fiction', as Bauckham and others would maintain. In the end, the testamental hypothesis, which has been broadly accepted as an interpretive framework for understanding 2 Peter, may be judged to be possible—and this with certain highly restricted qualifications—but by no means conclusive,[123] in spite of arguments to the contrary.

---

121. Green, *2 Peter and Jude*, p. 34.

122. So Ellis, *Prophecy and Hermeneutic*, p. 235.

123. Thus the summary statement of purpose by Chester and Martin needs some modification: 'One of the surest conclusions as to why the letter was composed is based on the evidence of 1.13-15, according to which the writer viewed the approach of his death as a sign that he should leave his written testament for posterity' (*Theology*, p. 134). The evidence, as we have sought to demonstrate, points not foremost to a testament for posterity's sake, but rather to apostolic paraenesis that is urgently needed in a local situation. That the writer may stand before death adds to the urgency of the moment.

2 Peter and Jude: A Contrast in Social Location

It is customary for commentators to focus on the intriguing question of literary relationship between 2 Peter and Jude. Who was dependent on whom and what were the reasons? Which work has priority? Was a common source being used? Frequently missing, however, is an exploration of literary strategy, that is, taking into consideration the literary building-blocks representing authorial intent whereby the two writings are to be differentiated. While the provenance and destination of both letters allude any certainty, 2 Peter and Jude contain numerous textual indicators pointing to two concrete local situations in which a prophetic-pastoral word is urgently needed. Resisting the strong pull to investigate the epistles' similarities at this point, we shall instead probe several of their differences.

Jude is generally acknowledged to reflect a Palestinian Jewish-Christian milieu. Its relationship and indebtedness to a Jewish cultural matrix is much more pronounced than that of 2 Peter. As a sample of apocalyptic paraenesis, Jude manifests a strongly Semitic lexical and stylistic cast, an incomparably strong eschatological perspective, a notable lordship Christology, day of the Lord imagery, overwhelming dependence on Old Testament tradition, and borrowing of extracanonical tradition-material from sectarian Judaism.

Old Testament motifs that figure prominently in Jude are the ungodly–faithful antithesis with attendant cataloging of moral paradigms, the coupling of theophany and judgment, judgment-by-fire symbolism, an accent on divine foreknowledge and election, and divine glory.[124] The moral paradigms in Jude appear as prophetic types, several of which are listed in groups of three, and simultaneously admonish the faithful while condemning the faithless.

One fascinating stylistic element of the epistle of Jude is the writer's rampant use of triplets.[125] The validity of testimony in the Old Testament was confirmed by the mouth of two or three witnesses, thus establishing a matter (Num. 35.30; Deut. 17.6; 19.15). The same principle of μαρτυρία is affirmed in the New Testament as well (Mt. 18.16; Jn 5.31-33; 8.17-18; 2 Cor. 13.1; 1 Tim. 5.19; Heb. 10.28). Ultimate testimony to the truth is lodged within the very triune nature of the

124. Charles, *Literary Strategy*, pp. 30-162.
125. See Mayor, *Jude and Second Peter*, pp. lvi-lvii, and Charles, *Literary Strategy*, pp. 40-41, 124-25.

godhead itself. Diverse in their functions, the members of the godhead in essence are one, their witness fully agreeing. The unsurpassed use of triplets in Jude—all told, 20 sets of triplets appear within the letter's mere 25 verses[126]—serves both a literary and theological function. In a very Jewish and calculating way, Jude corroborates evidence by saturating his polemic with instances of threefold witness. This feature applies to (1) his presentation of prophetic types, (2) his explanation of those types, (3) epistolary features of his address, and (4) the grammatical-lexical particularities of his writing style. His testimony is valid, securely buttressed by the cords of multiple witnesses.

The combined effect of Jude's theological motifs, use of prophetic typology through moral paradigms, reliance on Old Testament and non-canonical Jewish tradition-material, and peculiar literary style is to define the contours of his readers' social location. For example, the spate of Old Testament characters that parade before the audience is striking, especially considering the brevity of the epistle. Even more conspicuous is Jude's nearly verbatim citation of *1 Enoch*. All of which suggests that his readers are not living in Rome or Asia Minor or Alexandria, but in Palestine, where haggadic traditions associated with Old Testament characters and events or the apocalyptic pseudepigraphal traditions ascribed to Enoch would have circulated. Jude thus adapts his literary strategy to the cultural as well as pastoral needs of his audience.[127] Enochic literature would have had minimal effect outside of Palestine, assuming that 2 Peter is addressed to the Christian community in a pervasively Gentile environment. Similarly, the use of triplets, pregnant with significance to the Jewish mind, would have had less effect on a Gentile convert to the faith.

In our consideration of continuity and discontinuity between Jude and 2 Peter, one moral paradigm almost evades our notice. The unusually brief description of the fallen angels presents us with a most intriguing—and in some respects, revealing—example of how social

---

126. See Charles, *Literary Strategy*, pp. 40-41, 124-25; *idem*, 'Literary Artifice in the Epistle of Jude', *ZNW* 82.1,2 (1991), pp. 122-23.

127. Various aspects of the writer's literary arsenal, which shed light on the historical setting, are examined in Charles, 'Literary Artifice', pp. 106-24; *idem*, '"Those" and "These": The Use of the Old Testament in the Epistle of Jude', *JSNT* 38 (1990), pp. 109-24; and *idem*, 'Jude's Use of Pseudepigraphal Source-Material as Part of a Literary Strategy', *NTS* 37 (1991), pp. 130-45.

location in 2 Peter and Jude differ. Noting the seemingly minor differences in wording between the two underscores the nuances of literary 'brick and mortar'.

Εἰ γὰρ ὁ θεὸς ἀγγέλων ἁμαρτησάντων οὐκ ἐφείσατο ἀλλὰ σειραῖς ζόφου ταρταρώσας παρέδωκεν εἰς κρίσιν τηρουμένους (2 Pet. 2.4).

ἀγγέλους τε τοὺς μὴ τηρήσαντας τὴν ἑαυτῶν ἀρχὴν ἀλλὰ ἀπολιπόντας τὸ ἴδιον οἰκητήριον εἰς κρίσιν μεγάλης ἡμέρας δεσμοῖς ἀϊδίοις ὑπὸ ζόφον τετήρηκεν (Jude 6).

Aside from 'the angel of the Lord', angels generally receive less prominence in the Old Testament before the Exile. The angelology of the intertestamental period, however, is markedly different. Significantly, neither the Old Testament nor the New Testament makes any explicit statements as to the fall of rebellious angels, although the latter strongly implies the notion of Satan as a fallen angel chief among many who was cast down.[128] Corresponding typology to the fallen angels of 2 Peter and Jude might be drawn from several somewhat cryptic prophetic oracles in the Old Testament—for example, Isa. 14.5-23, a taunt against the king of Babylon; Isa. 24.21-22, a symbolic representation of Yahweh's judgment; and Ezek. 28.1-19, a prophetic funeral dirge against the king of Tyre. What unites these three figures with the angels of 2 Peter and Jude is their status: they become stripped of their exalted rank.

While the idea of imprisoned spirits in the Old Testament is undefined, in Jewish apocalyptic literature it is pronounced,[129] along with the notion of an 'abyss'.[130] Within apocalyptic mythology, a frequent pattern tends to emerge: (1) war erupts in heaven, often depicted in astral terms (cf. Jude 13), followed by (2) a spilling over of this rebellion to earth, then culminating in (3) ultimate vindication and punishment by the king of heaven.[131]

---

128. Cf. Lk. 10.18; Jn 12.31; Rev. 12.4, 7, 9, 10. Moreover, the New Testament gives no clear indication of the time of the fall.

129. For example, *1 En.* 10.4, 12-14; 13.1; 18.14-16; 21.3, 6, 10; 67.4; 69.8; 88.1, 3; 90.23; *2 Apoc. Bar.* 56.13; *Jub.* 5.10; cf. also Jude 6; Rev. 18.2; 20.7.

130. For example, *1 En.* 10.4; 18.11; 21.7; 22.1-2; 54.4; 56.3; 88.1, 3; 90.24, 26; cf. also Rev. 20.3.

131. P.D. Hanson, 'Rebellion in Heaven, Azazel, and Euhemeristic Heroes in *1 Enoch* 6–11', *JBL* 96 (1977), p. 208.

Jude's allusion to the disenfranchised angels is best understood in light of contemporary apocalyptic notions of imprisoned spirits. Thus, the similarities between Jude and *1 Enoch* are not superficial, given the epistle's likely Palestinian setting. In the latter, we find graphic accounts of the 'Watchers' of heaven who abandon the high heaven and are bound in chains of darkness, awaiting the great day of judgment.[132]

The inner contours of Jewish thought and culture in tension with the Hellenistic *Zeitgeist* during the last three centuries BCE have been thoroughly traced by Martin Hengel.[133] The tendency toward assimilation noted by Hengel is to be found even among the most devoutly religious Jews.[134] Accordingly, there is much to be said for T.F. Glasson's thesis that the second-century BC apocalypticist may well have drawn from Greek titan mythology. Indeed, the presence of δεσμοί and ζόφος in Hesiod's *Theogony*, appearing in Jude 6 and 2 Pet. 2.4, constitutes for Glasson concrete evidence.[135] While the relation of Jewish to Greek mythology remains outside the scope of this examination,[136] several features stand out which distinguish the reference to the fallen angels in 2 Peter from Jude. One is the absence of the apocalyptic designation 'the great day';[137] only judgment (κρίσις) in the generic sense is mentioned. The expression 'the great day', if the recipients of the letter are predominantly Gentile Christians, would more than likely have been unknown and thus meaningless. In addition, the writer appears to show no interest in the speculative details associated with the 'Watchers' in Enochic literature. Furthermore, while no mention in Jude is made of the angels sinning, only that they are being 'kept', in 2 Peter, however, they are explicitly said to have sinned (ἁμαρτησάντων), that is, they desert their exalted position. Similarly, while the emphasis in Jude is on 'keeping' the angels (the verb τηρέω appears twice), in 2 Peter,

132. *1 En.* 10.4, 6, 12; 12.4; 15.3; 54.4; 84.4; 94.9; 98.10; 99.15; 104.5.

133. M. Hengel, *Judaism and Hellenism: Studies in their Encounter in Palestine during the Early Hellenistic Period* (2 vols.; trans. J. Bowden; Philadelphia; Fortress Press, 1974).

134. Hengel, *Judaism and Hellenism*, I, pp. 261-314.

135. T.F. Glasson, *Greek Influence in Jewish Eschatology* (London: SPCK, 1961), pp. 63-67.

136. Numerous commentators, both ancient and modern, associate the fallen angels of 2 Peter and Jude with Gen. 6.1-4 and the 'sons of God'. Elsewhere this linkage, which I believe to be mistaken, is examined at greater length (*Literary Strategy*, pp. 108-16, 206-207 n. 111).

137. Cf. Joel 2.31; *1 En.* 10.6; 22.4, 11; 54.6; *Jub.* 5.10; Rev. 6.17; 16.14.

by contrast, the angels are said to be 'not spared' (οὐκ φείδομαι). Each letter establishes contrast through word play—in Jude, the wicked and the righteous are 'kept', and in 2 Peter, respectively, they are 'not spared' and indeed 'spared'. While the allusions to the angelic world in both epistles are similar, the subtle nuances suggesting how the illustration functions are significant.

A final peculiarity is the vocabulary of consignment. Jude speaks of the angels as being reserved in chains of 'nether gloom' (ζόφος) in Hades, whereas in 2 Peter the angels are said to have been cast into Tartarus (ταρταρόω), that is, the Greek hell, in 'pits' (σιροί). Typically, the verb ταρταρόω occurs in connection with Greek titan mythology,[138] where Tartarus represents the place of punishment for the worst of the wicked. The appearance of σιροί in this context is also intriguing, given both its use as a technical term for underground storage and its association with Greek hell. Fornberg is correct to suggest that in 2 Peter the writer is sensitive to Greek mythological vocabulary.[139]

What might we conclude from these nuances? Are we engaged in mere gnat-straining, or do these distinctions together tell us about the two respective audiences? For our present purposes, the allusion to the fallen angels as a moral paradigm in 2 Peter is highly instructive. The writer combines an awareness of the readers' cultural-social location with pastoral sensitivities in a way that infuses his literary-rhetorical strategy.

Other contrasts in the two epistles are worthy of note. Pagan proverbs illustrate in 2 Peter the gravity of denying moral truth, whereas a citation from Jewish apocalyptic literature serves as the appropriate exemplar in Jude. Unlike Jude, 2 Peter does not plunge directly into condemnation; rather, the initial one-third of the epistle is given to moral exhortation, couched in paraenetic reminder terminology. In

138. Examples of which are listed by B. Pearson, 'A Reminiscence of Classical Myth at II Peter 2.4', *GRBS* 10 (1969), pp. 75-78.

139. Fornberg, *Early Church*, p. 52. Just as Jude employs conventional apocalyptic imagery for pastoral purposes without necessarily endorsing highly speculative apocalyptic-Jewish theology, the writer in 2 Peter is employing popular Greek mythological imagery without necessarily endorsing its substance. Social location and pastoral sensitivity combine to inform literary strategy. By way of illustration, see this writer's discussion of Jude's use of *1 Enoch* in Charles, *Literary Strategy*, pp. 153-71, a condensed version of which is found in Charles, 'Jude's Use of Pseudepigraphal Source-Material', pp. 134-37.

2 Peter, it is Noah's and Lot's 'righteousnesss' and the perseverance of the saints, culminating in the promise of divine rescue, that is the theological direction of the moral paradigms; in Jude, by contrast, the faithless depart and are categorically judged.[140] In 2 Peter, moreover, an important distinction is the expansion of the Balaam typology (without any reference to Cain or Korah), which serves a pronounced didactic function. Balaam was seduced by the heathen to work against Israel. He is a moral farling and to be considered 'dangerous' insofar as he leads others into apostasy. And in 2 Peter, the *human* face of moral development presses to the fore—a development that is described in consciously pagan (that is, Stoic) terms; Jude, in comparison, accentuates *God's* ability to 'keep' and 'guard' the saints from moral blemish and fall.

Thus, despite the obvious literary relationship existing between the two epistles, one encounters cumulative evidence of a unique social setting in both letters. This distinctiveness deserves our careful attention. Material is chosen and structured as literary 'brick and mortar' for the purpose of addressing the needs of the community in its given social context. The *mode* of the Christian message is indivisible from its *content*[141] and is informed by the unique pastoral needs in the community.[142]

140. Note the future tense of the verbs in 2 Pet. 2.1-3 ('There will be false teachers who will. . . who will. . . Many will. . .') as compared with the verbs in Jude, which are past tense ('certain persons infiltrated. . .'; 'they walked. . . they strayed. . . they perished. . .'). This suggests that 2 Peter is a warning, whereas Jude is a lament, the implications of which might point in the direction of a possible early dating for the former.

141. On the stylistic peculiarities of 2 Peter, see Mayor, *Jude and Second Peter*, pp. xxvi-lxvii. From a linguistic standpoint, the Greek of 2 Peter has been described as in accord with technical prose (L. Rydbeck, *Fachprosa, Vermeintliche Volks sprache und Neues Testament* [SGU, 5; Uppsala: Uppsala University, 1967], pp. 186-99), 'elegant', 'rhythmical', and, in the end, 'too sophisticated' to belong to the vernacular Koine (N. Turner, 'The Literary Character of New Testament Greek', *NTS* 20 [1974], p. 107). That 2 Peter has the highest percentage of *hapax legomena* in the New Testament (J. Chaine, *Les épîtres catholiques* [Paris: Gabalda, 2nd edn, 1939], p. 15) suggests that the writer is well-read, a literary master (Bauckham, *Jude, 2 Peter*, p. 136), and the architect of a well-calculated literary strategy. In his volume *Invention, Arrangement and Style: Rhetorical Criticism of Jude and 2 Peter* (SBLDS, 104; Atlanta: Scholars, 1988), D.F. Watson seeks to apply the canons of ancient rhetorical practice to these two New Testament documents. The strength of Watson's work is its premise that the writing of the New Testament did not occur in

In 2 Peter, as in Jude, theological truth is uniquely clothed in literary arguments of the day.[143] Whereas Jude exemplifies a conspicuously Palestinian Jewish-Christianity, 2 Peter mirrors with considerable force—and stylistic flare—the church's encounter with 'the strongly syncretistic and pluralistic environment of the decline of antiquity'.[144] Fornberg nicely summarizes the challenges of the cultural environment that, in turn, required a culturally relevant response on the part of the church:

> 2 Peter demonstrates a situation in which the Church is in the process of being grafted into a pluralistic and syncretistic society constituted by the Mediterranean world of late antiquity. The dependence on Judaism gradually declined. Instead a large proportion of the religious terminology of the Church was derived from her heathen environment, at the same time as the Christians were profoundly aware of being a 'third race', set apart from Jews and heathen. The Church faced, and had to answer, new questions, but preserved her uniqueness without being absorbed by syncretism.[145]

More specifically, being reflected in 2 Peter are the twin peaks of moral relativism—the void of which the Stoa sought to fill—and hardened skepticism regarding the possibility of moral accountability after death—a notion alien to Epicureans and most Stoics. Belief in the Olympian pantheon is no longer strong, the emperor cult is a foremost political phenomenon, and mystery religions—through whose initiation a sense of immortality is reaffirmed—seek to fill the spiritual vacuum.

a cultural vacuum. Its weakness is that it makes no attempt to tie literary-rhetorical, sociological and theological perspectives together for the sake of the interpretive enterprise.

142. Entirely plausible is Fornberg's view that 2 Peter derives from a situation in Asia Minor (*Early Church*, p. 125). Moreover, that 2 Peter contains no allusions to the civil authorities suggests that persecutions were not yet present or widespread, in which case an earlier rather than late dating for the epistle is plausible. This squares with the picture conveyed in the New Testament Apocalypse, which may be taken to mirror Domitian persecution of the saints taking place in the 90s.

143. Consider the adaptation of pagan literary sources elsewhere in the New Testament: Acts 17.28-29 (Epimenides, Aratus and resonances of Cleanthes), 1 Cor. 12 (the Esclepius cult), 1 Cor. 15.33 (Menander), Tit. 1.12 (Epimenides and Callimachus), Jas 1.22-25 (Plutarch and Epictetus), and possibly Jude 13a (the Aphrodite myth).

144. Fornberg, *Early Church*, p. 88. Parallels between the social environment being mirrored in 2 Peter and mid-first-century Corinth provide a useful comparison. Both are pluralistic, cosmopolitan, lacking in moral constraints and offering little or no evidence of a Jewish understanding of creation, faith, law or morality.

145. Fornberg, *Early Church*, p. 124.

2 Peter offers the reader glimpses into the moral world and philosoph-ical discourse of Greco-Roman paganism.[146] It is to this moral world that I now wish to turn.

---

146. Whereas Chester and Martin make note of '2 Peter's rigidity and somewhat mechanical reaction to innovation and theological enterprise' (*Theology*, p. 163), we would argue that the writer is enormously innovative in the way he addresses moral lapse in the community—so much so that critical scholarship, precisely on account of style and rhetorical flourish, rejects the possibility of the letter being Petrine.

Chapter 3

ETHICS AND VIRTUE IN 2 PETER

The Virtuous Life: Tracing a Petrine Theme

Probing literary strategy in the epistle allows us to sharpen our focus:
What is the intent behind the ethical categories and paraenetic language
employed in 2 Peter 1? Throughout the whole epistle? Precisely what
is it that should be so urgently 'recalled' by the readers (1.12-15)? The
burden of the writer is that his readers cultivate an ethos which 'offers
proof' (ποιεῖσθαι βεβαίαν, 1.11) of a virtuous lifestyle—proof, that
is, both to the one who has provided abundant resources for life and
godliness (1.3-4, 11) and to the moral skeptic (3.3-7). 'What sort of
persons should you be in holy conduct and piety?' (3.11) is the ringing
question that the readers are left to ponder.

Following the epistolary greeting, the accent of which is received
righteousness and grace, a catalog of virtues (1.5-7) is introduced by
means of philosophic and conspicuously pagan religious formulations
(vv. 3-4). Significantly, the language of the mysteries surfaces again in
1.16, where the writer speaks of himself as ἐπόπτης, 'an eyewitness',
of the Transfiguration 'while we were on the holy mountain'. It is noteworthy that in spite of three Synoptic narratives recording the Transfiguration, 2 Pet. 1.16 is the only New Testament appearance of
ἐπόπτης. The reason may well lie in the fact that the term used in a
technical sense signified the highest degree of enlightenment in the
Eleusinian mysteries.[1] And if 2 Peter is addressed to an audience in
Asia Minor, use of the term ἐπόπτης may also have a strategic
rhetorical effect.[2]

---

1.   Thus J. Klinger, 'The Second Epistle of Peter: An Essay in Understanding',
SVTQ (1973), pp. 161-62. Cf. BAGD, p. 305, for examples of technical usage.
2.   1.16-18 is typically adduced as proof that the letter is pseudo-Petrine. Thus
Fornberg: 'The historical Peter hardly needed to express his authority as a witness so

The catalog of virtues itself (1.5-7), meant to outline the contours of Christian 'life and godliness' (v. 3), includes several commonly cited features that appear in standard Stoic virtue lists and are adapted to the Christian paraenetic tradition. Although Stoic categories are utilized, they serve a distinctly Christian purpose. The letter's greeting clarifies and highlights grace, an acute departure from the Stoic understanding of ultimate things. Both Stoic and Christian moral traditions compel moral progress, the προκοπή (cf. Phil. 1.25; 1 Tim. 4.15). The latter, however, can be said to be less rigorous and absolute, based on the fact that it is predicated on divine grace and not human achievement per se.[3]

To possess these things (vv. 8, 9)—that is, the virtues—in the mind of the writer is to prevent an ineffective and unfruitful life. To lack them, however, is analogous to blindness resulting from a neglect of truth. At issue is moral responsibility.

The language of paraenesis presses to the fore throughout 2 Peter 1: 'for this reason' (v. 5); 'if these things are yours' (v. 8); 'anyone lacking these things' (v. 9); 'if you do these things' (v. 10); 'for this reason I intend to remind you, even though you know them already and are established[4] in the truth that has come to you' (v. 12); 'I think it right to stir you up' (v. 13); 'recall these things' (v. 15). Being reflected in 2 Peter 1 is a markedly Gentile social environment in which the Christian community finds itself.[5] The rhetorical effect of this ethical

strongly' (*Early Church*, p. 11). The personal encounter with the historical Jesus was not merely essential to the subapostolic era, that is, 'at a time when the apostles had died' (p. 11); rather, it was the test of apostolicity *during the apostolic age*, as Paul emphatically asserts in 1 Cor. 15.1-11. Hence, there is no need to relocate 2 Pet. 1.16-18 to a period generations removed from the apostles, unless the text itself warrants such. The declarations 'we had been eyewitnesses (ἐπόπται)' (1.16), 'we were with him' and 'we (ἡμεῖς) heard his voice' (1.18), if not authentic, together constitute a boldly exaggerated claim to Petrine identity by the pseudepigrapher that scarcely can be judged as noble in motive.

3.   To illustrate, compare Clement's reflections on Stoic moral philosophy (*Strom.* 7.7.44) over against Stoic discourse on right actions and human autonomy (*SVF* 1.179). See also the fuller discussion of Stoic worldview in Chapter 4.

4.   It may well be, as Hillyer (*1 and 2 Peter, Jude*, p. 170) suggests, that if the epistle is genuine, the use of the verb 'firmly establish' (στηρίζω) is a conscious (or unconscious) and poignant echo of the word Jesus spoke to *Peter* years prior at a time when he would be tempted toward denial.

5.   This is the guiding assumption of Fornberg's thorough study (*Early Church*) discussed in the preceding chapter.

terminology, though easily lost on the modern reader, would have
been unmistakable to its intended audience. Theirs is not a faith that is
void of the moral life; rather, the distinctly Christian ethic is to shine
forth in bold contrast to surrounding culture. Tragically, in the view of
the author, some have disregarded the divine 'promises' (1.4; implied
in 1.9, 12, 15) and as a result of their intercourse with surrounding
culture have 'forgotten' their 'cleansing from past sins' (1.9). These are
to confirm their election through a robust Christian ethic (1.10). Worse
yet, some are even aggressively propagating that there is *no* moral
authority before which they must account (2.1; 3.3-5).

Moral typology as well as a detailed sketch of the opponents are featured in 2 Peter 2. The allusion to ψευδοπροφῆται and ψευδοδιδάσκαλοι in connection with αἱρέσεις in 2.1-3 is a sure indication for
most exegetes that 2 Peter was written for the purpose of combatting
heresy. Although we have dealt with this objection elsewhere,[6] several
remarks concerning the vocabulary of ch. 2 are in order. Against the
interpretative tendency of most commentaries, 'false teachers' and
'heresies' are to be understood in a non-technical sense, as the emphasis
on moral quality throughout 2 Peter 2 indicates. Ἁίρεσις is not required to carry the sense of 'heresy' or 'false doctrine' as it would later
acquire. Rather, the primary meaning is that of *choice*, and strictly
speaking, the promoting of dissensions, factions and opinions.[7]

The verb tenses in 2.1-2, moreover, indicate a *future* time in which
the ψευδοδιδάσκαλοι will manifest their destructive pattern. (By contrast, Jude 4 speaks of individuals who have already 'wormed their way
in'[8] and who are presently active.) The picture being presented in 2.1,
οἵτινες παρεισάξουσιν αἱρέσεις ἀπωλείας, is one of spies or traitors
infiltrating the enemy camp. That the word 'destruction', ἀπώλεια,
occurs three times in 2.1-3 is indicative of a struggle at hand that is
foremost moral. That ethics rather than doctrine is the burden of the
writer can be seen by the effects of this struggle—licentiousness
(ἀσέλγεια), reviling truth (ἡ ὁδὸς τῆς ἀληθείας βλασφημηθήσεται),
greed (πλεονεξία) and deception (πλαστοῖς λόγοις ὑμᾶς). Before false
doctrine can proceed, it typically is introduced by moral departure,
that is, a denial of absolute authority (δεσπότην ἀργέομαι). The present struggle in the community involves the flight of those who had

6. See the section 'Paraenesis and 2 Peter' in Chapter 1.
7. BAGD, p. 24.
8. Thus Kelly, *Commentary*, p. 248.

been been purchased by—and thus, were the property of—the Master (τὸν ἀγοράσαντα αὐτοὺς δεσπότην ἀρνούμενοι, 2.1).[9] Significantly, the slave-market metaphor appears again in 2.19.[10]

In addition, the link between 2.1-3 and 2.4-10a—including the material that follows—is decidedly ethical. The defining features of the pastoral problem, delineated in 2.10b-18 following the examples from the past, are 'licentiousness' [twice], 'defiling passion', 'squalor', 'moral depravity', 'corruption', 'seduction' and 'lawlessness'. The paradigms of 2.4-10a are united by the moral depths to which they sank and are relevant to the present, given the description of the reprobate who appear to be revelling in a like condition (2.13).

Complementing the allusions to the fallen angels and Sodom and Gomorrah that resemble Jude[11] is flood typology—notably absent from Jude—which is intended to be prototypical of eschatological judgment.[12] In 2 Peter, Noah and Lot become types of faithful Christians who are to expect deliverance from God (φυλάσσω, 2.5; ῥύομαι, 2.7, 9) despite enormous social obstacles.[13] The catchword 'savior',

9. Cf. Jude 4: τὸν μόνον δεσπότην καὶ κύριον ἡμῶν Ἰησοῦν χριστὸν ἀρνούμενοι.

10. Cf. 1 Cor. 6.20; 7.21-23; Gal. 3.28-29; 1 Pet. 1.18-19; and Rev. 5.9.

11. While M. Desjardins ('The Portrayal of the Dissidents in 2 Peter and Jude: Does it Tell Us More about the "Ungodly" than the "Godly"?', *JSNT* 30 [1987], pp. 89-95), in speaking for most New Testament scholars, is right to conclude that it is only natural that Jude and 2 Peter be viewed together due to the sizeable literary correspondence, this very tendency has prevented fresh inquiry into both epistles. Is it possible, indeed useful, to look past the correspondences to the uniquenesses (without becoming over-speculative) and thus gain new insight into the meaning and message of both?

12. In *3 Macc.* 2.3-7, the flood, Sodom and Pharaoh together serve as a παράδειγμα of judgment, similar to the angels, flood and Sodom in 2 Pet. 2, where they function as a ὑπόδειγμα of the ungodly (2.6). L. Goppelt (*TYPOS: The Typological Interpretation of the Old Testament in the New* [trans. D.H. Madvig; Grand Rapids: Eerdmans, 1982], p. 159) makes the distinction between type and symbol or analogy, identifying the fallen angels and Sodom as the latter.

13. Noah's generation is prototypical of a faithless generation in Jesus' teaching as well (Mt. 24.37-39; Lk. 17.26-28). In Luke's Gospel, Noah's and Lot's generations appear side by side, where both are united by a common thread: life proceeding as normal in spite of pending judgment. For a thorough examination of the use of flood typology in both Jewish and Christian literature, see J.P. Lewis, *A Study of the Interpretation of Noah and the Flood in Jewish and Christian Literature* (Leiden:

occuring five times in the epistle—1.1,11; 2.20; 3.2,18—is intended to have more than a christological thrust. God saves a righteous remnant:

> For in this way abundant entrance has been provided for you to the eternal kingdom of our Lord and *Savior* Jesus Christ (1.1, 11).

> For if, after having escaped the defilements of the world through the knowledge of our Lord and *Savior* Jesus Christ, they are again entangled. . . (2.20).

> Remember the past words spoken by the holy prophets and the commandment of the Lord and *Savior* spoken through your apostles (3.2).

> But grow in grace and knowledge of our Lord and *Savior* Jesus Christ (3.18).

The message of 2 Peter, unlike Jude, is not mere condemnation; rather, it is the assurance of rescue from the midst of the cultural 'furnace'.[14] This use of moral typology, however, requires a qualification. While Noah is a herald of righteousness[15] both in the Old Testament and intertestamental literature,[16] Lot is by no means a righteous model in the Old Testament.[17] Lot's 'righteousness'—thrice he is depicted as δίκαιος[18] in 2 Pet. 2.4-10—is developed more in Jewish intertestamental literature,[19] although it can be indirectly attributed to Abraham's pleading with God recorded in Gen. 18.16-33. Contrast, not essential nature, is the point of the Lot typology,[20] as clarified by the

Brill, 1968). On Noah and Lot as types in the Synoptic tradition, see J. Schlosser, 'Les jours de Noé et de Lot. A propos de Luc xvii,26-30', *RB* 80 (1973), pp. 13-36.

14. While 2 Peter shares the same eschatological outlook as Jude, the paradigms in 2 Peter have a different function.

15. See J.C. VanderKam, 'The Righteousness of Noah', in J.J. Collins and G.W.E. Nickelsburg (eds.), *Ideal Figures in Ancient Judaism* (SBLSCS, 12; Chico, CA: Scholars Press, 1980), pp. 13-22.

16. For example, Sir. 44.17-18; Wis. 10.4; *1 En.* 106–107; *Jub.* 5.19; Jos. 10, *Ant.* 1.3.1; *Gen. Rab.* 30.7; cf. Heb 11.7.

17. According to the Gen. 19 narrative, Lot appears to be fully acculturated in Sodom. In the end, he must be removed from the city by physical force (19.16).

18. The frequent occurrence of δίκαιος/δικαιοσύνη in 2 Peter (seven times: 1.1, 13; 2.5, 7, 8, 21; 3.13) has a distinctively ethical quality, as Hillyer (*1 and 2 Peter, Jude*, p. 158) points out. Moreover, δικαιοσύνη occurs often in Hellenistic catalogs of virtue, even when its sense is wholly anthropocentric ('justice') as opposed to theocentric with social implications ('righteousness').

19. Wis. 10.6; 19.17; also Philo, *Vit. Mos.* 2.58.

20. Therefore, some modification is needed in T.D. Alexander's statement that

structural pattern οὐκ ἐφείσατο... οὐκ ἐφείσατο... ἐρρύσατο.[21] Important touch-points exist between the social environment of the readers and the days of Noah[22] and Lot. Norman Hillyer captures the sense of these verses in considering the significance of the flood typology:

> Peter thus maintains his pastoral purpose of encouraging his readers to keep faith with God in their own situation. Such a loyal stand will neither go unnoticed nor fail to attract a similar divine protection from the consequences of sin of the godless. . . Yet, as God kept Noah and his family from perishing in the Flood which carried off the wicked of those times, so the same God will protect believers who remain faithful to him in later generations.[23]

In the typology of 2 Peter, the flood performs two functions: it both saves and judges.[24]

Lot, by contrast, is not Noah. He was 'tormented' (καταπονέω) in his soul by unrestrained, lawless men day after day. And in spite of it all, in spite of his comfort in Sodom (cf. Gen. 19), he too is rescued by God, which only serves to underline *the sheer unmerited grace* of God's merciful action.[25] The catastrophe that befell the cities of the plain is intended to be didactic. The visitation of divine judgment made Sodom and Gomorrah 'an example' or 'pattern' (ὑπόδειγμα)[26] for succeeding generations. And what is the pattern? Sin (which is moral lapse), when it is allowed to take root and be justified, leads to a moral departure and darkening of one's heart, which (sooner or later) incurs judgment.

'for the author of 2 Peter there could have been little doubt that Lot. . . clearly deserved the epithet "righteous"' ('Lot's Hospitality: A Clue to his Righteousness', *JBL* 104.2 [1985] p. 289). This premise is based on rabbinic understanding, according to which Lot was willing to offer shelter and food to strangers in Sodom (in which regard, cf. Ezek. 16.49; 22.29).

21. 2 Pet. 2.4-9 contains language, moral paradigms and a structural pattern that are very much akin to Sir. 16.7-11: οὐκ ἐξιλάσατο περὶ τῶν ἀρχαίων γιγάντων. . . οὐκ ἐφείσατο περὶ τῆς παροικίας Λωτ. . . οὐκ ἠλέησεν ἔθνος ἀπωλείας (16.7-9).

22. The 'days of Noah' and the flood also appear in 1 Peter in a similar context—suffering for doing right amid an evil age (1 Pet. 3.20). Moreover, 'imprisoned spirits' surface in both epistles (1 Pet. 3.19; 2 Pet. 2.4).

23. Hillyer, *1 and 2 Peter, Jude*, pp. 188-89.

24. In 1 Pet. 3.20-21 the flood has a chiefly salvific function, where it prefigures baptism.

25. So Hillyer, *1 and 2 Peter, Jude*, p. 190.

26. Cf. Jude 7: πρόκεινται δεῖγμα πυρὸς αἰωνίου δίκην ὑπέχουσαι.

While the moral paradigms in 2 Peter address both the apostate and the faithful, their thrust—consistent with moral exhortation—is to encourage the latter. God continues to be 'savior', amid the community's overwhelming cultural struggles.

The description accorded the adversaries in 2.10b-21 both contains significant parallels to Jude and is differentiated by a notable expansion of the Balaam typology (2.15-16). The moral corrosion that characterizes these individuals in 2 Peter is striking. They act as irrational beasts, they slander, they revel in their corruption. They are boastful, irreverent, disobedient and scornful. They are adulterous, insatiable in their appetite for sin, and actively seducing others.

Moreover, whereas only a brief standardization of type appears in Jude ('the error of Balaam', v. 11), in 2 Peter these individuals are more fully typologized and depicted as 'having abandoned the upright way and gone astray' (καταλείποντες εὐθεῖαν ὁδὸν ἐπλανήθησαν), following the road of Balaam son of Bosor, who 'loved the wages of wrongdoing' (v. 15). The language being employed strongly suggests apostasy. A paradigm of self-seeking and greed in Jewish tradition,[27] Balaam more importantly (for the immediate context) was seduced by pagans, the fruit of which meant apostasy for Israel. Balaam is prototypical of some in the community, and with Balaam these are depicted as actively pursuing wickedness.[28] The downfall of a prophet of God is a singular phenomenon—and one that is highly instructive. Balaam over time became ethically divorced from the message that he bore. The psychology and character of apostasy are such that a moral skepticism and cynicism cause one actually to loathe what was formerly embraced; in the end, one 'loves the rewards of wrongdoing'. Such a tragic case is not only a possibility that can befall the individual; it is also a cancer that threatens everything around it.

27. See G. Vermes, 'The Story of Balaam', in *Scripture and Tradition in Judaism* (Leiden: Brill, 1973), pp. 127-77; also, Charles, *Literary Strategy*, pp. 120-24.

28. Note a similar link to Balaam in the message to the church at Pergamum (Rev. 2.12-17). Significantly, idolatry and fornication are the two identifying characteristics in Pergamum (2.14), as in Thyatira, which is said to be under the influence of 'Jezebel' (Rev. 2.20-22). Balaam and Jezebel, given the trajectory of the related Old Testament narratives, are symbols for apostasy in the early church. See G. Forkman, *The Limits of the Religious Community* (ConBNT, 5; Lund: Gleerup, 1972), pp. 157-58.

The Noah and Balaam typology indicate that not doctrinal strife but ethical lapse is the focus of the writer's polemic. In addition, two further clues in 2.19 and 2.20-22 magnify the the pastoral problem. The opponents are antinomian in character and boast of their freedom from moral constraints. In casting off divine moral authority, these individuals end up as slaves (2.19) to their own lusts (ἐπιθυμίαι, v. 18) and pleasure (ἡδονή, v. 13). In the Pastoral epistles this very linkage of ἐπιθυμία and ἡδονή by means of the slave metaphor is also used in illustrating the Christian's servitude to the former life.[29] This combination, well known in Hellenistic ethics, for the Christian looking back on his pre-conversion state would have had even greater meaning than for the Greek moralist.[30] 2 Pet. 2.19, as 2.20-22, describes moral degeneration that characterizes pagan lifestyle, a decidedly pre-Christian condition. The implication for the readers, rhetorically speaking, is that even moral pagans are better off than some in the community.[31]

The language found in vv. 20-22 adds to the picture in a way that should give the readers pause. The adversaries, tragically, had previously escaped worldly defilement but have become entangled and overpowered therein once more—a horrendous state of affairs in which the latter condition eclipses the original. The picture that follows, though conventional, is meant to shock. A double proverb (v. 22) consisting of one part Old Testament (the dog returning to its vomit, Prov. 26.11) and one part extrabiblical tradition (the pig returning to the mud, Arabic, Syriac and Armenian versions of *The Story of Ahiqar*)[32] is employed. The readers are struck by the graphic simplicity of proverbial wisdom and will appreciate its appropriateness to the situation. The use of common proverbial stereotyping resonates with the audience, especially in a pagan social environment.

As already noted, traditional commentary has read 2 Peter 3 through the lens of eschatological frameworks, normally interpreting this material to be evidence of *doctrinal* deformation that is in need of adjustment. Viewed structurally, 3.1-13 consists of the following components: an exhortation to remembrance, a caricature of the hardened

---

29. Cf. Jas 4.1-2 and Tit. 3.3, where both elements are associated.

30. So D. Guthrie, *The Pastoral Epistles* (TNTC, 14; London: Tyndale Press, 1957), p. 203.

31. Cf. Tit. 3.3-5, which has a similar rhetorical function.

32. *APOT*, II, p. 772.

moral skeptic, the declaration that moral accountability is incontro-
vertible, pastoral remarks concerning theodicy, and concluding admonitions. Viewed theologically, not the *timing* of the Parousia but its
inescapable *fact* is that which is being vigorously asserted. The day of
moral reckoning and death, as aptly stated by Mayor,[33] removes the
skeptic from the realm of illusion and into the sphere of reality. On this
basis, paraenetic language can be inserted once more for the sake of
warning the saints. The writer thus concludes: 'I am arousing you by
way of reminder' (v. 11); 'what sort of people should you be?' (v. 11);
'therefore... make every effort' (v. 14).

Destruction of the cosmos by fire, alluded to in 3.10-13, mirrors
the Stoic belief that the universe underwent periodic renewal by means
of burning (ἐκπύρωσις). This restoration was understood to take place
over and over again, without end. While the author of 2 Peter does not
endorse this view of the universe and advances an apocalyptic eschatological perspective, he would seem to be borrowing Stoic ideas and
imagery for the sake of his argument.[34] These are marshalled not with
a view of emphasizing chronological timing but in order that the *certainty* of divine judgment be firmly established.[35] Moreover, the opponents not only question the reality of the Parousia, they challenge the
very stability and preservation of the cosmos.

Our encounter in ch. 3 with the writer's apologetic leads us to a conclusion contrary to that proposed by Käsemann. The literary units of
the epistle are not in fact disconnected or haphazardly assembled, nor
do they 'betray embarrassment rather than force'.[36] Neither does the
epistle close 'with the admission that the doctrine of the Last Things is
already landing the Church in difficulties, and her apologia is in fact

33. Mayor, *Jude and Second Peter*, p. 211.

34. Thus Neyrey, 'Form', pp. 407-31; Riesner, 'Der zweite Petrus-Brief',
pp. 124-43; Thiede, 'Pagan Reader', pp. 79-96; and M.E. Boring *et al.* (eds.), *Hellenistic Commentary to the New Testament* (Nashville: Abingdon Press, 1995),
pp. 537-38. A most useful discussion of the nature and origins of Stoic cosmology
is found in D.E. Hahm, *The Origins of Stoic Cosmology* (Columbus: Ohio State
University Press, 1977), pp. 200-15.

35. J. Chaine ('Cosmogonie aquatique et conflagration finale d'après la Secunda
Petri', *RB* 46 [1937], pp. 207-16) captures the proper sense of the use of eschatology in 2 Pet. 3 and, not unlike Neyrey, adduces several classical Stoic texts that
concern themselves with cosmic conflagration.

36. Käsemann, 'Apologia', p. 194.

the demonstration of a logical absurdity'.[37] Such rather are the mis-guided conclusions that issue out of faulty assumptions about the text of 2 Peter. The material in ch. 3 is a calculated response to the current moral state of affairs in which some have forgotten the binding power of Christian truth-claims, resulting in various levels of embracing the old, that is, heathen, way of life. An alternative reconstruction of 2 Peter 3, such as those proposed by Neyrey, Riesner and Thiede and alluded to earlier,[38] are to be preferred, insofar as they preserve the unity and literary arguments of the letter.

The affirmation of cosmic renewal in 3.13 mirrors interplay of pagan and Judeo-Christian cosmology, behind which stands a fundamental question—to wit: What is the relationship of man to matter? And yet behind this question stands an even more fundamental question, namely: What is the relationship of *moral* man to matter? Cosmology and eschatology in the strictest sense, however, are not being show-cased. Rather, the author's purpose is to develop a response to a cari-cature of the moral skeptic (v. 4). Because the opponents are cham-pioning moral self-determination (2.1, 2, [implicit in 4-10a], 13, 15, 18, 19), they must justify their ethical departure; hence, the function of the caricature in 3.3-5, which presents the moral question from the standpoint of someone on the outside.[39] What's more, they 'deliber-ately ignore' (λανθάνει γὰρ αὐτοὺς τοῦτο θέλοντας) past examples of divine retribution (3.5-6), which typologically point to the ultimate day of moral reckoning (3.7). The occurrence twice in ch. 3 of the verb, both future passives (vv. 10 and 14), is significant. In 3.10, the text reads: 'and the earth and all deeds done on it will be revealed'. The point of the teaching is not to adjust theology; rather, it is to stress that judgment will be the expression of a *judicial* process and a *moral* reckoning.[40]

From the standpoint of the faithful, that is, the 'beloved' of v. 8, this divine 'delay' is disconcerting and requires a proper perspective.

37. Käsemann, 'Apologia', p. 194.

38. See the section 'Social Location in 2 Peter' in Chapter 2.

39. S.S. Smalley ('The Delay of the Parousia', *JBL* 83 [1964], p. 54) correctly sees in these verses a concern not to adjust eschatology but to address the moral sceptic, that is, the 'outsider'.

40. This important exegetical and contextual point is made by H. Lenhard, 'Ein Beitrag zur Übersetzung von II Ptr 3.10d', *ZNW* 52 (1961), pp. 128-29, and F.W. Danker, 'II Peter 3.10 and Psalm of Solomon 17.10', *ZNW* 53 (1962), p. 84.

Contrary to the regnant assumptions of 'early Catholicism', there is no disappearance or 'fading' of the eschatological hope in 2 Peter 3; rather, it is the matter of *timing* that invites clarification. The faithful, like Noah and Lot (2.5-8), will be rescued at the appointed time. Until then, however, they must resist the social forces at work within culture that would undermine faith and morality. Theodicy and divine longsuffering, not a fading Parousia hope, constitute the pastoral burden of the writer (3.8-13). His is a response not to a warped eschatological framework or theology per se, but to a militantly resistant skepticism that denies any moral claims over one's life. For the faithful, patiently enduring (vv. 12 and 15) in a hostile social environment is part of God's call to 'holiness and godliness' (v. 11). The final exhortation in the epistle is instructive, for it clarifies the writer's priority: 'You, then, beloved, since you have been forewarned, be on guard, so that you are not carried away by the error of the morally depraved (ἄθεσμοι)' (v. 17).[41]

A unitary reading of 2 Peter brings us to an important determination. Ethical lapse and apostasy—by no means necessarily confined to the second century—and not the doctrinal emphasis presupposed by 'early Catholic' proponents is that which plagues the community to whom the epistle is addressed. The combined ingredients of literary style and paraenetic language, Stoic and mystic categories, the catalog of virtues, moral typology, and caricatures of the adversaries all add up to a cultural setting that is permeated by Hellenistic influence.[42] Moral corruption, licentiousness, antinomianism and irreverence vex the church set within a pluralistic society. For this reason, moral skepticism, not dissatisfaction with orthodoxy,[43] is the object of the author's highly stylized polemic. It is for this reason that piety and immorality, virtue and wickedness, are juxtaposed throughout the epistle.[44]

41. Three times in the epistle (2.7, 8 and 3.17) the opponents are characterized as 'morally depraved' (ἄθεσμος) or 'lawless' (ἄνομος). Twice, in 2.12 and 2.19, they are depicted as creatures or slaves of moral 'corruption' (φθορά).

42. Thus Fornberg: '2 Peter reflects a conflict in the church within a pluralistic, Hellenistic society' (*Early Church*, p. 116).

43. Contra Kelly (*Commentary*, p. 305) and others. Orthopraxy, not orthodoxy, is the problem.

44. Thus P. Perkins, *First and Second Peter, James, and Jude* (IBC; Louisville: John Knox Press, 1995), p. 163.

Given the community's need for orthopraxy which in turn informs the author's literary strategy, the introductory material in 2 Peter may be understood as presenting a window into the social location of the audience. Strongly suggested throughout the epistle is a fundamental denial of moral self-responsibility. In its advanced stages, this denial has resulted in the apostasy of certain members of the community. While it is true that 'theological' justification (that is, 'heresy') necessarily accompanies any departure from the faith, apostasy—which is to say, an ethical departure from the moral truth of Christian revelation—is that which is the scourge of the community. The present situation calls for a roundly prophetic, and eminently pastoral, word of exhortation—exhortation that is aimed foremost at enunciating the ethical foundations of the Christian faith.[45]

The Virtuous Life: Setting the Context

The addressees in 2 Peter are undesignated—'to those who have received a faith as precious as ours' (v. 1). Vague as this address may appear, it suggests nevertheless that a perception exists whereby some in the community doubt that the faith of the apostles is on the same level playing field as that of the average Christian believer. This exegetical suspicion is strengthened by the meticulous care with which the writer, in 1.3-4, stresses the exceeding abundance of divine resource accessible to all. While a setting of Asia Minor, Syria and Rome are variously speculated to lie behind the epistle, both the origin and the destination elude any certainty.[46] The lack of concrete description as to destination, however, belies the character of the epistle, which, already noted, contains clear markings of a concrete local situation where serious problems are already established.[47] In this narrower sense, then,

45. The situation being addressed in the epistle may be reasonably compared with that encountered by Paul in Corinth in AD 55. Moral lapse, credibility of confession and cultural idolatry—matters thoroughly discussed in 1 Cor. 1–11—all have a bearing on theological perspective (cf. 1 Cor. 15). The burden of Paul's letter, however, is foremost ethical.

46. Given some of the lexical parallels to 2 Peter found in inscriptions from Asia Minor (some discussion of which follows), an Asian destination for the epistle is entirely plausible. See Chapter 6.

47. Cf. 3.1.

the designation 'general epistle' is misleading, since by definition it connotes a literary trajectory that is broader or 'catholic' in scope.[48]

Three general redactive interests can be detected throughout ch. 1. The first of these relates to lifestyle and moral character (1.3-11). The author, by way of introduction, places notable emphasis on the fact that divine resources are available to the Christian for living a godly life. Divine power and promises have been provided so that the readers might escape moral corruption in the world around them. This demarcation, the writer takes great pains to point out, depends not merely on the promises themselves (great as they are), but on the ethical response of the Christian. To this end, the author employs a Hellenistic rhetorical device, a catalog of virtues, to exhort his readers to a higher ethical plane. The net effect of the catalog should not be lost on the reader: human cooperation with God, while it does not *cause* righteousness, nevertheless 'confirms' or validates the believer's 'call and election' (1.10).

A second note of pastoral concern is reflected in the surplus of reminder terminology (1.12-15). The writer intends 'to keep on reiterating these things', even though the readers 'already know them and are established in the truth that formerly had come' to them. The author deems it necessary to 'refresh the memory' of his audience. He seeks to 'make every effort' in admonishing them 'to recall these things'.[49]

The third emphasis in 2 Peter 1 is the accent on the writer's own moral authority. If it is assumed from the outset that the letter is from an individual other than the apostle, 2 Peter is then read with a view of ferreting out evidence that would support the notion of pseudepigraphy. The result is, *inter alia*, that the self-referential allusions such as one finds in 1.1 ('Simon Peter,[50] an apostle')—and 1.16-18 (eyewitness

---

48. Thus Kelly (*Commentary*, pp. 227-28) over against Moffatt (*Introduction*, p. 368), who states that 'there is an entire absence of any personal relationship between the writer and the church or churches'.

49. To this end, 'knowledge' and 'knowing' receive particular emphasis in 2 Pet. 1, not because of a purported second-century Gnostic threat (contra Moffatt, *Introduction*, pp. 361-63, and others) but because of the grace the Christian community has already received (1.1-4).

50. Συμεών occurs also in Acts 15.14. The double name Συμεών Πέτρος and its significance for the church in Acts and Paul are the subject of J. Schmid's inquiry in 'Petrus der "Fels" und die Petrusgestalt in der Urgemeinde', in J.B. Baur (ed.) *Evangelienforschungen* (Graz: Verlag Styria, 1968), pp. 170-75. Although he held 2 Peter to be inauthentic, M.R. James, whose primary focus of scholarship earlier this

testimony of the Transfiguration event) are to be viewed as literary hubris at best and forgery at worst. In the end, one is left, like Käsemann, to hypothesize about 'Gnostic intrusion' in the second century.

If, on the other hand, the writer is defending himself as well as the integrity of the Christian gospel (as Paul was forced to do on occasion),[51] his own authority rests on nothing less than his historical relationship to Jesus. That (a) the writer seems not dependent on Synoptic accounts of the Transfiguration and (b) the pseudepigraphal *Apocalypse of Peter* makes use of 2 Peter together have been interpreted as casting doubt on 2 Peter's authenticity. Despite the overwhelming consensus of biblical scholarship in rejecting Petrine authorship, satisfactory explanations of the 'eyewitness' language in these verses have yet to be offered. Michael Green calls to attention 'the apostolic "we"' in 'We were eyewitnesses'—indeed, a necessary accent if Christian truth is being undermined.[52] It is supremely difficult to envision moral authority resting in the literary product of one who, even though well intentioned, must resort to specious statements such as 'we were there with him on the holy mountain'. Such requires too much from the reader.

Should the epistle in fact be a pseudepigraphon, the writer has overextended himself in seeking to be identified as the apostle Peter.[53] This exaggeration by a pseudepigrapher is all the more astounding in light of the fact that Peter's position was secure in the mind of the church, even outside of his own geographical area.[54] A less strained attempt at explaining these verses would be to view them as a logical and, depending on the urgency of the occasion, necessary device—one that would have been deployed by any of the apostles in validating Christian truth-claims.[55]

Having briefly considered the epistle's three introductory redactive elements, we may proceed onward with a view to examine the moral

---

century was Jewish-Christian pseudepigrapha, was able to concede that the double name 'Simon Peter' was evidence pointing in the direction of the epistle's authenticity (*The Second Epistle General of St Peter and the General Epistle of Jude* [Cambridge: Cambridge University Press, 1912], p. 9).

51. 1 Cor. 4 is a striking example.

52. Green, *2 Peter and Jude*, p. 93. Cf. 1 Cor. 15.3-8; 1 Jn 1.1-3; 4.14.

53. Thus Green, *2 Peter and Jude*, pp. 95-97.

54. J. Lowe, *St Peter* (London: SPCK, 1962), p. 10.

55. Cf., for example, the elaborate defenses by Paul in 1 Cor. 4 and 9.

grammar that lies behind 2 Peter 1. Verses 3-7 have been said to constitute a page out of 'current pagan textbook morality'.[56] In what way does this material reflect the social location of the readers? How does the language of paraenesis bear on the purpose of the letter? What is to be inferred about the recipients' spiritual and moral health from the author's vocabulary?

Ethics, godliness and moral tone do not develop in a vacuum. Rather, they are molded by the social forces at work in culture. It is hoped that in the following chapter the cultural milieu of the readers begins to take shape. If clearer definition of these forces emerges, important light will be shed on the language and logic of virtue in 2 Peter.

56. Kelly, *Commentary*, p. 306.

Chapter 4

THE MORAL WORLD OF GRECO-ROMAN PAGANISM[1]

Virtue and the Stoic Worldview

It is chiefly with the philosophical monism of the Stoa that we have to do as we assess moral philosophy in later Hellenism. Not only are the Stoa heirs of classical philosophical reflection, they are the primary propagators of ethics during this period. Consequently, the early Christians were frequently in conversation with Stoic doctrine as they carved out a cultural apologetic that would be ever more needful with the church's proliferation in the Gentile world.

But first it is necessary to ask precisely what it is of which the Stoa were heirs. There is a shift that occurs in the movement from Homeric ethics, with its primacy of bravery and courage (ἀνδρεία), to post-Homeric ethics. The Socratic man is still brave,[2] but he is also temperate, pious, just and prudent. Temperance (σωφροσύνη) is virtuous because it knows no limits as bravery does. An awareness of limits comes to characterize the thinking or knowing man, the man of sound or sensible mind.[3] The Socratic man, moreover, is pious ('οδιότης)[4], which is to say, his actions are pleasing to the gods. He is also just (δίκαιος);[5] that is, he discerns what is good in the context of the

1. Modern usage of the term 'pagan' may denote people who cannot embrace the stories, creeds and lifestyle of revealed religion, or it may simply designate colloquially a worldly—and perhaps even slightly barbarian—majority. Christians first ascribed to others the name *pagani* in the early fourth century. *Pagani* were 'civilians' not enlisted through baptism as soldiers of Christ against the powers of Satan and the world (R.L. Fox, *Pagans and Christians* [New York: A.A. Knopf, 1987], pp. 30-31).

2. *Laches* 190e4-6.

3. *Protagoras* 333d. Temperance is calmness (ἡσυχία) in *Charmides* 159b2-3, modesty (ἄδιος) in *Charmides* 160e3-5.

4. *Protagoras* 331a6-b8.

5. Aristotle, *Eth. Nic.* 1129b11-1130a5.

community. And the Socratic man is prudent or wise (φρόνιμος);[6] he exercises forethought and sensibility in his actions.[7]

Both Platonic and Aristotelian ethics assume that man possesses λόγος, the power of reasoning and speech. Platonic discussions of ethics are devoted primarily to the notion of justice/rightness/righteousness (δικαιοσύνη). Plato's teachings convey the firm sense that true virtue is found only in the realm of academic philosophy.[8] Aristotle stresses with even greater resolve the ethical life, the spine of which is the community, the πόλις. For Aristotle, the human is a ζωή πολιτική, a social and political being.[9] A striking difference between Aristotle and his master Plato is that whereas the latter passionately strove to see the unity and interdependence of all human knowledge, the former was concerned to observe what differentiates diverse spheres of ἐπιστήμη. Of the three domains delineated by Aristotle—the theoretical (θεωρητική), the productive (ποιητική) and the practical (πρακτική)—the theoretical was observed to be the highest and purest form. It seeks truth for truth's sake; hence, the priority of metaphysics in his writings.

Virtue, for Aristotle, consists of two kinds—intellectual and moral. While intellectual virtue derives from pedagogy, moral virtue is formed by habit, ἦθος. Moral virtue is not implanted within human nature; rather, it must be cultivated.[10] Moreover, the same habits that produce virtue and moral excellence can destroy it, as is true of the art of playing an instrument.[11] The nature of the moral virtues is such that they can be ruined by either defect or excess. Conversely, they are cultivated and strengthened by exercise. The virtuous person becomes habituated. By abstaining from pleasure one becomes self-controlled, and by means of self-control one abstains from pleasure.[12]

At the time of the Christian advent, the dominant ethical teachers of the Hellenistic world were the Stoa, who absorbed Socratic thought and expanded it. Stoic philosophy takes its departure from the intellectual

6. Thucydides 3.37.3.

7. Plato appears to be the first to designate 'cardinal' virtues.

8. *Theaet.* 176. See T. Irwin, *Plato's Moral Theory: The Early and Middle Dialogues* (Oxford: Clarendon Press, 1977).

9. *Pol.* 1253; *Eth. Nic.* 1102a; 1106a36-b3.

10. *Eth. Nic.* 1103a.

11. *Eth. Nic.* 1103b.

12. *Eth. Nic.* 1104b-1105b.

developments attending the socio-political changes at the end of the fourth century BC. It was the Stoa who had found an adequate world-view explanation for the era.[13] Whereas Plato and Aristotle had attracted a more or less aristocratic circle of disciples, philosophy of the middle and later Hellenistic era was increasingly democratic in its mold.[14]

For the Stoic, things have their origin and essence from within; they are not 'received'.[15] In contrast to the idealism of Platonic thought and the detached hedonism of Epicurean thought,[16] Stoic philosophy is rooted in nature, in the φύσις.[17] Two traits broadly characterize and sum up Stoic worldview: it is rational and it is dogmatic. Reason begins at approximately the age of fourteen—that is, at the time when one begins discovering a relationship between motive and action, when one begins to analyze, critique and judge.[18] The virtuous man, consequently, strives to live according to reason, according to the divine λόγος which was understood to permeate all things.

The intelligible and perceptible world is represented as the λόγος, the sum-total of that which permeates the physical world and gives it meaning. λόγος is the mediating force for divinity in an essentially unified world;[19] every human being is understood to have received the

13. What factors are responsible for calling Stoic philosophy into existence? Perhaps more than anything it was the social-political exigencies of the era—a socio-political world stripped of its insulation by Alexandrian conquests and a consequent exceedingly expanded polity. Thus argues M. Hadas in the introduction of his volume, *The Stoic Philosophy of Seneca* (Garden City: Doubleday, 1958). It is the Stoic whose worldview best spoke to the question of how one makes sense of the vastly expanded world.

14. See P. Wendland, *Die hellenistisch-römische Kultur in ihren Beziehungen zu Judentum und Christentum* (HNT, 1.2; Tübingen: Mohr, 1907), pp. 39-43.

15. Cf. 2 Pet. 1.1.

16. Whereas withdrawal from society is a necessary means of attaining 'happiness' for the Epicurean, the Stoic can involve himself in human affairs, inasmuch as happiness and virtue are not dependent life's circumstances.

17. With the use of φύσις in 2 Pet. 1.4 and φυσικός in 2 Pet. 2.12, the writer employs the vocabulary of Hellenistic piety. Jas 3.7 also demonstrates similar usage. See H. Koester, 'φύσις', *TDNT*, IX, pp. 251-77.

18. *SVF* 3.188.

19. The relationship of man to matter, and to λόγος, is the subject of a fascinating volume by A.P. O'Hagan, *Material Recreation in the Apostolic Fathers* (TU, 100; Berlin: Akademie Verlag, 1968). O'Hagan makes 2 Pet. 3.13 his starting point before analyzing the λόγος-speculation in the early fathers.

λόγος by nature.[20] Because humans are fully integrated with the
cosmos, the Stoic ethos can be summed up in the expression ὁμο-
λογουμένως ζωήν, in accordance with nature.[21] The Stoic way of life
is to let one's moral character shine through one's actions. Given the
exalted place of reason in the Stoic view of things, the individual is
self-responsible; people make moral choices.[22]

   At the center of Stoic ethics stands the all-pervasive λόγος-prin-
ciple.[23] The foundation of Stoic ethical teaching, framed by the Stoic
founder Zeno and his disciple Chrysippus, can be stated in the following manner: 'the true goal (τέλος) of moral action is to live in agreement with the Reason (λόγος) or nature (φύσις)'.[24] Hence, ethics in
Stoic thought is necessarily linked to cosmology. 'Right reason' (ὀρθὸς
λόγος), which is identified with and the equivalent of nature and deity,
is the power by which one attains virtue. To become virtuous, one
allows the λόγος to be fully realized in oneself. The individual, co-
extensive with the world, is connected to the cosmos by reason. It is in
this light that 'providence' is to be understood. Inasmuch as the cosmos
itself is divine, there is no personal god that is separate from the
cosmos. After death, the individual is understood as 'returning to', that
is, becoming one with, the cosmos.

   Stoic cosmology,[25] while it can be adapted to the language of Christian theism, has the consequence of obscuring any notion of original
sin, and thus, moral reckoning. The Stoic belief in moral progress is
rooted in the notion of οἰκείωσις [26] (from οἰκεόω: 'to adopt as one's

   20. Epictetus, *Diss.* 1.20.5; 2.20.21.
   21. In Stoic thought, φύσις is always, philosophically speaking, the highest court
of appeal, reality that is uncreated. A most helpful discussion of the Stoic tenet of
harmony between nature/reason and human action is J. Stelzenberger, *Die Beziehungen der frühchristlichen Sittenlehre zur Ethik der Stoa* (Munich: Beck, 1933), pp.
307-54.
   22. On the Stoic 'way' as it is seen through ethics, see L. Edelstein, *The Meaning of Stoicism* (Cambridge, MA: Harvard University Press, 1966), pp. 71-98.
   23. See A. Aall, *Geschichte der Logosidee in der griechischen Philosophie*
(Leipzig: Reisland, 1896).
   24. *SVF* 1.85; 2.37,38,41,43,70; 3.189.
   25. See D.E. Hahm, *The Origins of Stoic Cosmology* (Columbus: Ohio State
University Press, 1977), pp. 200-15.
   26. See T. Engberg-Pedersen, *The Stoic Theory of Oikeiōsis: Moral Development and Social Interaction in Early Stoic Philosophy* (SHC, 2; Aarhus: Aarhus
University Press, 1990).

own', and thus, 'to acquire'). At birth a person's soul is understood to be a sort of *tabula rasa*. There is movement in Stoic ethics from the pre-rational and irrational to the rational (cf. 2 Pet. 2.12)[27]. Character is cultivated, virtue is acquired; hence the Stoic view of moral advancement. The wise and prudent individual becomes free from irrational impulses and thereby develops into a sage.[28] Good and evil are understood only in the sense that one possesses virtue—the one true good—or one is given to vice.[29]

The implications of Stoic anthropology are readily grasped. The Stoic ethos is void of the soteriological and eschatological elements which form the heart of Christian revelation. The reader senses this fundamental differentiation in Paul's work in Athens. In his Areopagus speech, the apostle makes use of Stoic poets' praise of Zeus[30]—'in him we live and move and have our being' and 'for we are his offspring' (Acts 17.28)—and applies it to theistic creation. While he masterfully finds common linguistic and philosophical ground, radical discontinuity follows in the proclamation of (a) repentance and (b) judgment by the one who was raised from the dead (vv. 30-31).

Because Stoicism in its essence is pantheistic, it can tolerate religion: God and the cosmos are one and the same. The Olympian pantheon, broadly speaking, can symbolize virtues such as wisdom and justice[31]

27. Here the opponents are depicted as ἄλογα ζῷα.

28. *SVF* 1.205, 211; 2.828; 3.412. On the Stoic theory of moral development, see chapter 6 in B. Inwood, *Ethics and Human Action in Early Stoicism* (Oxford: Clarendon Press, 1985), pp. 182-215, and Engberg-Pedersen, *Oikeiōsis*.

29. *SVF* 1.231; Epictetus, *Diss.* 1.8.16; 1.29.1; 2.10.25. On Stoic categories and their uses, see J.M. Rist, *Stoic Philosophy* (Cambridge: Cambridge University Press, 1969), pp. 152-72.

30. 'Zeus' would be understood as the personification of fate or reason.

31. The legend that stands behind ὁ Ἄρεοις πάγος is instructive. With the passing of the centuries a canonical twelve gods were thought to hold power on Olympus. Religion and culture, it would appear, were ineluctably intertwined, as evidenced by surviving literature. In a speech dating c. AD 155 by Aelius Aristides at the Panathenaic festival, the author recounts a legal battle of the gods that is significant for an understanding of Athenian history—and thus, for Hellenism in general. In his pursuit of justice, Poseidon sued Ares over the murder of his son, ultimately winning the case in the presence of the gods (A. Aristides 1.40-48). As a record of the event, the purported site of disputation took on Ares' name. For this reason, throughout Greece's illustrious history this was a hallowed location; it was here that justice was eternally manifest. Thus it was that Athenians—indeed all cultured Hellenists—looked to the Areopagus as a fount of knowledge, wisdom, reason and justice. Although Luke

which constitute the core of the Stoic ethos. While able to tolerate the religious syncretism of the day, Stoicism also provides an adequate philosophical rationale. Moreover, in contrast to the mystery cults whose proliferation was evidence of a 'cosmic pessimism' in the Hellenistic world, Stoics proffered a 'cosmic optimism'. It is entirely plausible to suggest, as one historian has done, that if asked the difference between his own life-view and the Christian equivalent, a first-century pagan probably would have responded that it was the difference between λογισμός and πίστις, between reasoned logic and blind faith, since the latter generally (though by no means exclusively) was associated with the uneducated and illiterate.[32] And should Christians have been recognized as possessing ἐγκράτεια (self-control), φιλαδελφία (brotherly affection), εὐσέβεια (piety) or ὑπομονή (perseverance), they may have been accused of lacking φρόνησις (intellectual insight) and γνῶσις (knowledge).[33] At the same time that the Stoic is keenly aware of his duty to fate and the world, he is stubbornly independent of others and self-sufficient (αὐτάρκης).[34] The latter issues out of a conviction of the former.

Although the thread of 'knowing' and reflecting was shared by all the major Greek philosophs,[35] the Stoa more than others stressed moral

gives no indication that Paul's ministry at Athens—whether his 'dialoguing' in the marketplace or his address to the Council of the Areopagus—was marked by notable 'success', the details contained in the Lukan narrative (Acts 17.16-34) tantalize the reader enough to suggest two things: (1) that this was an eyewitness report and (2) that this may have been an apologetic 'highpoint' in Paul's ministry (to the extent that the apostle to the Gentiles is entering into philosophical and moral discourse with the cultural 'elite' of day).

32. E.R. Dodds, *Pagan and Christian in an Age of Anxiety* (Cambridge: Cambridge University Press, 1965), p. 114.

33. Perhaps it is with this in mind that the writer in 1 Pet. 3.15 exhorts his readers: 'Always be ready to offer a defense (ἀπολογία) to anyone asking from you a reason for the hope that is within you'.

34. This very independence accounts for suicide as the respectable means of release from undignified circumstances. In Paul, αὐτάρκεια denotes a sufficiency that is rooted in *divine* resources (2 Cor. 9.8; Phil. 4.11; 1 Tim. 6.6).

35. Whereas in Epicurean thought all human beings have a basic commitment to ἡδονή, pleasure (= happiness), which could lead to withdrawal or a negation of social responsibilities, all humans in Stoic thought have a basic commitment to ἀρετή, virtue.

behavior, intention and motive.[36] Stoic ethical thought was based on certain foundational assumptions that may be summarized as follows: (1) morally right acts depend on virtue, ἀρετή; (2) virtue is the highest level of human development, the goal to which all things must converge; (3) virtues are acquired and not inherent;[37] and (4) virtues are culti-vated by exercise.[38]

That Stoics were committed to a theory of moral progression in the personal life is significant for the present study, for it is this very as-sumption that 2 Peter exploits and baptizes for distinctly Christian purposes.[39]

The Interaction of Stoic and Christian Worldviews

Although by the time of the church's birth Stoicism was almost 300 years old, the first century—the period of the Caesars—was the period in which Stoic ethical *Massenpropaganda* blossomed.[40] This was spawned in no small part by the excesses, despotism and moral bankruptcy that attended this era. The ethical preaching of the Stoics may be rightly viewed as a calculated reaction to the moral depravity of the day. It is for this reason that the relationship of philosophical ethics during this period to Christianity is by no means incidental, for the aforementioned moral-cultural and social conditions served to create fertile soil among the masses for the Christian message. Thus it is only natural that one can detect numerous touch-points between Stoic and Christian life-views. The New Testament is not without evidence of the interaction between Christian and Stoic philosophy. Both groups

36. See G. Kidd, 'Moral Actions and Rules in Stoic Ethics', in J.M. Rist (ed.), *The Stoics* (Berkeley: University of California Press, 1978), pp. 247-58.

37. By definition, it is impossible for children to possess virtue, since it signifies moral completion (τελειότης), according to Chrysippus (*Gal.* 437ff). Moreover, once it is achieved, it cannot be lost (Zeno 148; Cleanthes 75), in contrast to the moral element requiring both cultivation and preservation in Christian discipleship.

38. For a thorough discussion of ethics and moral action in Stoic thought, see Inwood, *Ethics*.

39. Although the Platonic ideals of prudence, fortitude, temperance and justice were acknowledged, Stoic ethics did not presupppose a rigid hierarchy of virtues. On the individual Stoic virtues as ideals, see K. Campbell, *A Stoic Philosophy of Life* (Lanham, MD: University Press of America, 1986), pp. 23-59.

40. By the first century, Stoics and Cynics were viewed as the popularizers of ethics.

were active in the marketplace, propagating their views for consumption by broader audiences. Both utilized diatribe, paraenesis, epistles and ethical lists. It is not purely coincidental that they shared a common moral vocabulary, as 2 Peter 1 illustrates.[41]

Perhaps the most lucid demonstration of recorded early Christian interaction with Stoic worldview and ethical discourse is Paul's ministry in Athens—particularly his address to the Council of the Areopagus, the essence of which is preserved by Luke in Acts 17. Luke initially frames the narrative in a way that shows Paul 'dialoguing' in the marketplace with Epicurean and Stoic philosophers. Luke further depicts Paul as following in the Socratic mold by being accused of introducing 'new gods'—an imputation attributed not only to Socrates but Anaxagoras, Protagoras and the Stoic master Chrysippus. From Luke's perspective this is not bad company to keep, apologetically speaking. In his ensuing Areopagus speech, Paul's rhetorical arsenal includes several strategies. Among these are: (1) an appeal to 'nature' in contending for the God who has made himself known; (2) exploiting common philosophical ground (namely, reason, the highest expression of nature) to bridge the gap between Stoic and Christian understanding of the cosmos; (3) stressing continuity with Stoic belief (kinship with God) while emphasizing radical discontinuity (divine transcendence) with Hellenistic worldview thinking; and (4) enlisting conventional literary sources (namely, citations from well-known 'poets') that illustrate Stoic belief in kinship with God.[42]

---

41. Neyrey proposes that the material in 2 Pet. 1 be subsumed under the rhetorical rubric of praise and shame (*2 Peter, Jude*, pp. 5-6). The interpretive schema applied by Neyrey to 2 Peter is a welcome adjustment to the 'early Catholic' thesis that traditionally has been advanced virtually lock-step by critical scholarship, even when Neyrey views the material in 2 Peter as having a more Epicurean rather than Stoic cast.

42. Acts 17.16-34. For a fuller treatment of Paul's accommodation to philosophical and moral discourse in Athens, see W. Eltester, 'Gott und die Natur in der Areopagrede', in *Neutestamentliche Studien für R. Bultmann* (Berlin: Töpelmann, 1954), pp. 202-27; B. Gärtner, *The Areopagus Speech and Natural Revelation* (ASNU, 21; Uppsala: Almquist, 1955); F. Mussner, 'Anknüpfung und Kerygma in der Areopagrede (Apg 17, 22b-31)', in *Präsentia Salutis: Gesammelte Studien zu Fragen und Themen des Neuen Testaments* (Düsseldorf: Patmos Verlag, 1967), pp. 235-43; G. Schneider, 'Anknüpfung, Kontinuität und Widerspruch in der Areopagrede. Apg. 17,22-31', in P.G. Müller and W. Stenger (eds.), *Kontinuität und Einheit* (Freiburg: Herder, 1981), pp. 173-78; and more recently, J.D. Charles,

A comparison of Acts 17.16-34 and 2 Peter 1 is useful for the purposes of illuminating the mode of apostolic witness in Gentile culture.
Both texts are marked by several features which facilitate the bridging
of core Stoic and Christian philosophical assumptions. First, while neither the writer in 2 Peter nor Paul in Acts 17 adopts the materialist-
rationalist assumptions of the intended audience, both demonstrate an
understanding of—and hence, an ability to interact with—Stoic cosmology.[43] Secondly, both find common philosophical ground with Stoics
in their acknowledgment—explicit in Acts 17 and tacit in 2 Peter—of
reason as the highest expression of human existence. In Acts 17, reason
(λόγος) is used by Paul to lead beyond the 'unknown God' to the 'God
who has made himself known'; in 2 Peter, it is implicitly recognized
as the vehicle that (a) facilitates moral development based on what the
readers already know (1.3-15; 3.11-13) and (b) distinguishes humans
from 'irrational beasts' (2.12).

Thirdly, both engage Hellenistic outlooks on immortality and moral
accountability. Epicureans wholly rejected the notion of an afterlife,
while Stoics viewed human life as eventually reabsorbed into the
cosmos, the divine Reason. By the account in Acts 17, after having
affirmed continuity with the Stoic notion of kinship with God, Paul
establishes radical discontinuity by emphasizing divine transcendence
and the certitude of a day on which the world is to be judged by the
God-man risen from the dead, Jesus Christ. In 2 Peter 3, the Stoic
concept of ἐκπύρωσις, cosmic destruction by fire, appears in the background of the author's polemic. It is very possible that in responding
to the rationale of the hardened moral skeptic (which is the focus of 2
Pet. 3), the author vigorously asserts the *inescapable fact* of moral
accountability and divine judgment by contrasting the Stoic understanding of ἐκπύρωσις—by which a reconstituted cosmos was to be

'Engaging the (Neo)Pagan Mind: Paul's Encounter with Athenian Culture as a Model
of Cultural Apologetics', *TJ* 16 NS (1995), pp. 47-62.

43. See R.B. Todd, 'Stoics and their Cosmology in the First and Second Centuries A.D.', in W. Haase (ed.), *Aufstieg und Niedergang der römischen Welt:
Geschichte und Kultur Roms im Spiegel der neueren Forschung* (Berlin: de Gruyter,
1989), II.36.3, pp. 1365-78. For a survey of broader Stoic thought during this
period, see M. Pohlenz, *Die Stoa* (2 vols.; Göttingen: Vandenhoeck & Ruprecht, 4th
edn, 1972), II, pp. 277-99.

expected[44]—with the Jewish-Christian apocalyptic eschatological framework—by which a wholly *new* creation (καινὸς οὐρανὸς καὶ γῆ καινῆ, 3.13) would appear.[45]

Fourthly, both Paul in Acts 17 and the letter of 2 Peter demonstrate the ability to be conversant with literary currents of the day. In Athens, Paul exploits the well-known tradition of the 'unknown God' with a monotheistic adaptation. Furthermore, theological 'common ground' is sustained by two citations from well-known 'poets'—literary asser- tions about kinship with the divine and the divine filling the universe— which no Stoic philosopher worth his salt could deny.[46] In 2 Peter, two conventional proverbs illustrating the absurdity of rejecting the truth are cited for rhetorical effect (2.20-22). Moreover, if Neyrey is correct in his hypothesis for the eschatological argument appearing in 2 Peter 3,[47] a secular work of apologetics may be supplying the writer a format with which to denounce entrenched skeptics who are denying a moral day of reckoning in the afterlife.[48]

From the standpoint of ethics, Christian revelation distinguishes itself from the Stoic doctrine on the basis of anthropology, soteriology and eschatology. The Christian analog to the Stoic notion of oneness with— and assimilation into—the divine is discipleship and ethical progress.

---

44. Cosmic cycles in Stoic teaching are thought to have beginning- and end- points, yet the end-points are not developed clearly and remain virtually impenetrable to the modern reader. Ancient evidence suggests ἐκπύρωσις—the Stoic doctrine of destuc- tion of the cosmos by fire—to refer to a burnt up rather than reconstituted universe (*SVF* 2.617).

45. Although commentators are by no means unified as to this interpretation of the eschatological polemic in 2 Pet. 3, it seems to be the most plausible and has been argued persuasively by Riesner ('Der zweite Petrus-Brief', pp. 124-43) and extended by C.P. Thiede ('A Pagan Reader', pp. 79-96). Neyrey's provocative essay, 'The Form and Background', pp. 407-431, antedates those of Riesner and Thiede and attempts to construct an alternative starting-point in 2 Peter interpretation to the traditional 'early Catholic' model by suggesting that the epistle is an apologetic inter- action with Epicurean rather than Stoic cosmology. See the section 'Social Location in 2 Peter' in Chapter 2.

46. On the tradition of an 'unknown god', to which a vast amount of literature has been devoted, see Charles, 'Engaging the (Neo)Pagan Mind', p. 58 n. 65; on Paul's use of literary traditions at the Areopagus, see pp. 57-58.

47. See Chapter 2.

48. While aspects of Neyrey's argument are convincing, the depiction in 2 Pet. 3 of ἐκπύρωσις, coupled with the writer's own 'logos-speculation', would seem to mirror Stoic rather than Epicurean cosmology.

Yet, while the goal may appear similar, the motive and means are radically different.[49] It should be reiterated that while Paul borrows and masterfully exploits the language of Stoic ethics and cosmology in Athens, he does not speak of ἀρετή in general or of any ἀρεταί in particular. The issue for him is to clarify the need for faith, repentance and conversion[50]—concepts that are alien, indeed scandalous, to the cultured Hellenist.[51]

This stark contrast can be observed both in the New Testament and in the writings of Philo and Clement of Alexandria. Because Philo writes not with Jews or Pharisees but primarily Gentiles in view, he can be seen as attempting to conceptualize moral virtue in the service of promoting a Jewish notion of righteousness. Philo strives to be at home in both worlds.[52] And for him, much liked the writers of the New Testament, grace is the supreme virtue.[53] In Philo, the manifestation of virtue begins with the awareness of God[54]—an awareness and search that is planted within the soul.[55] It thus follows that reason (νοῦς), with its moral agency, is God-given.[56] Essential components of Philo's worldview are divine mercy for sinners, divine wrath, judgment and the necessity of conversion. As a result, ontology and soteriology form indivisible cords of a tether to which all of reality must be anchored.

The framework for constructing worldview in Philo clearly assumes the need for special revelation; it is precisely God's self-disclosure that sets Israel apart. Nevertheless, Philo can place Israel's revelation against the backdrop of creation and the natural world. Utilizing the language and thought-world of cosmic origins and human virtues allows him to engage pagans on philosophically common ground. For example, in his writings he will employ the Stoic attributes of εὐεργέτικος (doing good deeds), φιλάνθρωπος (benevolent), προνοήτικος (having

49. See E.F. Osborn, *Ethical Patterns in Early Christian Thought* (Cambridge: Cambridge University Press, 1976).
50. Acts 17.30-31.
51. Acts 17.18, 32.
52. Thus W.A. Meeks, *The Moral World of the First Christians* (Philadelphia: Westminster Press, 1986), p. 84.
53. The volume by D. Zeller, *Charis bei Philon und Paulus* (SBS, 142; Stuttgart: KBW, 1990), is devoted to tracing this theme in Philonic literature.
54. *Leg. alleg.* 1.38.
55. *De plant.* 23.
56. *De plant.* 23.; also *Quod deus immut.* 45-50.

foresight) and κηδεμών νεκρῶν (respecting the dead) in order to illuminate a theology of creation.[57]

As a result of this accent on grace—χάρις and χάριτος appear nearly one hundred times in Philonic literature[58]—the differences between Stoic and Christian ethics are rendered transparent. In Stoic literature, grace is displaced in the cosmos,[59] to which Philo responds by arguing that grace is necessary in the very act of creating.[60]

It is almost universally agreed that Stoic doctrine exerted major influence on Clement of Alexandria and that he adapted Stoic categories to his Christian presuppositions.[61] This is readily understood when considering the context of Clement's writings: namely, the need to relate Christian truth-claims to a pervasively Hellenistic culture.

D.J.M. Bradley has assessed Clement's adaptation of Stoic thinking to Christian assumptions. Notable examples in Clement are a personalization of the divine λόγος, the exaltation of wisdom, frequent allusion to the 'Christian Gnostic', and affirmation of the cardinal virtues. In his commentary on the Stoic virtue αὐτάρκεια (self-sufficiency or contentment), however, an important modification is made. For the Stoic, right actions are to be understood apart from any outside help.[62] For the Christian, by contrast, right actions are important but only as they are accomplished by means of divine grace.[63] The Stoic ethos, then, for Clement is far more rigorist and absolutist than its Christian counterpart, due not in small part to the *Christian distinctive*.[64] While both Stoic and Christian ethical theory can be seen to espouse moral progress, one assumes human achievement as the means, the other divine grace.

The Stoic view of moral actions and moral development has eschatological consequences, as Clement observes. For the Stoic, it is how one dies, not what occurs after death, that counts. In response, Clement

57. For example, *SVF* 2.1115; 2.1021, 1126.
58. Zeller, *Charis*, p. 33 n. 1.
59. *SVF* 2.310, 323.
60. *Leg. alleg.* 3.78.
61. See D.J.M. Bradley, 'The Transformation of the Stoic Ethic in Clement of Alexandria', in E. Ferguson (ed.), *Christian Life: Ethics, Morality, and Discipline in the Early Church* (New York: Garland, 1993), pp. 41-66.
62. *SVF* 1.179.
63. *SVF* 7.7.
64. The rigidity of Stoic morality can be seen as a response—a logical response—to surrounding culture.

notes that indeed man can become like God (ὁμοίωσις)—reminiscent of Stoic and mystical thought[65]—to the extent that an increase in the knowledge of God conforms us to our Creator.[66] Yet in the end, the Stoic sage is but a dim foreshadow of divine-human οὐσία, for he lacks the Christian distinctive of grace. Nonetheless, Clement's theology, for apologetic reasons, is colored by the philosophical and moral vocabulary of his day.

Pagan ethics knows nothing of the conceptual realities of sin, guilt and redemption that lie at the heart of the Christian belief-system. Where 'wisdom' is lauded, it is only insofar as it stands in relationship to righteousness.[67] Pagan virtues such as courage, temperance, prudence or justice are the extension of a naturalistic ethic and rational reflection. They presuppose human autonomy and self-sufficiency, whereas the Christian ethic is rooted in divine grace and sufficiency in Christ.[68] Law to the virtuous pagan is autonomic, while law for the Christian is theonomic.[69]

For Paul, transcending the wisdom of this world is a triad of what have been called 'theological virtues'—faith, hope and love—the latter of which is said to be the highest expression of human character (1 Cor. 13.1-13). All other qualities are subsumed under this priority, suggesting a hierarchy that is wholly foreign to pagan ethics. Agape is *the* prerequisite for all action, a motivation that vanishes from pagan ethical teaching. The Christian's behavior at bottom is rooted in the Christ-event.[70] It is the teaching of the New Testament that love and eschatology are bound together, forming what H. Preisker has termed the *Telostatsache*.[71]

---

65. *Strom.* 2.19.102.

66. *Strom.* 6.9.78.

67. In James, true wisdom is qualified as that 'which is from above' (3.17).

68. Unquestionably, pelagianism receives part of its inspiration from Stoicism, which subsists in the understanding that the human being can fulfill divine standards apart from grace. It is against this backdrop that one may better appreciate Augustine's strong response in *De natura et gratia*. The Christian ethic depends wholly on pneumatic inspiration; grace, a component of the universe, cannot be acquired.

69. A thorough contrast between Stoic and Christian ethical teaching is found in J. Stelzenberger, *Die Beziehungen der frühchristlichen Sittenlehre zur Ethik der Stoa* (Munich: Beck, 1933), pp. 307-54.

70. H. Preisker, *Das Ethos des Urchristentums* (Darmstadt: Wissenschaftliche Buchgesellschaft, 1968), pp. 145, 169.

71. Preisker, *Ethos*, p. 148.

Chapter 5

THE ETHICAL CATALOG AS A PEDAGOGICAL DEVICE

The Language and Logic of Virtue

The grouping of ethical values into lists surfaces in diverse cultures of antiquity. One encounters, for example, in Egypt, India and Iran documented crime registers and similar lists of offenses. To the extent that religion as practiced by ancient civilizations is characterized by the striving and performance of its adherents, the function of the ethical list can be seen as a natural extension. To be sure, it is precisely in the realm of human striving that Israelite religion distinguishes itself from that of the nations: Yahweh's self-disclosure establishes a covenant, with corresponding obligations, that nevertheless are predicated on grace and forgiveness (that is, atonement for sins). Yet even though Israel (and the Christian church to follow) was governed by a distinct awareness of covenantal grace, the format of the Decalogue as an expression of the will of God has antecedents in lists of antiquity. It suggests the function of the ethical list as a public memory device, notwithstanding the fact that material in Exodus 20, 22–23, 33, Leviticus 18 and 19, for example, is framed in casuistic language.[1] These lists make concrete the ethical principles that are an extension of a particular worldview.

The recording of ethical lists in the Hellenistic world extends formally from the Homeric era. Their usage is by no means restricted to the domain of philosophy, even when moral-philosophical discourse appears to be the *Sitz im Leben* of the ethical catalog. Catalogs occur in very diverse literary—and non-literary—contexts. A rather large number of inscriptions—notably, grave-sites and memorials—list

---

1. In general, a listing of ethical or godly virtues does not appear in the Old Testament to the extent that vice lists do. Ethical lists become more commonplace in later Jewish literature, under the influence of Hellenism.

virtues in honor of the said individual. Honors were typically bestowed upon military generals, doctors, judges and office-holders.[2]

Use of the ethical list abounds both in literary and non-literary contexts. In Hesiod, for example, we encounter two types of catalogs— name registers and ethical lists (the latter containing both transgressions against the gods and transgressions of the children against the parents).[3] The ethical catalog finds its way into the work of poet/playwright Aristophanes, in whose intellectual satire—a parody of the Eleusinian mysteries—the stereotypes of ξένοι, μητραλῶαι, πατρολῶαι, and ἐπίορκοι are held in contempt.[4] And in Seneca vice lists are used to explain why, in bald contrast to Aristophanes, he cannot even *recommend* going to the theater. By his own account, he returns home (after the theater) 'greedier', 'more envious', 'more sensual', 'crueler' and 'more inhuman' than before. The reason? He has just been in the presence of 'ambitious people', 'proud despisers', 'arrogant winners', 'cunning liars' and 'careless spendthrifts'—all of which depict quite adequately his fellow-Romans, who 'indulge only in the discovery of new vices'.[5]

In spite of this diversity of setting, however, the pre-Socratic traces of paraenetic listing come to full bloom in the Socratic philosophers, and particularly, in the teaching of the Stoa. The emergence of ethical catalogs in the Hellenistic period can be seen as the result of philosophical reflection, initially within an 'academic' but later a more popular context.[6] In time, however, the focus of philosophical ethics moves from the theoretical basis for ἀρετή, 'virtue' or 'moral excellence',[7] in the direction of its concrete and practical expression. Rhetorically speaking, the ethical list has an epideictic function; that is, as a form of speech it is intended to instill praise or shame in the hearer or listener. Vice and virtue lists perform this practical rhetorical function

2. Numerous examples are cited in Vögtle, *Die Tugend- und Lasterkataloge*, pp. 89-92.

3. Hesiod, *Theog.* 77-79, 240-64. Name-catalogs served for Hesiod the purpose of succinctly summarizing genealogies of the gods. Examples are reproduced in H. Trüb, *Kataloge in der griechischen Dichtung* (Zürich: Buchdruckerei Winterthur, 1952), pp. 7-43.

4. *Frogs* 5.145.

5. *Brev. vit.* 10.4.

6. Thus Vögtle, *Die Tugend- und Lasterkataloge*, pp. 58-62.

7. Ἀρετή also can denote the manifestation of divine power, the sense of which is conveyed in 2 Pet. 1.3.

equally in both Stoic and Christian usage. Because the ethical contours
of both were shaped against the backdrop of Greco-Roman moral-social
conditions, touch-points between Stoic discourse and the New Testament are numerous. While the two systems are radically different in
the way each perceives the *means* to the ethical life, they nonetheless
share common ethical categories. It is in the broader context of Paul's
'natural theology' in Romans 1 that a stereotyping of pagan moral
depravity and an ethical catalog are employed. Human guilt is said to
be universal because of the fact that humans do not see fit to acknowledge God (1.28). The vice list of 1.29-31—the lengthiest in the New
Testament—is intended both to encompass every stereotype of human
corruption imaginable as well as mirror conditions in the Imperial seat.
There are no theoretical components to Paul's discussion of ethics in
Romans. It is flatly assumed that all 'know' (ἐπιγινώσκω, 1.28, 32) the
truth. The result is that all are guilty.

Whether ἀρετή conceptually derives originally from the verb αἴρω
('lift upward', 'take up', 'pick up') or ἀρέσκω ('to strive to please', 'to
be pleasing'), the early sense of ἀρετή conveys bravery or valor in
battle. In time the term was extended to other realms: the state, family
life, friendships, art and ethics. From the standpoint of learning, ethical
lists—by which the ethical life is organized, accented and stereotyped—
serve a very practical and pedagogical function. They standardize a
type of attitude or behavior and thus are a common feature of the
paraenetic tradition.

The virtues ἀνδρεία, φρόνησις/σοφία, σωφροσύνη and δικαιοσύνη
individually play a central role in the ethical teaching of Socrates.
Schematization first presses to the fore in Plato, who is the first to designate four 'cardinal' ἀρεταί.[8] Although formal presentation of the
'cardinal' virtues appears first in Plato's *Republic*, similar formulations of the moral ideal predate this by over a century—for example,
in Aeschylus.[9] Xenophon, who on occasion in his writings stresses the
need for exercising one's spirit,[10] appears not to have been much taken
by the fourfold schema as Plato. This is in spite of the many ethical

---

8.   In Plato's earlier dialogues (e.g., *Laches*, *Charmides* and *Protagoras*), virtue
is an essentially singular phenomenon. In his later dialogues, however, the fourfold
schema surfaces.
    9.   *Sept.* 610: a man who is σώφρων, δίκαιος, ἀγαθός and εὐσεβής.
    10.   For example, *Mem.* 1.2.19.

topics found in his writings, for example, ordering of the home, healthy outside relationships, the treatment of slaves, and civilian duties toward political and military obligations. Aristotle, as already noted, distinguished between practical and ethical virtues, although on occasion he fails to make this demarcation. In *Rhetorik*, for example, he lists together δικαιοσύνη, ἀνδρεία, σωφροσύνη, μεγαλοψυχία, ἐλευθεριότης, πραότης and σοφία without any differentiation.[11] Otherwise, the classification of virtues in Aristotle proceeds in a two-fold manner. Books 3–6 of *Nicomachean Ethics*[12] arrange the virtues according to (a) ethical virtues: the individual virtues of ἀνδρεία and σωφροσύνη; the political virtues of ἐλευθεριότης, μεγαλοπρέπεια, μεγαλοψυχία, φιλοτιμία and πραότης; the social virtues of φιλία, ἀληθευτικός, εὐτραπελία and ἐπιδεξιότης; the highest social-political virtue δικαιοσύνη; and (b) intellectual virtues: ἐπιστήμη, τέχνη, φρόνησις, σοφία and νοῦς. For the most part Aristotle resisted the fourfold schema that had arisen largely out of the Pythagorean love of the number four, considered to be symbolic of life's completeness.

The classical period of ethical lists begins with Zeno (mid-third century BC), founder of the Stoa, and is expanded under the Stoic teachers who followed.[13] The early masters, notably Chrysippus (280–210 BC), tended to use 'virtue' and 'knowledge' (ἐπιστήμη) interchangeably,[14] a practice that is significant for the understanding Stoic ethical discourse. Consider Stoic definitions of the cardinal virtues: justice is knowledge of what is due, what is right and fitting; temperance is knowledge of what to choose or not to choose; prudence is knowledge of what to do or not to do in a given situation; courage is knowlege of what should or should not be feared.[15]

In the moral doctrine of the Stoics, one encounters a return to the tetradic schema that characterized Socratic-Platonic ethical teaching. Organization serves an important recall function in Stoic pedagogy. Proceeding from the four cardinal virtues, Stoic teaching derives

11. *Rhetorik* 1366b.
12. 1115a-1145a.
13. On the relationship between Aristotelian and Stoic ethics, see F.H. Sandbach, *Aristotle and the Stoics* (Cambridge: Cambridge Philological Society, 1985), pp. 24-30.
14. Examples are found in Dyroff, *Ethik*, p. 81.
15. The Stoic mindset is elucidated by the very useful discussion found in Dyroff, *Ethik*, pp. 82-84.

multiple subsets of virtues. Chrysippus divides the ἀρεταί into two groups of cardinal (πρῶται) and subordinate (ὑποτεταγμέναι) virtues, with a long list of subordinates attached to the cardinal virtues. One of the most comprehensive catalogs of virtue comes from the Stoic Andronikos, who compiled the writings of his master Chrysippus and whose list contains no fewer than 20 ἀρεταί.[16] All in all, precise grouping of ethical traits plays nowhere near the role in Aristotelian discussions of moral philosophy as it does in Stoic discussions.

To the Stoic mind, where there exists an antithesis of one virtue, the same must apply to others. For example, the health of one's soul suggests the possibility of psychological sickness. Similarly, the experience of wisdom points to folly; contentment, anxiety; brotherly kindness, enmity; and so on. Just as the virtue can be standardized or personified, so can the corresponding vice. A typical construction in Stoic ethics is the listing of four primary ἀρεταί—that is, the four cardinal virtues—and, in juxtaposition, four types of 'cardinal' vices: injustice, cowardice, intemperance and folly.[17] This tetradic schema of organizing vice and virtue for didactic purposes seems to occur more frequently in the earlier Stoic lists.[18] Zeno presupposes four chief vices that plague human existence—sorrow, fear, greed and lust. Later Stoic teachers not infrequently divided these into further subspecies, exemplary lists appearing in Andronikos, Cicero and Diogenes Laertius.[19] Once more we encounter in Andronikos extraordinary variety and detail—he lists no less than 27 kinds of ἐπιθυμία, 27 kinds of λύπη, 13 kinds of φόβος and five kinds of ἡδονή[20]—even when his list pales by comparison to that of Philo, where 147 vices personify the 'friends' of the 'hedonist' (φιλήδονος).[21]

We observed that use of the ethical list—which concretizes the rigorous moral struggle of the Stoic lifeview—was not merely confined to philosophical literature. It appears as well in the poets (relatively

16. The text of which is reproduced in *SVF* 3.64.
17. *SVF* 3.20,24.
18. For example, *SVF* 3.17,18.
19. Numerous examples are reproduced in Vögtle, *Die Tugend- und Lasterkataloge*, pp. 32-36, and Wibbing, *Die Tugend- und Lasterkataloge*, pp. 14-23.
20. *SVF* 3.397, 401, 409, 414. Varieties of Stoic catalogs are compiled in *De Stoicorum catalogis affectum* and cited by Vögtle, *Die Tugend- und Lasterkataloge*, pp. 58-88.
21. *De sacr. Ab. et Caini* 32.

frequently in Vergil[22] and Horace[23]) and in popular literature. The more popularized form of vice and virtue lists, while sharing a common ethical vocabulary with Stoic philosophers, loses the schematization that had characterized the 'scholastic' masters. Two lists from first-century Asia Minor inscriptions that describe the ideal wife are remarkably close to the model one finds in Titus 2 describing the older women in the community: φιλανδρία, φιλοτεκνία, κάλλος, σωφροσύνη ἀδιήγητος (list #1) and φιλοσοφία, φιλανδρία, φιλοπαιδία, φιλοπατρία (list #2)[24] versus φιλάνδρους, φιλοτέκνους, σώφρονας, ἁγνάς, οἰκουργούς (Tit. 2.4-5).

In this regard, it is instructive to note the growth of the genre diatribe,[25] for ethical lists constitute an important element in its content and style.[26] Although in its evolution the diatribe derives initially from the pedagogy of the philosophical schools (frequently developed in the context of lectures or treatises on providence, cosmology or virtue), it could be adapted as well to a literary style[27] and, over time, to the more popular treatment of ethical topics in a way that was designed to move people to action.[28] From the standpoint of style, the diatribe and the epistle converge quite readily, given the didactic and hortatory character of each. Ethical lists, quotations, anecdotes and rhetorical questions are frequently integrated into both.[29]

An impressive array of literature provides a window into the world of dialogical discourse, which by its hortatory character serves as ethical 'propaganda through the living word with [practical] personal

22. For example, *Aen.* 6.732.

23. For example, *Ep.* 1.1.33-40.

24. *CIG* 1.1452-53 and 2.2384.

25. In his discussion of the diatribe's setting, S.K. Stowers assumes usage and definition of the term in a 'scholastic' rather than popular context ('The Diatribe', in D.E. Aune [ed.], *Greco-Roman Literature and the New Testament* [Atlanta: Scholars Press, 1988], pp. 71-83 [73-74]). This distinction, however, is not always clear in much of the literature.

26. Stowers cites four primary forms of pedagogical activity in the philosophical schools: (1) lectures that are cast as hortatory sermons, (2) exegesis and discussion of texts, (3) general group discussion, and (4) dialogue ('Diatribe', pp. 74-75).

27. Stowers, 'Diatribe', p. 75.

28. Malherbe, *Moral Exhortation*, p. 129.

29. Diatribe in the New Testament is most readily identified in Romans and the letter of James.

effects'.[30] One may cite as examples the letters of Heraclitus (c. 250 BCE), the dissertations of Epictetus (c. 50–130 CE), the lectures of Musonius Rufus (c. 65–80 CE), and the writings of Philo (c. 20 BCE–50 CE), Seneca (early- to mid- first century), Dio Chrysostom (c. 40–120 CE), and Plutarch (50–120 CE).

As a pedagogical tool, the ethical list was seen to derive its force from a standardization of human or behavioral types. Preliterary types of the catalog that can be cited include crime registers (already noted), character traits of those born under certain constellations, memorials to the deceased and decrees of honor.[31]

While it is difficult to pinpoint with precision the origin of the dualistic format of vice and virtue in juxtaposition, one of the earliest traces is the use of allegory by Heraclitus,[32] in which a struggle between πλοῦτος and ἀρετή occurs. Typically, the personified features which accompany πλοῦτος in these allegorical tales are τύχη (fortune), ἡδονή (pleasure), ἐπιθυμία (lust), ἔρος (passionate love), and τρυφή (self-indulgence).[33]

The *Sitz im Leben* of the dualistic schema is generally agreed to be the propaganda of the moral philosophers. Accordingly, those heeding their advice are considered to be wise, those who cast it aside are ignorant and foolish. This dualism allows easy incorporation into Hellenistic Jewish as well as New Testament literature. In many respects, a conversion to Judeo-Christian faith is conceived of in terms not unlike a 'conversion' to the wisdom of philosophy. Consequently, the ethical list has a useful role in Hellenistic-Jewish and early Christian post-conversion paraenesis.[34]

Over time, popular moral philosophers expanded the form of ethical catalogs to include new concepts—particularly, additional vices. Preaching moral uplift in the marketplace, peripatetics found ethical lists to be a practical and effective rhetorical tool. The lists were far from the complicated, convoluted philosophical constructs that had been advanced by 'scholastic' moral philosophers. People saw themselves in

---

30. Thus Wendland, *Die Hellenistisch-Römische Kultur*, p. 84.

31. See Vögtle, *Die Tugend- und Lasterkataloge*, pp. 84-91.

32. Cited by Berger, 'Hellenistische Gattungen', p. 1090.

33. Philo allegorizes in a similar fashion. Contradistinguished from the eleven vices, represented as 'friends' of Lust, are 34 attendants of Virtue (*De sacr. Ab. et Caini* 20-45).

34. Thus Berger, 'Hellenistische Gattungen', pp. 1091-92.

these lists—whether by vice or virtue. Practical needs of the masses propelled the use and extension of ethical lists in a popular format. Stoic ethical catalogs do not possess a rigid hierarchy of virtues so as to suggest a moral progression leading to an ethical climax. All the virtues stand in close connection with each other; all constitute a natural unity. No particular order or arrangement of virtues came to characterize popular usage of lists, although paronomasia was frequently achieved through the word-order. Stoic vice or virtue lists were not meant to be all-inclusive, and the presence or absence of particular virtues in the list simply reflected the values of the author.[35]

Ethical Catalogs in Jewish Literature and the New Testament

While vice and virtue lists in the narrower sense do not occur in the Old Testament, the tradition of ethical catalogs finds a secure place in the literature of Hellenistic Judaism. Frequently, these are vice catalogs that are related in some way to sins delineated in the Decalogue. In reading this literature one senses both polemical and non-polemical interaction between Stoic and Jewish worldviews. Vögtle's description of Philo reflects an individual who is at home in both worlds: 'By the sheer number and length of virtue and vice lists, Philo seems to have achieved the measure of the Stoic popular philosophers'.[36] Indeed, this impression is confirmed by a survey of Philonic literature. Philo develops the Stoic ethical schema in both public and private domains. In his contrast of ἀρετή with ἡδονή, he uses the metaphor of two women.[37] Lust, that ever-wandering prostitute, surrounds herself with the friends of πανουργία, προπέτεια, ἀπιστία, κολακεία, ἀπάτη, ψευδολογία, ψευδορκία, ἀσέβεια, ἀδικία and ἀκολασία.[38] The friends of the virtuous woman, however, are even more abundant. At this point, Philo lists 34 such 'friends', beginning with εὐσέβεια and ending with ἀγαθότης.[39]

Philo frequently refers to the four cardinal passions: lust, sorrow, greed and fear.[40] The number four is so important to him that the four

35. Malherbe, *Moral Exhortation*, p. 138.
36. Vögtle, *Die Tugend- und Lasterkataloge*, p. 107.
37. *De sacr. Ab. et Caini* 20-21.
38. *De sacr. Ab. et Caini* 22.
39. *De sacr. Ab. et Caini* 27.
40. For example, *De praem. et poen.* 419.

headwaters of the river flowing through Eden (Gen. 2.8-14) point to four cardinal virtues.[41] The largest stream is ἀρετή, out of which all others flow. Elsewhere in Philo, the four cardinal virtues and the four cardinal vices are presented as issuing from the nature of the soul. If the soul is possessed by vice and ἡδονή, it manifests ἐπιθυμία, ἀφροσύνη, ἀκολασία and ἀδικία; should it be governed by virtuous transformation, however, the soul is as a 'pure woman' with innumerable laudable qualities.[42] Philo always manages to return to the Stoic emphasis on struggling against vice; yet at the same time he is anchored to the ethical teaching of the Old Testament. While it is true that human passions arise, these are not detached from one's life in God.[43] Obedience is important because it produces virtue, just as disobedience and unbelief have a negative spiral.[44] Stoic categories and Old Testament ethics can thus stand side-by-side. Philo is a poignant reminder of the extent of Stoic influence during the last two centuries BC and through the first century CE. He also demonstrates graphically how religious truth could be clothed in relevant literary and philosophical arguments of the day, even when Philonic allegorizing (by our standards) over-extended itself in its attempt to reconcile Hellenistic moral philosophy and the Old Testament.

The Wisdom of Solomon is another relevant example of Hellenistic literary influence on Judaism. In this work we encounter the four cardinal virtues, whose tutor is said to be the wisdom of God.[45] Correlatively, serving false gods is the equivalent of ignorance, ἄγνοια, and must be countered with the γνῶσις of God.[46] In 14.25-26 a lengthy list of vices proceeds which characterizes the life that is absent the knowledge of God. It manifests: αἷμα καὶ φόνος, κλοπὴ καὶ δόλος, φθορά, ἀπιστία, τάραχος, ἐπιορκία, θόρυβος ἀγαθῶν, χάριτος ἀμνηστία, ψυχῶν μιασμός, γενέσεως ἐναλλαγή, γάμων ἀταξία, μοιχεία καὶ ἀσέλγεια (blood and murder, theft and fraud, depravity, faithlessness, disorder, perjury, suppressing the good, ingratitude for what is given, soulish defilement, sexual confusion, marital disorder, adultery and licentiousness). Stoic influence in Wisdom

---

41. *Leg. alleg.* 1.19.56; 2.23.24.
42. *De exsecr.* 159-60.
43. *De Spec. leg.* 3.63.
44. *De ebr.* 19.
45. Wis. 8.4, 7.
46. Wis. 14.22.

can also be seen in the admonitions toward reflection.[47] The author is not concerned, however, to correct the sins that he catalogs; rather, he is content merely to list the depths of depravity to which Gentiles have descended.[48]

The use of the ethical catalog by New Testament writers[49] derives from its function in Hellenistic and Jewish literature. With some exceptions, the theological motivation behind use of the catalog can be seen as due primarily to the thought-world of Hellenistic Judaism, in which the dualism of the righteous and unrighteous comes to expression. In the New Testament, both strands—Hellenistic form and Jewish theological assumptions—merge in the Christian paraenetic tradition.

The intellectual element of Greek philosophical reflection, it should be emphasized, is not carried over into the New Testament by its writers. The reason for this, already discussed in the preceding chapter, can be traced to the fundamental Stoic outlook. To the Greek mind, ethical requirements do not issue from a source of transcendent moral authority; rather, they are the fruit of rational education and knowledge, by which one comes to realize the fullness of human nature.[50] Acquiring virtue for the Stoic is an absolute good, a goal in and of itself. Hence the categories of sin and guilt have no real place in Stoic thought. While the Stoic is called to reflect, the Christian is called to repent and be redeemed—what the human mind is incapable of producing. Punishment for the Stoic consists of the imminent consequences of foolish behavior; thus, its ethic is without any eschatological ramifications. For this reason, 2 Peter 3 is significant, insofar as it clarifies the author's use of Stoic categories with a distinctly Christian qualification.[51] The writer will underscore the inevitability of eschatological judgment and moral accountability.

---

47. For example, Wis. 4.11 and 12.10.

48. So B.S. Easton, 'New Testament Ethical Lists', *JBL* 51 (1932), pp. 10-12.

49. See Easton, 'Ethical Lists', pp. 1-12, and N.J. McEleney, 'The Vice Lists of the Pastoral Epistles', *CBQ* 36 (1974), pp. 203-19.

50. J.N. Sevenster, 'Education or Conversion: Epictetus and the Gospels', *NovT* 8 (1966), p. 247.

51. Wibbing's contention that 2 Pet. 1.5-7 constitutes the only echo of the Stoic catalog form in the New Testament (*Die Tugend- und Lasterkataloge*, p. 86) can be moderated. It is certainly one of the clearest structural echoes in the New Testament, when not the sole one.

Ethical catalogs appearing in the New Testament take on two syntactical arrangements.[52] They can be polysyndetic, such as the list in 1 Cor. 6.9-10, where members are bound together rhetorically through the use or repetition of conjunctions in close succession.[53]

> Do not be deceived; neither fornicators nor idolaters nor adulterers nor prostitutes nor sodomites nor thieves nor greedy persons nor drunkards nor revilers nor robbers will inherit the kingdom of God.

Catalogs can be asyndetic as well, such as in Gal. 5.22-23a, where no connective particle is used: 'But the fruit of the Spirit consists of love, joy, peace, patience, kindness, generosity, faithfulness, humility and self-control'.[54] The lists distributed throughout the New Testament are fairly evenly divided between polysyndetic and asyndetic forms.

Thirteen virtue lists appear in the New Testament, all but two of which are found in epistles: 2 Cor. 6.6; Gal. 5.22-23; Eph. 4.23, 32; 5.9; Phil. 4.8; Col. 3.12; 1 Tim. 4.12; 6.11; 2 Tim. 2.22; 3.10; Jas 3.17; 1 Pet. 3.8; 2 Pet. 1.5-7. Twenty-three vice lists are found in the New Testament, all but two of which also occur in the epistles: Mt. 15.19; Mk 7.21-22; Rom. 1.29-31; 13.13; 1 Cor. 5.10-11; 6.9-10; 2 Cor. 6.9-10; 12.20-21; Gal. 5.19-21; Eph. 4.31; 5.3-5; Col. 3.5,8; 1 Tim. 1.9-10; 2 Tim. 3.2-5; Tit. 3.3; Jas 3.15; 1 Pet. 2.1; 4.3,15; Rev. 9.21; 21.8; 22.15.[55]

The Pastoral epistles contain the most dense usage of ethical lists in the New Testament. Here we find four virtue lists and four vice lists, all of which suggest a social location not unlike that of 2 Peter in which the foundations of morality are being called into question. N.J. McEleney, in his examination of the four vice lists, observes the presence of five basic elements as part of a literary strategy: references to the law, a background of pagan idolatry, transfer of Hellenistic conceptions of

---

52. See Vögtle, *Die Tugend- und Lasterkataloge*, p. 13, and Wibbing, *Die Tugend- und Lasterkataloge*, p. 78.

53. All but three of these New Testament catalogs have the items linked by the conjunctions καί, ἤ or οὔτε.

54. D.E. Aune (*The New Testament in its Literary Environment* [Philadelphia: Westminster Press, 1987], pp. 194-95), following Wibbing, suggests a third category—'amplified' lists that are more discursive in form—and cites 1 Thess. 4.3-7 as an example.

55. In the Pastoral Epistles, the lists of various responsibilities on the part of elders in the church are not ethical catalogs in the strict sense.

vice and virtue to the Christian context, moral dualism and eschato-logical punishment.[56]

Despite the variety found in the ethical lists of the New Testament, there seems to be an 'early Christian paraenetic formula', if we may call it thus, that constitutes numerous vice lists in the New Testament. Those which share this schema[57] have the function of reminding the audience of what characterized their former life; thus Paul to the Corinthians: 'And this is what some of you used to be' (1 Cor. 6.11a).

> For out of the human heart within comes evil: fornication, theft, murder, adultery, greed, wickedness, deceit, licentiousness, envy, slander, pride folly (Mk 7.21-22).

> Let us live modestly, not in revelling or drunkenness, debauchery and licentiousness, quarreling or jealousy. Instead, put on the Lord Jesus Christ, and make no provision for the flesh with its lusts (Rom. 13.13).

> Don't you know that wrongdoers will not inherit the kingdom of God? . . . neither fornicators nor idolators nor adulterers nor male prostitutes nor sodomites nor thieves nor the greedy nor drunkards nor revilers nor robbers will inherit the kingdom of God (1 Cor. 6.9).

> For we ourselves were once foolish, disobedient, led astray, slaves to various passions and pleasures, passing our days in malice and envy, despicable, hating one another (Tit. 3.3).

> You have already spent enough time doing what the Gentiles like to do, living in licentiousness, passions, drunkenness, revellings, carousing and lawless idolatry (1 Pet. 4.3).

Not infrequently, idolatry (εἰδωλολατρία) and sexual impurity (πόρνος, ἀκαθαρσία or ἀσέλγεια) are featured together in the vice lists of the New Testament, for example, 1 Cor. 6.9-10; Gal. 5.19-21; Eph. 5.5; Col. 3.5; 1 Pet. 4.3; Rev. 21.8; 22.15. This may well correspond to the twin stereotypes of pleasure (ἡδονή) and lust (ἐπιθυμία) which frequently occur in pagan lists. There is reason to believe, as Easton suggests, that the Hellenistic-Jewish literary form of denouncing Gentile practice via lists of grossly depraved deeds was carried over into the practice of the New Testament writers.[58] As a conventional formula, it served a useful purpose. Gal. 5.19-21, however,

56. McEleney, 'Vice Lists', p. 218.
57. To this group could be added Rom. 1.29-31 and 1 Tim. 3.2.
58. Easton, 'Ethical Lists', pp. 4-5.

departs somewhat from this pattern. Although several of the stereo-typical gross sins appear (for example, idolatry, fornication, sorcery, revelling), the remaining vices reflect quite precisely the Galatian sit-uation—enmities, strife, jealousies, wraths, factions, divisions, cliques, envyings. These, in turn, form an ethical counterpart to the virtues that follow—love, joy, peace, and so on. The vice catalog, therefore, can be seen as Paul's own construction, injected into a rhetorical con-vention.[59] Once more, as in Romans 1, euphony (rather than progres-sion) is the prominent characteristic. Of the vice lists in the New Testa-ment, Romans 1 and 2 Timothy 3 give the greatest indication of a direct, non-Jewish precedent. Most of the other lists show some debt to Hellenistic-Jewish catalogs.

A regularly appearing feature in the Christian paraenetic tradition, used in connection with several vice lists, is the formula ἀποτίθημι ('put off') plus a list of vices. For example, preceding the list in Rom. 13.13 is the imperative 'Cast off the works of darkness'; in Eph. 4.22: 'Put off the old nature which belongs to your former lifestyle that is corrupted by deceitful lusts', and again in 4.25: 'Therefore put away falsehood'; in Col. 3.8: 'But now put away all such things'; and in 1 Pet. 2.1: 'Therefore, put away all malice'.[60]

Furthermore, several New Testament vice lists seem to give evidence of a Christian paraenetic schema for addressing sins that quench or inhibit Christian love:

> Remove from yourselves all bitterness and wrath and anger and wrangling and slander together with all malice (Eph. 4.31).

> But now get rid of all wrath, anger, malice, slander and foul talk from your mouth (Col. 3.8).

> Therefore, put away all malice and guile and hypocrisy and envy and all slander (1 Pet. 2.1).

The longest vice list in the New Testament is found in Rom. 1.29-31 and bears notable similarities to 2 Tim. 3.2-5.[61] It serves as a climax to the Pauline argument that humans stand guilty and without excuse

---

59. Easton, 'Ethical Lists', p. 5.

60. See also Jas 1.21.

61. Easton ('Ethical Lists', p. 7) correctly identifies the difference in the two catalogs. In Rom. 1 the list functions as a general stereotype, whereas in 2 Timothy a concrete situation is being addressed.

before their Creator, before whom they have rejected truth and consequently have had their minds and hearts darkened. Euphony rather than
logic or moral progression is the prime feature of this list. Paul would
seem to be adopting the technical language of Stoic moralists in the
phrasing by which he introduces the catalog—τὰ μὴ καθήκοντα.[62]

In comparing the virtue lists in the New Testament,[63] one observes
both similarities and differences. Fewer conventional formulas appear
in virtue than in vice lists. This may be attributed to the fact that for
Jewish and Christian writers righteousness rather than moral goodness
is essential. In Jewish thinking, discussions of ethics proceed normally
in terms of one's obedience to the law, since law defines one's relationship to God. In point of fact, the New Testament's most noteworthy
listing of 'virtues' (which we have not included as an ethical catalog
per se) is the recording of 'Beatitudes' in Matthew 5, which is of conspicuously Jewish-Christian origin and to which none of the other New
Testament lists share any affinity. One striking parallel to pagan catalogs noted by both Martin Dibelius[64] and B.S. Easton[65] deserves
mention. The qualities of an elder listed in 1 Timothy 3 are reminiscent of qualities that are necessary of a military general. In a similar
vein, it can be argued that the lists in Phil. 4.8, Tit.1.7-8, 3.1-2 and 1
Tim. 3.2-3 diverge very little from pagan ethical lists.[66] Quite the
opposite, however, can be said of the virtue lists in Gal. 5.22-23 and 1
Tim. 6.11.

Vice and virtue lists in the New Testament function paraenetically
in different contexts. They may be used for the purpose of antithesis
(for example, Gal. 5.19-23 and Jas 3.13-18), contrast (for example,
Tit. 3.1-7), instruction (for example, 2 Pet. 1.5-7) or polemics (for
example, 1 Tim. 1.9-10; 6.3-5; 2 Tim. 3.2-5). These lists resist any
attempts at being reduced to a single *Urkatalog* or set pattern. Occasionally, though not necessarily, alliteration or assonance, cadence and
inclusio enhance their descriptions. A unified structure is hard to detect,
and rhetorical motivation is not always apparent, with the notable
exception of Phil. 4.8. Vögtle links together 2 Cor. 6.6, Gal. 5.22,

---

62. Easton, 'Ethical Lists', pp. 3-4.
63. Easton ('Ethical Lists', pp. 1-12) has summarized these.
64. M. Dibelius, *Die Pastoralbriefe* (Tübingen: Mohr, 2nd edn, 1931), p. 100.
65. Easton, 'Ethical Lists', p. 10.
66. Thus Easton, 'Ethical Lists', p. 11.

Eph. 4.2-5 and Col. 3.12-14 as having a 'logical-psychological' function,[67] whereby the virtues are thought to build on one another and
demonstrate a progression of sorts. Although Vögtle does not see a
logical progression in the virtue catalog in 2 Pet. 1.5-7, he does rec-
ognize that in a distinctly Christian sense, each successive virtue listed
issues from the one that precedes. Thus, faith can be seen as the foundation of the Christian ethic and love as the climax.[68] At the very least,
one may assume that the rhetorical effect created by the progression
and climax of the virtues in 2 Peter 1 is mirroring a concrete situation
in which there has been fundamental ethical breakdown. In order to
address this crisis, the writer is utilizing a standard hortatory device
to underscore the necessity of the moral life as proof of one's profession both to the community and to the world.

Paul shows himself to be quite capable in adopting Hellenistic ethical
categories for his own purposes. In virtually all of the Pauline and in
each of the Pastoral Epistles, an ethical catalog is employed. The reason
that Greek ethical terminology is particularly applicable in Paul and
the pastorals is not difficult to grasp. Gentile converts would have been
already familiar with it. The utility of the ethical lists in the New Testament would appear dependent upon the social location of the readers
and the writer's ability to adapt them to the said social situation.
Unlike Stoic lists, which demonstrate no discernible unity and an at
times bewildering array of detail, Christian virtue lists by contrast
derive from their relationship to faith and love, a prime example of
which is 2 Pet. 1.5-7. The classical fourfold schema of φρόνησις,
ἀνδρεία, σωφροσύνη and δικαιοσύνη is eclipsed in the New Testament by δικαιοσύνη, ἁγιασμός, ἀπολύτρωσις and σοφία.[69] In stark
contrast to the Stoic emphasis on, the Christian's boast is 'in the Lord'
(1 Cor. 1.30-31).

While the New Testament writers show an aptitude for borrowing
catalogs from Hellenistic moral philosophy, to speak of Christian
'virtue' in the New Testament is to speak of the three 'theological'
virtues (1 Cor. 13.13; Col. 1.4-5; 1 Thess. 1.3; 5.8).[70] These represent
the primary modalities of the Christian's experience of redemption.
Though not ἀρεταί in the technical sense, they constitute the foundation

---

67. Vögtle, *Die Tugend- und Lasterkataloge*, p. 47.
68. See the commentary in Chapter 6.
69. This wisdom, James notes, is a 'wisdom from above' (3.17).
70. Implied also in Jude 20-21.

of all virtues and the wellspring of the Christian life. Further clarifying this triad, in continuity with the Old Testament, is Paul's assertion that love is the sum and fulfillment of the law (Rom. 13.10; Gal. 5.14; 1 Tim. 1.5). By extension, the ethical life may be summed up in the Christian distinctive of love.

Given the considerable variety with which virtue catalogs appear in Jewish and early Christian literature, the repetition of particular virtues in New Testament and sub-apostolic lists[71] may point to an additional function. The inclusion of πίστις, ἀγάπη and ὑπομονή in 2 Pet. 1.5, Rev. 2.19, *Barn.* 2.2ff. and *1 Clem.* 62.2 are evidence to Vögtle of the possibility that virtue catalogs may have acquired in the apostolic paraenetic tradition a catechetical function.[72] While the form is distinctly Hellenistic, the content is uniquely Christian. That Christian catechesis may have been preserved in such a format is not implausible. A catalogical format is faintly suggested by confessions of faith such as are found in 1 Tim. 3.16 and 2 Tim. 2.11-13. Regardless of whether virtue lists may have functioned in this manner catechetically, for the writers of the New Testament, virtues are no artificial mechanism. Rather, they are a natural expression of one's organic union with Christ, the fruit of divine grace.[73]

71. A catalog of seven virtues, including πίστις and ἀγάπη, appears in *Herm. Vis.* 3.8.

72. Vögtle, *Die Tugend- und Lasterkataloge*, p. 54. Cf. also *1 Clem.* 64 and *Herm. Man.* 8.9. πίστις and ἀγάπη occur in a list from Ignatius to the Ephesians (14.1).

73. Cf. Mt. 15.13; Jn 15.1-7; Rom. 7.4; 1 Cor. 3.9; Gal. 5.19-24; Col. 1.10. On the notion of fruitfulness in the New Testament, see J. Bommer, *Die Idee der Fruchtbarkeit in den Evangelien* (Pfullingen: Mohn, 1950), and F. Böckle, *Die Idee der Fruchtbarkeit in den Paulusbriefen* (Fribourg: Fribourg Universität, 1953).

Chapter 6

THE CATALOG OF VIRTUES IN 2 PETER 1.5-7

In Chapter 3 the theme of the moral life was traced throughout the epistle. A modest attempt was made to demonstrate that the various components to the writer's literary strategy were subordinated to this thematic development. The epistle's opening material, which contains several catchwords that point in the direction of the main theme,[1] is a particularly strong witness to the priority of ethics and virtue, as the structural arrangement of 1.3-11 below suggests:

> [Because] everything has been given to us. . .
>   [in order that] through this . . .
> [For this very reason] make every effort. . .
>   [For] if these things are yours. . .
>   [For] anyone who lacks these things. . .
> [Therefore all the more] be diligent. . .
>   [For] thus will be supplied. . .

We have already observed the absence in 2 Peter of three elements that constitute testamental pseudepigraphy: (1) a high-profile introduction that describes the imminent death of the patriarchal figure, (2) apocalyptic visions or dreams, and (3) blessings or curses. Regarding the introduction of 2 Peter, it was noted that both the veiled allusion to the writer's death and its placement in the epistle (1.14)—injected parenthetically well after (a) the letter's greeting and introduction (1.1-4), (b) didactic block of teaching (1.5-7) and (c) hortatory statement of purpose (1.8-11)—undercuts the certainty that we have to do with the genre of 'last will' or 'testament' as it is normally conceived. In order to underscore how 2 Peter distinguishes itself from the genre testament, it is useful to consider by way of contrast the introductions to several exemplary testaments:

---

1.   'Knowledge', 'righteousness', 'piety' and 'savior'.

A copy of the testament of Reuben: the things which he commanded to his sons before he died in the one hundred twenty-fifth year of his life. . . And he said to them, 'My children, behold I am dying, and I am going the way of my fathers. . . Raise me up so that I can tell my brothers and my children the things that I have hidden in my heart, for behold I am departing from you now.'[2]

Now on the day when, having fallen ill, he began to settle his affairs, he called his seven sons and three daughters. . . And when he had called his children he said, 'Gather around, my children. . . so that I may show you the things which the Lord did with me and all the things which have happened to me'.[3]

Abraham lived the measure of his life, 995 years. All the years of his life he lived in quietness, gentleness, and righteousness. . . But even to him came the common and inexorable bitter cup of death and the unforeseen end of life. Therefore the Master God called his archangel Michael and said to him, 'Commander-in-Chief Michael, go down to Abraham and tell him about his death, so that he may arrange for the disposition of his possessions'.[4]

In terms of strict genre, that 2 Peter is both epistolary and testamental remains possible but inconclusive.

The Basis for Virtue (1.1-4)

The epistle's opening, despite its seeming lack of data, identifies the writer and audience and hints at important subthemes in the epistle—moral authority and knowledge. The writer identifies himself as 'Simon Peter, a servant and apostle', which will underscore his authoritative role,[5] given the weighty issues that must be treated in the letter. Similar to Jude (δοῦλος, ἀδελφός, v. 1) 2 Peter combines spiritual authority and humility (δοῦλος καὶ ἀπόστολος, 1.1) in a way that allows the writer to achieve identity with his audience, even while he is constrained by the prophetic burden.

2. *T. Reub.* 1.1-5 (the introduction to the pseudepigraphal *Testaments of the Twelve Patriarchs*).

3. *T. Job* 1.1-4.

4. *T. Abr.* 1.1-5.

5. Cf. Acts 15.14, the context of which is the Council of Jerusalem. Significantly, this double name does not occur in the pseudo-Petrine literature of the second century. For those who see here an over-reaching by a pseudepigrapher, Συμεὼν Πέτρος is a nice 'old-fashioned, Semitic touch' (thus Kelly, *Commentary*, p. 296).

While the matter of authorship has already been taken up in the discussion of testamental genre in Chapter 2, several remarks remain to be made. To commentators, the use of the double name Συμεὼν Πέτπος seems strange, as it occurs elsewhere only in Acts 15.14. It is noteworthy that 'Simon Peter' does not occur in any pseudo-Petrine writings of the second century. Earlier this century M.R. James, in his examination of apocalyptic pseudepigraphy, conceded that despite his doubts about the authorship of 2 Peter, the use of Συμεὼν Πέτπος was a mark *in favor of* authenticity.[6] Guthrie's comments in this regard are in order:

> We should certainly expect that an imitator of 1 Peter would have kept closer to his model in the salutation, since in 3.1 he is going to imply that his present letter is in the same sequence as the first. It is not possible in this case to treat the variation as an unconscious lapse on the part of the author, for he would hardly have begun his work with a lapse and, in any case, would not have lapsed into a primitive Hebrew form no longer in use in his own day. The only alternative is to assume that the use of the name Simeon was a deliberate device to give a greater impression of authenticity. In that case it would be necessary to suppose that the author had been studying the book of Acts or else that the form had independently survived orally in the author's own circles. On the whole, the author's name presents much greater difficulty for the pseudepigraphic writer than for Peter himself, who, in any case, would enjoy greater liberty in varying the form.[7]

The recipients of the letter are identified as 'those who have received a faith of equal standing as ours through the righteousness of our God and Savior Jesus Christ'. This 'faith' which has been imparted to the readers is described in two ways. First, it has been freely offered by God through Christ's righteousness, λαχοῦσιν πίστιν ἐν δικαιοσύνη[8] τοῦ θεοῦ ἡμῶν καὶ σωτῆρος[9] Ἰησοῦ χριστοῦ. The frequent occurrence of δίκαιος/δικαιοσύνη in 2 Peter (seven times: 1.1,13; 2.5, 7, 8, 21; 3.13) has a distinctly ethical quality, as Norman Hillyer points out,[10] and is

6. M.R. James, *The Second Epistle General of St Peter and the General Epistle of St Jude* (Cambridge: Cambridge University Press, 1912), p. 9.

7. Guthrie, *Introduction*, pp. 820-21.

8. The δίκαι- word group in 2 Peter: 1.1, 13; 2.5, 7, 8 (twice), 21; 3.13.

9. 'Savior' occurs five time in the epistle (1.1, 11; 2.20; 3.2, 18). As a corollary, 'escape' (ἀποφεύγω) appears three times in 2 Peter (1.4; 2.18, 20), but nowhere else in the New Testament.

10. Hillyer, *1 and 2 Peter, Jude*, p. 158.

all the more significant because of its frequency in Hellenistic ethical lists, though with an entirely different inflection. Nevertheless, it is a righteousness imparted by God, not produced by human effort. The initial obligation that the gospel places upon us is not to achieve something but to receive something. Not what we do before God, but what Christ has done—this is the basis for faith.

Secondly, this is a 'faith of equal standing with ours', τοῖς ἰσότιμον[11] ἡμῖν λαχοῦσιν πίστιν. The sense of equality expressed by ἰσότιμος resonates with the Greek mind, given its importance in law and politics.[12] From a political standpoint, all citizens have the same position and rights; they are thus ἴσος καὶ ὅμοιοι.[13] Political connotations carry over into the legal domain, infusing law with a principle of judicial right; the law is no respector of persons.[14] It is then quite natural that these legal connotations are translated into the covenantal language of the New Testament, illustrated by 2 Pet. 1.1.

Insofar as a reference to ἰσότιμος in Hellenistic culture reassures the citizen of his or her rights and privileges, its application to equality of spiritual allotment in the Christian life is equally meaningful. This has the effect of reassuring the recipients of 2 Peter that they stand on the same footing as the apostle and share in the very same divine provisions, irrespective of calling or stature in the faith. Such an 'equal opportunity' faith makes no distinctions or cleavages between apostles and lay persons, between those possessing spiritual authority and the rest of the church.[15] The implication is patent: 'there are no second class citizens in God's kingdom'.[16]

But the expression also can be seen as a veiled warning. Israel, in the words of Jude, was delivered once for all ἅπαξ from the land of Egypt but afterward (δεύτερον) destroyed because of unbelief (Jude 5). Israel was chosen to be a blessing to the nations. Her history, however, is

11. Kelly, *Commentary*, p. 297, misplaces the sense of by an interpretation that infers the juxtapositon of the apostles and Christians two and three generations removed.

12. See G. Stählin, 'ἴσος', *TDNT*, III, pp. 343-55.

13. Xenophon, *Hist. Graec.* 7.1.1.

14. Thus Aristotle, *Eth. Nic.* 1129a.

15. Verse 1 already hints at the difficulties that attend an 'early Catholic' reading of 2 Peter. It is equality and unlimited accessibility of the Spirit's resources, not the Spirit's power being concentrated in the ecclesiastical office, that the writer wishes to emphasize.

16. Green, *2 Peter and Jude*, p. 68.

littered with faithlessness and apostasy. Great blessing, such as has been given the saints (2 Pet. 1.3), means proportionate responsibility.

Already in the letter's opening (1.2, 3), a key term, 'knowledge', is repeated for the sake of emphasis. As it turns out, 'knowledge' is an important catchword throughout 2 Peter. The writer's prayer is that grace and peace might be multiplied to the readers via the ἐπίγνωσις of God. What role does 'knowledge'—and more pointedly, 'thorough knowledge'[17]—play in the writer's literary arsenal? In the moral self-responsibility of the audience?

'Knowledge' is important in pagan Hellenism, whether we are speaking of its central place in Stoic ethical lists (cf. the virtue of γνῶσις in 1.5) or its value to the one being initiated into the higher mysteries of cultic life (cf. the use of γνωρίζω, 'to make known' or 'to disclose' in 1.16). That, however, is not to say that the Christian counterpart is the pagan equivalent. Indeed, grace has come to believers (λαχοῦσιν πίστιν), and the knowledge—the practical awareness—of this grace is liberating, indeed salvific, in nature. Thus, 'knowledge' in 2 Peter is stripped of any misconception whereby the distinction between Christian revelation and pagan rationalism might be obscured. The writer speaks of 'knowledge of God and of Jesus our Lord' (v. 2), and it is by means of this knowledge that 'grace and peace might be multiplied'.

The implications thereof should not be lost on the readers and are twofold. First, the knowledge of God makes possible their growth in grace and peace. This axiom both opens and closes the letter: χάρις ὑμῖν καὶ εἰρήνη πληθυνθείη ἐν ἐπιγνώσει τοῦ θεοῦ καὶ Ἰησοῦ τοῦ κυρίου ἡμῶν (1.2); αὐξάνετε δὲ ἐν χάριτι καὶ γνώσει τοῦ κυρίου ἡμῶν καὶ σωτῆρος Ἰησοῦ χριστοῦ (3.18a). Secondly, this grace operating through the knowledge of God has the consequence of providing everything in the way of divine resources needed for life and godliness

17. Conflicting views on the etymology of ἐπίγνωσις notwithstanding, the writer's own use of terms would appear to determine their inflection. Sometimes, a distinction regarding the use of ἐπιγινώσκω is found in the New Testament—for example, in Johannine literature, where certain linguistic-theological developments are probably being mirrored. Other times ἐπιγινώσκω and νινώσκω are used indifferently. R.E. Picirelli ('The Meaning of "Epignosis"', *EvQ* 47.2 [1975], pp. 85-93) examines both sides of the argument. He concludes that there are sufficient grounds for giving ἐπιγινώσκω an intensive force in *some* of its New Testament occurrences (p. 90). Mere γνῶσις represents a knowledge already existing, whereas ἐπιγινώσκω represents a point at which one experiences this (p. 91). In 2 Peter, this 'knowledge' is decisive, given the issues at stake.

(1.3-4). The message of Christian grace in the pagan world is a radical reconstruction of human nature. No philosophical abstraction, this χάρις ἐν ἐπιγνώσει τοῦ θεοῦ cuts against materialistic rationalism on the one hand and philosophical mysticism on the other. The powers of the universe are henceforth no longer to be understood as impersonal and distant; the power over death and life, verified in the incarnation and the resurrection, forever changes human psychology and soteriology. Furthermore, lest the readers misinterpret the ethical admonitions to follow as a form of 'works-righteousness' or striving that is rooted solely in the power of the human will, the writer emphasizes that the power to lead an ethical life resides not in mere human strength but in the power of God.

'On account of these things' (καὶ αὐτὸ τοῦτο, v.5; διὸ μᾶλλον, v. 10) the writer is calling back to their memory concerns which they already 'know' (οἶδα, 1.12)—'truth that has already come to you'. The individuals who are roundly condemned in 2 Peter are said to have had 'full knowledge' (ἐπίγνωσις)[18] of 'the Lord and Saviour Jesus Christ', then, astoundingly, have become entangled again in (and overpowered by) the world, so that the current state is worse than the first. It would have been better for these had they never 'fully known' (ἐπιγινώσκω) the way of righteousness than, having 'fully known' it (ἐπιγινώσκω), later turned back and disavowed what had been previously passed on to them (2.20-21).

That some in the community have actually departed the faith and are claiming moral autonomy is a weighty enough constraint upon the writer. A second factor, however, contributes to the exigencies of the moment: 'Knowing that my death [literally, 'the removal of my body'] will be soon',[19] 1.14a). The combined force of these two factors in writing—the eternal destiny of those in the community and the possibility of approaching martyrdom—are sufficient reason to account for the

18. While the compound ἐπιγινώσκω and γινώσκω are used interchangeably in classical literature, ἐπιγινώσκω becomes a virtual technical term in the New Testament for the decisive knowledge of God. Significantly, it does not occur in the Fourth Gospel or in the Johannine epistles, where one might expect it. This may suggest its graduation in time into protognostic distortions. See R. Bultmann, 'γινώσκω' *TDNT*, I, pp. 707-14.

19. ταχινή may denote 'soon' in a temporal sense as well as 'rapid' in a modal sense. If 1.14 is to be understood modally, then the writer is alluding to the manner in which he departs, reminiscent of Jesus' prophecy concerning Peter in Jn 21.18.

passion and force with which 2 Peter is written. Hence, it is all the more reason for reiterating that the readers 'know' these things. Twice in the opening three verses (1.2,3) the writer employs the word ἐπίγνωσις. The accent cannot possibly be any stronger. The virtuous life, rooted in the ἐπίγνωσις of God, is to *increase* (πλεονάζω) on their part, so that they are not rendered 'barren and ineffective in the knowledge (ἐπίγνωσις) of our Lord Jesus Christ' (1.8).

How important is 'knowledge' to the writer? Based upon his vocabulary, it is extremely important, and thus, an epistolary catchword. For this reason he can write that the experience of grace and peace in the believer's life is anchored in—indeed, predicated upon—knowledge (1.2). Not the philosophic reflection of contemporary ethicists and moral philosophers, not the protognostic speculation of pseudo-Christian mystics, but the knowledge 'of God and of our Lord Jesus Christ'. The correlation of virtue to knowledge, developed in the ethical catalog that follows (1.5-7), is not incidental. This affiliation points to a practical understanding of what righteousness should resemble.[20] And what is the *summum bonum* of the Christian life? It is to *know* God.

Thus, 'knowledge' is integral to literary strategy in 2 Peter.[21] A second key term, εὐσέβεια[22] ('godliness' or 'piety'), also appears in the opening context. Following the greeting, 'knowledge' and 'godliness' are united in 1.3-4 in a way that serves two strategic epistolary functions. (1) They preview together the foremost ethical burden of the writer ('You know these things' [1.12]; 'What sort of persons should you be in leading lives of holiness and godliness?' [3.11]). (2) They are couched together in language that is quite striking to the average reader.

Consider the language employed: 'According to the divine power everything necessary for life and godliness has been given to us through the knowledge of him who has called us by his own glory and goodness' (v. 3). The Christian truth expressed in this statement is being emphasized in a distinctly 'un-Christian' manner. Pagan philosophical categories are used to describe the nature of the full repository of faith

20. O. Zöckler (*Die Tugendlehre des Christentums* [Gütersloh: Bertelsmann, 1904], pp. 3-4) captures this nuance in his comments on the ethical list in 2 Pet. 1.

21. Other key words in the epistle include κρίσις (four times), κόσμος (four times), σωτήρ (four times), ὁδός (four times), ἀπώλεια or ἀπόλλυμι (five times), προσδοκάω (three times), and the rare ἐξακολουθέω (three times).

22. εὐσέβεια occurs in 2 Peter four times: 1.3, 6, 7 and 3.11.

already alluded to in the greeting.[23] God has provided lavish resources (τὰ τίμια καὶ μέγιστα ἐπαγγέλματα),[24] according to the writer, so that, stated negatively, the readers might thereby escape the world's corruption[25] and, stated positively, they 'might become partakers of the divine nature' (v. 4). The vocabulary in vv. 3-4 merits some consideration.

In speaking of suppressing fleshly lusts, the writer is borrowing heavily from Stoic ethical categories. In Stoic doctrine, one suppresses the passions of the flesh by cultivating virtue. Being virtuous, however, is an entirely rational rather than 'spiritual' exercise. While the Christian distinctive of grace is presupposed (πίστις ἐν δικαιοσύνῃ τοῦ θεοῦ, v. 1; χάρις καὶ εἰρήνη πληθυνθείη, v. 2), the will to deal with the flesh must be evidenced. As the rest of 2 Peter makes clear, not only is this 'will' to curb the passions to be questioned among some, there are even those in the community who are revelling in moral depravity.

In addition to the presence of Stoic vocabulary in vv. 3-4, the reader encounters the Platonic linkage of δόξα and ἀρετή[26] in the description of Christ's 'moral excellence';[27] two uses of the adjectival substantive θεῖος, 'the divine';[28] and the striking phrase 'partaking in the divine

23. A. Deissmann (*Bible Studies: Contributions Chiefly from Papyri and Inscriptions to the History of the Language, the Literature, and the Religion of Hellenistic Judaism and Primitive Christianity*[trans. A. Grieve; Edinburgh: T.& T. Clark, 1901], p. 367) is more inclined to see in 1.3 'the official liturgical language of Asia Minor'.

24. In classical Greek, ἐπαγγέλματα denotes voluntary or spontaneous promises (in contrast to ὑποσχέσεις, which are promises made in response to a petition).

25. Literally, 'the corruption that is in the world because of lust'.

26. The linkage of δόξα and ἀρετή surfaces in two works of Plato—*Meno* and *Republic*. For a discussion of pertinent philosophical background, see Y. Lefrance, *La théorie platonicienne de la Doxa* (Montreal: Bellarmin; Paris: Les Belles Lettres, 1981).

27. Rarely occurring in the New Testament (in 2 Peter thrice [1.3,5], Phil. 4.8 and 1 Pet. 2.9), ἀρετή is all the more striking due to its customary association in philosophical discourse with a pleasant temporal existence and not afterlife (thus, A. Hermann, *Untersuchungen zu Platons Auffassung von der Hedone: Ein Beitrag zum Verständnis des platonischen Tugendbegriffes* [Hypomnemata, 35; Göttingen: Vandenhoeck & Ruprecht, 1972], pp. 59-73).

28. For an analysis of Paul's presentation at the Areopagus of Christian revelation in culturally relevant categories, see M. Pohlenz, 'Paulus und die Stoa', *ZNW* 42 (1949), pp. 69-104; B. Gärtner, *The Areopagus Speech and Natural Revelation* (ASNU, 21; Uppsala: Almquist, 1955), pp. 73-241; L. Legrand, 'The Areopagus Speech: Its Theological Kerygma and its Missionary Significance', in J. Coppens

nature' (γένησθε θείας κοινωνοὶ φύσεως).[29] Stoics, unlike the academic and peripatetic philosophers, affirmed both human and divine virtue; thus, ἀρετή can be ascribed both to men and the gods. For Christian purposes, both δόξα and ἀρετή inhere in the character of God. Moreover, the glory and goodness of God are exhibited by his very acts and works.[30]

The linkage of divine δόξα and ἀρετή is found outside of the New Testament as well. Plutarch uses δόξα and ἀρετή together in a similar context as 2 Peter 1.[31] Philo alludes to the excellence (ἀρετή) and wisdom (σοφία) of God.[32] Josephus speaks of individuals who 'abuse the goodness (ἀρετή) of the divine'.[33] Plutarch elsewhere remarks on the qualities of the divine in a way that is relevant to the immediate context of 2 Peter:

> Divinity, to which men are eager to adapt and conform themselves, seems
> to have three elements of superiority—incorruption, power, and virtue
> [ἀρετή]; and the most impressive, the divinest of these is virtue'.[34]

Surely there is a resonation in the mind of the readers between the way in which ἀρετή is used here and its application to ethics immediately

---

(ed.), *La notion de Dieu* (Louvain: Gembloux, 1974), pp. 338-41; F. Mussner, 'Anknüpfung, Kontinuität und Widerspruch in der Areopagrede. Apg 17,22-31', in P.G. Müller and W. Stenger (eds.), *Kontinuität und Einheit* (Freiburg: Herder, 1981); and J.D. Charles, 'Engaging the (Neo)Pagan Mind: Paul's Encounter with Athenian Culture as a Model for Cultural Apologetics (Acts 17.16-34)', *TJ* 16 NS (1995), pp. 47-62.

29. The Platonic phrase θεῖα φύσις (*Rep.* 366c; *Phaed.* 230a; *Theaet.* 176ab), occurs also in Aristotle (*Part. Anim.* 4.10; *Apol.* 7.1.2), Seneca (*Ep. Mor.* 92.30), Josephus (*Apion* 26), Philo (*Dc.* 104; *Conf. Ling.* 154), and Diogenes Laertius (10.97.103). Philo distinguishes union with God as being initiated by God, not caused by humans (*Leg. All.* 1.38). Thus, it is only natural that in Lystra the Christian apostles attempt to dispell any notion that might mistake a man for a god ('Barnabas they called Zeus, and Paul they called Hermes', Acts 14.12). Contra Moffatt (*Introduction*, p. 360), who states that the use of θεῖα δύναμις and θεῖα φύσις in 1.3, 4 'is missed unless the writer is placed in the second century', the vocabulary is very much in accord with what early Christian apologists would have encountered—and perhaps coopted—in their interaction with Stoic counterparts.

30. So Mayor, *Jude and Second Peter*, p. 189.

31. *De vit. Pud.* 535.

32. *Leg. alleg.* 2.14.

33. *Ant.* 17.5.6.

34. *Arist.* 6.3 (cited in Kelly, *Commentary*, p. 301).

following (1.5). To wit: there exists a relationship between God's moral character and ours.

It is noteworthy that the use of θεῖος in the New Testament is limited to two instances—1.3-4 and Acts 17.29. The context of the latter is Paul's discourse before the Council of the Areopagus in Athens. Both social locations—cosmopolitan Athens and perhaps a very similar setting in 2 Peter such as Asia Minor—betray no evidence of Jewish Torah- or worldview-thinking such as one finds in the epistle of James or the huge cast of Jewish characters in Jude. The terminology employed in 2 Peter 1, reminiscent of philosophical mysticism and the mystery cults, is especially relevant if the epistle is addressed to a community in Asia Minor.

Not surprisingly, the adjectival θεῖος occurs with relative frequency in Hellenistic Jewish literature.[35] Philo, who also speaks of oneness with the divine,[36] distinguishes this union as being initiated by God, not caused by humans.[37]

Christian evangelists and writers would have been particularly sensitive about using language to denote becoming like God or mystical union with the divine, given contemporary connotations stemming from ever-present mysticism.[38] It is conceivable that Paul and Barnabas have something similar in mind following their ministry in Lystra (Acts 14.8-18). Reacting to the healing of an invalid, the crowd exclaims, 'The gods have come down to us in the likeness of men (ὁμοιωθέντες ἀνθρώποις)!' In reaction, Paul and Barnabas instinctively rend their garments and rush out among the people crying, 'Men, why are you doing this? We are also mere humans like you.' The rather unique problem confronting the apostles in Lystra, at least from Luke's point of view, is that a pagan understanding of ὁμοιοπαθής might hinder the crowd's grasp of the good news. Theirs is the challenge of dispelling any notion that might mistake a man for a god, especially where supernatural powers are on display. The narrative ends with this note from Luke: 'With these words [of disclamation] they scarcely restrained the people from sacrificing to them' (14.18).

---

35. Kelly, *Commentary*, p. 302, notes 25 appearances in *4 Maccabees*.

36. *Dec.* 104 and *Abr.* 107.

37. *Leg. All.* 1.38.

38. This language appears in a wide range of literature, from Plutarch (*De Is. et Os.* 358) to Philo (*Conf. Ling.* 154) to Ps.-Phocylides (103-104).

That the writer is making use in 2 Peter 1 of pagan metaphysical language reveals an underlying motivation: to demonstrate an awareness of and relevance to the social location of his audience.

The Catalog of Virtues (1.5-7)

Among Hellenistic philosophers, no one could consider himself rational without a pledge to be moral.[39] Such is implicit in Cicero's rhetorical question, 'Is not philosophy the law of life?'[40] Indeed, the real business of all philosophy, which performed a therapeutic function,[41] was viewed as moral conduct. Reason and virtue together are that which separates humans from wild beasts, write Epictetus and Seneca. Foundationally, virtue in the Stoic view is a corollary of knowledge (γνῶσις).[42] By this moral calculus, vice is to be equated with ignorance. It may well be that in 2 Peter the writer is exploiting this common epistemological assumption in his moral exhortation; hence his strategic use of the catchwords 'knowledge' and 'knowing' throughout the epistle.[43]

If 2 Peter is addressed to the Christian community in a Gentile social setting, as Fornberg has persuasively argued, the concepts of virtue, faith and love would be an appropriate method of countering immorality or amorality in a skeptical environment. In the hands of the writer, the foundations of pagan ethical life can be symbolically sanctified and utilized. No dichotomy exists between the temporal and the eternal, between the human cooperation and divine initiation. Christian truth, the writer wishes to emphasize, manifests itself in the Hellenistic ethical ideal[44] (even when the means to this ideal is antithetical to Christian

---

39. Thus Cicero, *Leg.* 1.12.33.

40. *Ep.* 39. To the extent that religion consists in wisdom and virtue, it does not differ with Hellenistic philosophy (thus, for example, Seneca, *Ep. Mor.* 95.47; idem, *Fr.* 123; Epictetus, *Ench.* 31.1; and Cicero, *De nat. deo* 2.71). It was of the more popular, 'irrational' forms of religion that Stoic philosophers were critical.

41. Seneca writes that philosophy 'tones the soul' (*Ep. Mor.* 15).

42. Because the Stoic virtues are all forms of knowledge, philosophy can be viewed as both a means and an end.

43. Consider the vocabulary: γινώσκω (1.20; 3.3); ἐπιγινώσκω (2.21 twice); προγινώσκω (3.17); γνωρίζω (1.16); οἶδα (1.12, 14); γνῶσις (1.5, 6; 3.18); and ἐπίγνωσις (1.2, 3, 8; 2.20). To Clement of Alexandria, accustomed to bridging culture and faith, γνῶσις is the intermediary between faith and love (*Strom.* 7.46.55).

44. Thus Klinger, 'Second Epistle', pp. 163-68.

grace). Indeed, it can be argued that where a people has no regard for moral authority in general, there can be no social bond, no common life, and no virtue.[45]

Not only would a catalog of virtues be an appropriate way of countering a deterioration of the moral life in the community, it would also be relevant based on the catalog's popular usage. One unusually striking parallel to 2 Pet. 1.5-7 comes from a first-century Asia Minor inscription said to be in honor of one Herostratus, son of Dorcalion.[46] Listed in this catalog, respectively, are πίστις (faith), ἀρετή (virtue), δικαιοσύνη (righteousness), εὐσέβεια (piety) and σπουδή (diligence).[47] A comparison of the two texts, which show verbatim similarities, is worth noting.

> ἄνδρα ἀγαθὸν γενόμενον καὶ διενένκαντα πίστει καὶ ἀρετῆ καὶ δ[ικ]αιοσύνη και εὐσεβείαι... τὴν πλεῖστ[η]ν εἰσενηνεγμένον σπουδὴν

> σπουδὴν πᾶσαν παρεισενέγκαντες ἐπιχορηγήσατε ἐν τῆ πίστει ὑμῶν τὴν ἀρετήν, ἐν δὲ τῆ ἀρετῆ τὴν γνῶσιν, ἐν δὲ τῆ γνώσει τὴν ἐγκράτειαν, ἐν δὲ τῆ ἐγκρατείᾳ τὴν ὑπομονήν, ἐν δὲ τῆ ὑπομονῆ τὴν εὐσεβειαν

2 Pet. 1.5 begins: 'For this very reason make every effort to add to your faith.' The Hellenistic thought-world, on display in 1.3-4, comes to expression in vv. 5-7 as well. Of the eight virtues listed in vv. 5-7, ἀρετή (moral excellence), γνῶσις[48] (knowledge), ἐγκράτεια (self-

---

45. As argued by R.L. Wilken, 'Serving the One True God', in C.E. Braaten and R.W. Jensen (eds.), *Either/Or: The Gospel or Neopaganism* (Grand Rapids: Eerdmans, 1995), p. 62.

46. The text appears in F. Dittenberger (ed.), *Orientis Graeci Inscriptiones Selectae: Supplementum Sylloges inscriptionum Graecarum* (Hildesheim: Georg Olms, 1970), pp. 12-13 (no. 438), and is cited due to its notable parallels in A. Deissmann, *Light from the Ancient East* (trans. L.R.M. Strachan; New York: G.H. Doran, 1927), pp. 317-18.

47. Cf. 2 Pet. 1.5, 10, 15; 3.14.

48. K.-W. Tröger ('Zum gegenwärtigen Stand der Gnosis- und Nag-Hammadi-Forschung', in K.-W. Tröger (ed.), *Altes Testament—Frühjudentum—Gnosis: Neue Studien zu 'Gnosis und Bibel'* [Gütersloh: Mohn, 1980], pp. 11-33) points to the considerable diversity and confusion surrounding use of the term 'gnosis'—usage that ranges from non-technical to religious. While γνῶσις in 2 Pet. 1 as part of a rhetorical strategy that reflects broader Hellenistic usage, popular understanding related foremost to knowing *oneself* (γνῶθι σαυτόν) and others (Dupont, *Gnosis: La Connaissance religieuse dans les épîtres de Saint Paul* [Louvain: E. Nauwelaerts; Paris:

control), ὑπομονή (perseverance), εὐσέβεια [49] (godliness) and φιλαδελφία (brotherly affection) all appear in one form or another in comparable (pagan) ethical lists, of which ἀρετή, γνῶσις, ἐγκράτεια and
εὐσέβεια are most common.[50] The individual virtues in the 2 Peter
catena that also appear in pagan lists give evidence that the letter orig-
inated in or was destined to a Gentile setting.[51] Moreover, the exhortation to virtue in 1.5-7 suggests a concrete local situation that is in
need of being addressed.

πίστις, normally conveying the sense of loyalty or trust in common
parlance, is to be understood as distinctly Christian in its conception.[52]
In comparable sub-apostolic lists, faith is also the foundation. Hermas's
list[53] begins with πίστις and ends with ἀγάπη, between which are found
ἐγκράτεια, ἀπλοτής, ἀκακία, σεμνότης and ἐπιστήμης. Barnabas[54]
begins with πίστις, upon which φόβος, ὑπομονή, μακροθυμία and
ἐγκράτεια follow. Clement has two short lists of three and four virtues respectively,[55] with πίστις beginning both and ἀγάπη included in
the second. πίστις in v. 5 is not the *fides quae creditur* of 'early Catholic' understanding, that is, the objective creedal dogma formulated in
response to second-century heresy.[56] It is rather the subjective trust
placed in the gospel—a faith procured ἐν δικαιοσύνῃ τοῦ θεοῦ ἡμῶν
καὶ σωτῆρος Ἰησοῦ χριστοῦ. It is, moreover, a faith 'received'
(λαγχάνω) and not 'handed down' (παραδίδωμι) by way of tradition,
which is to say, it is a free gift, bestowed upon all.[57]

In its earlier classical usage, ἀρετή denotes excellence or renown. In
time, it was applied to the sphere of ethics, to which it was henceforth

J. Gabalda, 1949], pp. 383-84). Note also Paul's word-play with 'knowledge' in
Acts 17.23 before the Areopagus Council concerning the ἀγνώστῳ θεῷ, ὃ οὖν
ἀγνοοῦντες εὐσεβεῖτε, τοῦτο ἐγὼ καταγγέλλω ὑμῖν.

49. Note the verb form εὐσεβεῖτε in Paul's Areopagus speech (Acts 17.23).

50. Even πίστις, understood as loyalty, occurs with relative frequency in popular
philosophical catalogs (Vögtle, *Die Tugend-und Lasterkataloge*, pp. 188-89).

51. So Fornberg, *Early Church*, p. 98.

52. Dupont, *Gnosis*, p. 403.

53. *Vis.* 3.8.1.

54. 2.2.3.

55. *1 Clem.* 62.2.43.

56. Represented, for example, by Schelkle, 'Spätapostolische Briefe', pp. 225-
32, and *idem, Die Petrusbriefe—Der Judasbrief* (HTKNT, 13.2; Freiburg: Herder,
1970), pp. 145-68, 241-48.

57. Thus Hillyer, *1 and 2 Peter, Jude*, p. 157.

more or less restricted. As one might expect, given the underlying Stoic belief that moral excellence was the result of human achievement (as opposed to righteousness and obedience to the Torah) without any consequence of afterlife, its occurrence in the LXX is rare. The term does appear with some frequency in Philo, Wisdom of Solomon and *4 Maccabees*, that is, Hellenistic Judaism. Although ἀρετή appears three times in 2 Peter 1,[58] its usage in 1.3, applied to divine manifestation, is similar to that found in 1 Pet. 2.9 ('that you might proclaim his mighty ἀρετή').[59]

Knowledge, γνῶσις, frequently begins or ends pagan ethical lists.[60] One is thus justified in concluding that its placement in the catalog immediately following ἀρετή reflects the Stoic belief that there is an organic and indivisible link between the two virtues. Where the Christian and Stoic views of knowledge differ is that the Christian view strips knowledge of its technical nuance so that it is not a goal in and of itself. In contrast to speculative philosophy,[61] by which γνῶσις underpins the acquisition of all the virtues, in the Petrine progression it is an extension and not the sole *basis* of one's faith and virtue. It is rather rooted in revelatory grace (v. 2). Apart from faith and virtue, knowledge is detrimental, a reality to which the community at Corinth bears striking testimony.[62] What the readers do with the knowledge imparted to them is decisive. In the present context γνῶσις signifies a practical manifestation or application of what is known to be true. In the moral progression of 2 Pet. 1.5-7, knowledge should progress toward greater self-control in the lives of the readers. Growth in knowledge, simply stated, will lead to an exemplary lifestyle—one that is virtuous and, in Hellenistic culture, necessarily restrained.

58. ἀρετή in the New Testament: Phil. 4.8; 1 Pet. 2.9; 2 Pet. 1.3, 5.

59. Cf. LXX Isa. 43.21.

60. Vögtle, *Die Tugend- und Lasterkataloge*, pp. 187-91, and Dupont, *Gnosis*, pp. 388-93.

61. Kelly, *Commentary*, p. 306, believes the reference to γνῶσις in 1.5 to be 'a critical side-glance at the speculative gnosis of the errorists'. More plausibly, the writer's vocabulary is simply a reflection of a broader Hellenistic and philosophical usage.

62. 1 Cor. 8.1-3, 7-13; 13.2. γνῶσις in succeeding generations would be possessed by the few 'who are capable of grasping it' (Clement, *Strom.* 1.13.1).

By the logic of virtue, knowledge motivates and moves the individual toward self-control,[63] ἐγκράτεια.[64] This is an organic connection that is not incidental; both elements go together naturally, just as their opposites, ignorance (ἄγνοια) and lust (ἐπιθυμία), find an irrepressible linkage both in pagan ethics and the New Testament: 'Like obedient children, do not be conformed to the desires (ἐπιθυμίαι) of your former ignorance (ἄγνοια) (1 Pet. 1.14). ἐγκράτεια is a cardinal virtue for Socrates,[65] and in his contrast of moral strength and weakness, Aristotle devotes a whole section to its importance in *Nicomachean Ethics*.[66] Stoics adopted the same exalted view of ἐγκράτεια,[67] although in the hierarchy of virtues it is subordinated to σωφροσύνη.[68] In Philo, it is a superior virtue,[69] though linked with asceticism,[70] which marks something of a shift from the classical view.

Defined in Stoic terms as 'self-discipline in all matters affecting the senses',[71] ἐγκράτεια[72] is perhaps best understood when set in juxtaposition to its antithetical twins—ἀκρασία (incontinence) and ἀκολασία (licentiousness). ἐγκράτεια, moreover, is a necessary component in the ethical life to counter any potential misunderstanding of Christian 'freedom'—a misunderstanding, for example, that might view the struggle against πάθος or ἐπιθυμία as unnecessary. It is not coincidental that ἐγκράτεια is frequently associated with sexual restraint, even within the Christian community (for example, Gal. 5.23).[73] A synonym of ἀκολασία, ἀσέλγεια occurs twice in 2 Peter (2.7, 18), alongside other linguistic indications of moral squalor that invade the community—φθορά (1.4; 2.12 [twice], 19), ἐπιθυμία (1.4; 2.10, 18; 3.3), ἄνομος (2.8) and ἄθεσμος (2.7; 3.17).

63. Clement notes this relationship as well in *Strom.* 7.46.
64. See W. Grundmann, 'ἐγκράτεια', *TDNT*, II, pp. 339-42.
65. Xenophon, *Mem.* 1.5.4.
66. Book 7 (1145b-1154b).
67. Stobaeus, *Ecl.* 2.61.11; Diog. Laert. 7.92.
68. Stobaeus, *Ecl.* 2.60.20.
69. *Spec. Leg.* 2.195.
70. *Leg. All.* 3.18.
71. Thus Kelly, *Commentary*, p. 306.
72. From the stem κρατ-, signifying power or lordship, and thus, dominion over oneself.
73. In his defense before Felix, Paul's discussion of ἐγκράτεια, δικαιοσύνη, and κρίμα (Acts 24.25) proves somewhat difficult for the governor.

2 Peter gives evidence not only that humans are capable of unbridled passion but also that such indulgence has a seductive effect on others (2.10-12, 15-16; 3.3). Thus it is that Stoic philosophy carved out its niche by a rigorous ethical program aimed at curbing the passions. While the power and motivation of the Christian ethic are distinct from the Stoic counterpart, they nevertheless share common ethical ground as well as a common moral grammar. Self-restraint is not only a mark of and prerequisite for a spiritual leader (Tit. 1.8), it is a fruit of the Spirit and a necessary part of any Christian's ethical arsenal (Gal. 5.23). With this in full view, Tertullian seeks to encourage Christians under persecution by citing the example of the athletes: *Coguntur, cruciantur, fatigantur* ('They are constrained, harassed, wearied').[74] Given the fact that the trajectory of much of the material in 2 Peter is aimed at the lawless and morally depraved, that is, those who revel in their 'freedom' (2.19), ἐγκράτεια is the practical manifestation of the ethical life.

From ἐγκράτεια develops ὑπομονή, endurance or perseverance. In its classical usage, ὑπομονή connotes 'courageous endurance that fully defies evil',[75] and thus, is active rather than passive. In Plato,[76] it is brave resistance that is honorable to a man. Aristotle subordinates ὑπομονή to ἀνδρεία,[77] a categorization that is carried over into Stoic ethics. Endurance has two sides: it expresses itself toward the world and toward God. Far from mere will power,[78] by which the Stoic deadens his sensibilities, endurance in the Christian scheme of things issues out of the deep confidence in the divine will and a submission to the hand of God. This quality allows the believer to bear up—or, more accurately, 'remain under'—difficulty and trial and remain unmoved. To endure temptation, suffering and hardship requires patience. It is, moreover, hope that allows one to 'endure all things' (1 Cor. 13.7)—a Christian hope anchored in a deep confidence that God the Father will not allow one to be tested beyond the capacity to stand firm. To endure is to demonstrate mature faith. This emphasis of enduring presses to the fore in much of the New Testament, particularly in Hebrews, James, 1 Peter and Revelation. Within the context of faith, the person who endures temptation is blessed (Jas 1.12). If we endure when we do right,

74. *Ad mart.* 3.
75. F. Hauck, 'ὑπομονή', *TDNT*, IV, pp. 581-88.
76. *Theaet.* 117b.
77. *Eth. Nic.* 1115a-1117b.
78. For example, *SVF* 3.65; Seneca, *Ep. Mor.* 67.10.

we have God's approval (1 Pet. 2.20). In persevering, it is important to remember that we have a model (Heb. 12.2).[79] In 2 Peter, ὑπομονή appears alongside the μακροθυμία of God (3.15). We endure because of God's longsuffering toward humans.

The connection between self-control, endurance and godliness (the next link in the Petrine catena) is transparent and logical in the Christian ethical progression. εὐσέβεια is to be interpreted in a broad sense. In late Hellenism it expresses general 'piety' or reverence and occurs in both religious and non-religious contexts. It may be used in the sense of reverence toward the gods, or it may denote respect for family, tradition or the social order.[80] Thus, in the wider sense of the term, it is not an expression of Greek religiosity.[81] In the New Testament it carries both Christian and broader Hellenistic connotations. Significantly, all the occurrences of εὐσέβεια are confined to the Pastorals[82] and 2 Peter,[83] where it serves to underscore a particular way of life, that is, the behavior that is worthy of praise. In a Hellenistic context, it bespeaks laudable behavior toward the gods and cultic duties[84] and thus is a pagan ideal. The soul of religion, after all, is its practice.

The virtue of piety expresses itself in our relationships with others—to the world and to the household of faith. Out of one's reverence toward God one learns to love others. Indeed, the Christian gospel is nothing if it does not affect one's relationships. How one relates to God will determine how one relates to others. φιλαδελφία, often appearing as φιλανθρωπία[85] in pagan texts,[86] describes a kindness or affection toward family members and toward others in general. Behind the term stands the Greek ideal of friendship, suggesting duties that attend our relationships.[87] For the household of faith, it acquires a special

---

79. The verb and noun forms of ὑπομένω occur six times in Hebrews, where trials and persecution require being addressed by the writer.

80. W. Foerster, 'εὐσέβεια', *TDNT*, VII, pp. 175-85.

81. So Fornberg, *Early Church*, p. 100.

82. εὐσέβεια occurs ten times in the Pastorals.

83. The εὐσεβ- word group occurs four times in 2 Peter: 1.3, 6, 7; 3.11.

84. Kelly, *Commentary*, p. 303.

85. Philo links φιλανθρωπία with εὐσέβεια in *Virt.* 51 and 95, while linking together ἐγκράτεια, εὐσέβεια and φιλανθρωπία in *Spec. Leg.* 4.97.

86. Vögtle, *Die Tugend- und Lasterkataloge*, p. 188, notes the rather scant use of the term φιλαδελφία outside of Christian literature.

87. See U. Luck, 'φιλανθρωπία', *TDNT*, IX, pp. 107-12.

meaning, though it can be taken for granted. It constantly needs to be refined by the work of the Spirit.[88]

The catalog achieves its climax in ἀγάπη, which distinguishes the Christian ethos and without which it would be incomplete. Christian morality is distinctly the morality of charity. It is the morality of fruit bearing, whereby one gives evidence of an internal work of grace, demonstrating gratitude through one's actions.[89] Seen in this way, Christian morality issues from a wholly unique motivation. Frequently in the New Testament this work of grace is depicted by exploiting the imagery of the farmer, the gardener, and the vinedresser. God is the cultivator, we are the field (1 Cor. 3.5-9). The Christian disciple exists to bear fruit—lasting fruit (Jn 15; Rom. 7.4). The Christian's life, if it is judged to be qualitatively different, must bear the fruit of the Spirit (Gal. 5). It is in this process of fruit bearing that we please God (Col. 1.10) and influence men (Mt. 5.16). Yet this is no rigorist asceticism; rather, it flows from a divine source. Inasmuch as ἀγάπη is the fount and the goal of Christian virtuous action,[90] therein lies the difference between the Christian and pagan ethos.

To the modern Christian reader the question might naturally arise as to why the writer does not include the third of the 'theological' virtues—hope—or why the many fruits of the Spirit, listed in Galatians 5, are omitted. Or, from the other direction, why did the writer omit three of the four 'cardinal' virtues (σωφροσύνη, ἀνδρεία and δικαιοσύνη)? Is the list arbitrary in its selection, as some commentators maintain?

While vice and virtue lists in the New Testament are not all of the same compositional variety, one peculiar feature which is absent from pagan catalogs is the occasional movement in a list toward crescendo or decrescendo. A prime example of this is 2 Pet. 1.5-7, which features an ethical progression that builds toward a climax in ἀγάπη.[91]

88. See, for example, Rom. 12.9-10; Eph. 4.1-3; Phil. 4.2, 5; Col. 3.12-15; 1 Thess. 4.9; Heb. 13.1; 1 Pet. 1.22; 1 Jn 5.1.

89. C. Spicq, *Théologie morale du Nouveau Testament* (2 vols.; Paris: Gabalda, 1970), I, pp. 50, 141.

90. Parallel to the over-arching mandate of love is doing the will of God. On this dual emphasis in the New Testament, see J. Stelzenberger, *Lehrbuch der Moraltheologie* (Paderborn: Schöningh, 1965), pp. 69-73.

91. Contra H. Windisch (*Die katholischen Briefe* [HNT, 4.2; Tübingen: Mohr, 2nd edn, 1930], p. 84) and Bauckham (*Jude, 2 Peter*, pp. 184-85), who see no

Each virtue, a fruit of the life of faith, facilitates the next; none is independent of the others, as is suggested by the ἐν δὲ τῇ syntactical arrangement of vv. 5-7. The virtues cannot stand in unrelated or unconnected juxtaposition. Because of this organic unity, which is rooted in the spiritual realities of faith and the righteousness of Christ, the catalog of virtues in 2 Peter is not largely random; rather, it demonstrates from a Christian standpoint a logical interconnection of virtues, all of which move toward the highest virtue, ἀγάπη. The relation between the individual virtues has been aptly summarized by Mayor:

> Faith is the gift of God already received; to this must be added (1) moral
> strength which enables a man to do what he knows to be right; (2) spiritual
> discernment; (3) self-control by which a man resists temptation; (4) en-
> durance by which he bears up under persecution or adversity; (5) right
> . . . behavior toward God [piety]; (6) toward the brethren [brotherly love];
> [and] toward all [love].[92]

Rather remarkable verbal and conceptual parallels to 2 Pet. 1.3-7 show up in an early first-century Asia Minor inscription. A decree issued by the inhabitants of Stratonicea in the Asian province of Caria[93] mirrors what is apparently commonplace liturgical language for that region. The affinities between the inscription and 2 Peter 1 are strong enough to suggest the possibility of literary dependence. Both the text of the decree and that of 2 Peter follow:

> . . . τὴν πόλιν ἄνωθεν τῇ τῶν προεστώτων αὐτῆς μεγίστων θεῶν
> [προνοίᾳ Διὸς Π]ανημε[ρίου καὶ Ἑ]κάτης ἐκ πολλῶν καὶ μεγάλων

logical progression in the virtue catalog, there *is*, from a uniquely Christian perspective, a logic, a cadence, a starting-point and a climax to the virtues listed. Bauckham is correct to observe that apart from πίστις and ἀγάπη the writer has chosen virtues from the Stoic and popular philosophical milieu that demonstrate ethical relevance in a Hellenistic cultural environment. His claim, however, that '[o]nly two virtues have a clearly intelligible place in the list' would indicate a lack of discernment as to their theological and organic union, which indeed at the very least is suggested by the syntax of vv. 5-7. Escalation can also be detected in Rom. 5.1-5, where the trajectory of grace moves from suffering to hope. Similarly, the list of hardships encountered by Paul recorded in 2 Cor. 6.6 moves from the general (afflictions and hardships) to the specific (sleepless nights and hunger). This rhetorical movement is analyzed in H.A. Fischel, 'The Uses of Sorites (Climax, Gradatio) in the Tannaitic Period', *HUCA* 44 (1973), pp. 119-51.

92. Mayor, *Jude and Second Peter*, p. 93.

93. Caria, known for its exportation of Aphrodisiac statues worldwide, comprised southwest coastal Asia Minor and was situated between Lycia and Lydia.

καὶ συνεχῶν κινδύνων σεσῶσθαι, ὧν καὶ τὰ ἱερὰ ἄσυλα καὶ ἱκέται
καὶ ἡ ἱερὰ σύνκλητος δόγματι Σε[βαστοῦ Καίσαρος ἐπὶ] τῆς τῶν
κυρίων Ῥωμαίων αἰωνίου ἀρχῆς ἐποιήσαντο προφανεῖς ἐναρνείας·
καλῶς δὲ ἔχι πᾶσαν σπουδὴν ἰσφέρεσθαι ἰς τὴν πρὸς [αὐτοὺς
εὐσέβ]ειαν καὶ μηδένα καιρὸν παραλιπῖν τοῦ εὐσεβεῖν καὶ λιτανεύιν
αὐτούς. καθίδρυται δὲ ἀγάλματα ἐν τῷ σεβαστῷ βουλευτηρίῳ τῶν
προειρημένω[ν θεῶν ἐπιφαν]εστάτας παρέχοντα τῆς θείας δυνάμεως
ἀρετάς, δι᾽ ἃς καὶ το σύνπαν πλῆθος θύει τε καὶ ἐπιθυμιᾷ καὶ εὔχεται
καὶ εὐχαριστεῖ... τοῖς οὕτως ἐπιφανεστάτοις θεοῖς κἀκ τῆς δι᾽
ὑμνῳδίας προσόδου καὶ θρησκείας εὐσεβεῖν αὐτοὺς [εἴθισται].[94]

'Ως πάντα ὑμῖν τῆς θείας δυνάμεως αὐτοῦ τὰ πρὸς ζωὴν καὶ
εὐσέβειαν δεδωρημένης διὰ τῆς ἐπιγνώσεως τοῦ καλέσαντος ἡμᾶς
ἰδίᾳ δόξῃ καὶ ἀρετῇ, δι᾽ ὧν τὰ τίμια καὶ μέγιστα ἡμῖν ἐπαγγέλματα
δεδώρηται, ἵνα διὰ τούτων γένησθε θείας κοινωνοὶ φύσεως
ἀποφυγόντες τῆς ἐν τῷ κόσμῳ ἐν ἐπιθυμίᾳ φθορᾶς. Καὶ αὐτὸ τοῦτο δὲ
σπουδὴν πᾶσαν παρεισενέγκαντες ἐπιχορηγήσατε ἐν τῇ πίστει ὑμῶν
τὴν ἀρετήν, ἐν δὲ τῇ ἀρετῇ τὴν γνῶσιν, ἐν δὲ τῇ γνώσει τὴν
ἐγκράτειαν, ἐν δὲ τῇ ἐγκρατείᾳ τὴν ὑπομονήν, ἐν δὲ τῇ ὑπομονῇ τὴν
εὐσέβειαν, ἐν δὲ τῇ εὐσεβείᾳ τὴν φιλαδελφίαν, ἐν δὲ τῇ φιλαδελφίᾳ
τὴν ἀγάπην.

The verbal affinities in the two texts are striking. Consider, for
example, the likeness of the common Greek idiom πᾶσαν σπουδὴν
εἰσφέρεσθαι[95] in the inscription to σπουδὴν πᾶσαν παρεισενέγκαντες in 2 Pet 1.5. Other parallels are noteworthy as well, for example, (1) the periphrastic reference to God, ἡ θεία δύναμις, in connection with ἀρετή—τῆς θείας δυνάμεως ἀρετάς versus τῆς θείας
δυνάμεως... καὶ ἀρετῇ (1.3); (2) the language of eternal lordship—
τῶν κυρίων αἰωνίου ἀρχῆς versus τὴν αἰώνιον βασιλείαν τοῦ
κυρίου Ἰησοῦ Χριστοῦ (1.11); (3) the introduction of a relative clause
following the word ἀρετή—τῆς θείας δυνάμεως ἀρετάς, δι᾽ versus
ἰδίᾳ καὶ ἀρετῇ, δι᾽ (1.3-4); (4) repetition of the term εὐσέβεια—τὴν
πρὸς αὐτοὺς εὐσέβειαν καὶ μηδένα καιρὸν παραλιπῖν τοῦ εὐσεβεῖν
versus τὴν εὐσέβειαν ἐν δὲ τῇ εὐσεβείᾳ τὴν φιλαδελφίαν (1.7); and
(5) use of the superlative μέγιστος in both texts (cf. 1.4).[96] Not merely
the isolated verbal correspondences, not only the listing of virtues, but
also the like syntax in which these parallels are found is quite significant. Evidently, we have here to do with stereotypical religious

94. *CIG* 3.2715a,b.
95. For example, Polybius, *Hist.* 21.29.12, and Josephus, *Ant.* 20.204.
96. It is worthy of note that the superlative of μέγας occurs nowhere else in the
New Testament.

language of the Imperial period.⁹⁷ Deissmann dates the above inscription as possibly prior to AD 22,⁹⁸ and should it in fact reflect the local color of the readers' situation, interesting light is thereby shed on the destination of 2 Peter.

In addition to the idiomatic σπουδὴν παρεισφέρω in 2 Pet. 1.5, the second verb of note in this sequence (also in 1.11) is singular due to its rich history and the cultural context from which it derives, as evidenced by its frequent usage by classical writers.⁹⁹ The color that it adds to the commentary is considerable. In Greek theater, large and costly choruses were often employed that required the assistance of a wealthy local benefactor, the χόρηγος, in helping to defray the costs. The relative extravagance attached to some of these productions is connoted by the verb-form χορηγέω, a strengthened form of which is used in 2 Pet. 1.5 (ἐπιχορηγέω).¹⁰⁰ Unfortunately, the richness of this picture is lost in its translation. The readers are not merely to 'add' or 'supply', they are to contribute *extravagantly* to their own moral development. Lest there be any misunderstanding, however, this is no mere 'works-righteousness', for two important reasons enunciated with considerable rhetorical flourish in the text: (1) a surplus of grace and divine resources has already been lavished upon believers for the ethical life (vv. 1-4), and (2) entrance into the divine kingdom will be 'richly' (πλουσίως) 'supplied' (ἐπιχορηγέω) by Jesus Christ himself (v. 11).¹⁰¹

The Necessity of Virtue (1.8-11)

The presence of the catalog of virtues leads to the following conclusion: 'For if you possess these things and they are increasing, they render you from being ineffective and unfruitful in the knowledge of

97. Deissmann, *Bible Studies*, p. 364.
98. Deissmann, *Bible Studies*, p. 367.
99. It occurs in Xenophon (*Mem.* 3.4.3) and Aristotle (*Eth. Nic.* 1100a-b), also in Plutarch (*Mor.* 13e), Polybius (*Hist.* 3.78.8), and Strabo (11.14.16). ἐπιχορηγέω is used with some frequency in the LXX (44 times) and appears five times in the New Testament (apart from 2 Peter, 2 Cor. 9.10; Gal. 3.5 and Col. 2.19).
100. Appearing 12 times in the LXX, ἐπιχορηγέω is used five times in the New Testament: 2 Cor. 9.10; Gal. 3.5; Col. 2.19, 2 Pet. 1.5, 1.11.
101. This imagery lends plausibility to F.W. Danker's thesis that 2 Pet. 1.1-11 bears some resemblance to later Hellenistic civic decrees, by which the generosity of local benefactors to a particular community was noted ('2 Peter 1: A Solemn Decree', *CBQ* 40 [1978], pp. 64-82).

our Lord Jesus Christ' (v. 8). Faith received, far from being passive in nature, requires of the believer active cooperation with the grace of God. Progress in one's moral development prevents one from being 'ineffective' (ἀργός). The same word is also used in two other New Testament texts, both of which convey the same notion of effective faith: Jas 2.20 ('Do you wish to be shown, you foolish person, that faith without works is ἀργός?') and Mt. 12.36 ('For I tell you that on the day of judgment you will have to give account for every ἀργός word you utter').

In the same way, the virtues prevent one from becoming ἄκαρπος, unproductive. In Jesus' parable of the sower, it is the seed choked out by the cares of the world, the deceit of riches and lust that are accorded the description ἄκαρπος (Mt. 13.22; Mk 4.19). Significantly, the very same linkage of bearing fruit, good works and the knowledge of God is found in Col 1.10: 'so that you may lead lives worthy of the Lord, fully pleasing to him, as you bear fruit in every good work and as you grow in the knowledge (ἐπίγνωσις) of God'. At issue in the Colossian epistle and in 2 Peter is the matter of a life *worthy of one's calling*.

In short, to be ineffective and unfruitful is to cause a Christian scandal. The scandal on the part of the readers consists in the fact that (1) to them has been granted much (v. 1), (2) on them has been bestowed much, and (3) to the saints everything has been given. The presence of futility and fruitlessness with ἐπίγνωσις, the knowledge of God, is a blatant contradiction.

Having stated the conclusion positively, the writer expresses it negatively: 'For anyone who lacks these things is blind and short-sighted and blind, having forgotten the cleansing of his former sins' (v. 9). Throughout the epistle imagery is utilized that is quite simple yet striking. The metaphor of blindness coincides with the images in ch. 2 of slavery, the dog returning to its vomit and the pig returning to the mud (2.19, 22). Its occurrence in the New Testament—for example, Mt. 15.14; 23.16; Jn 9.40-41 and Rev. 3.17—shows the blindness metaphor to be an integral part of the Christian paraenetic tradition. While a flat translation of τυφλός ἐστιν μυωπάζων ('blind and short-sighted') in 2 Pet. 1.9 loses it force, the more nuanced rendering of μυωπάζω (literally, 'to close the eye') by Mayor[102] and followed by Spicq[103],

---

102. Mayor, *Jude and Second Peter*, p. lxii.
103. C. Spicq, *Les épîtres de Saint Pierre* (Paris: Gabalda, 1966), p. 223.

Kelly[104] and Green[105] captures the correct sense.[106] The emphasis here
is moral self-responsibility. Some have shut their eyes to the truth, resulting in a blindness that is not inherited but *cultivated*. The same moral
dynamic is found in Paul. People suppress the truth that is already
known (Rom. 1.18-19). The result is a darkening of their foolish minds.
Such is the legacy of apostasy. In 2 Peter it is characterized by denial
(2.1), deception (2.3), boldness and willfulness (2.10b), a lust for sin
(2.14a) and seduction (2.14b, 18). Those individuals possessing these
traits are cast as antitypes of Balaam (2.15-16), who was seduced by the
heathen with a view to lead Israel astray.

Some in the community, astonishingly, have 'forgotten' that they
were forgiven and cleansed of their past.[107] The text of 2 Pet. 1.9 literally reads 'having received forgetfulness' (λήθην λαβών),[108] which
offers the faint suggestion of a *voluntary acceptance* of their deceived
and darkened condition. Like the dog returning to its vomit, like a pig
that has been washed and then returns to the filth, these persons, in a
revolting sort of fashion, return to the former way of life from which
they had been delivered. They have become slaves to a new tyranny
that is worse than the first (2.20-21).

Following the ethical argument presented in vv. 5-9, a strengthened
conclusion—'Therefore be all the more diligent (διὸ μᾶλλον σπουδάσατε) to confirm your calling'—introduces v. 10. The Aorist imperative σπουδάσατε points to decisive action, of which Hillyer captures
the urgency: 'Determine to put in all the more effort'.[109] Repetition
is important at this point. σπουδή was used in v. 5 ('make every
effort')[110] in the context of moral progression, while 'calling' points

104. Kelly, *Commentary*, p. 308.
105. Green, *2 Peter and Jude*, p. 82.
106. Fornberg, *Early Church*, p. 53, sees here the writer's exploitation of the language of the mystery cults.
107. This may be an allusion back to the 'cleansing' waters of baptism, but it need
not be restricted to this (against Bauckham, *Jude, 2 Peter*, p. 191). It can refer to the
expiatory cleansing of sins by Christ as expressed in Heb. 1.3. Forgetting one's baptism may stand in the background of Paul's teaching in Rom. 6.1-14.
108. This phrase also occurs in Josephus (*Ant.* 2.6.9; 4.8.44).
109. Hillyer, *1 and 2 Peter, Jude*, p. 170.
110. Note also the occurrence of the verb σπουδάζω in Eph. 4.3 ('striving to
keep the unity of the Spirit in the bond of peace') and Heb. 4.11 ('Let us therefore
strive to enter into that rest').

back to v. 3 ('him who called us by his own glory and goodness').[111] The tone by now has intensified from teaching to exhortation, from didactics to a warning.

The notion of confirming one's calling and election is a prominent feature of the Pauline epistles, for example, 1 Cor. 1.2; Gal. 5.13; Eph. 4.1; and 1 Tim. 6.12.[112] To confirm one's calling is to offer proof—or disproof—of one's profession.[113] As Calvin aptly puts it,

> purity of life is not improperly called the evidence and proof of election, by which the faithful may not only testify to others that they are the children of God, but also confirm themselves in this confidence.[114]

Moreover, the ethical tension contained within the phrase βεβαίαν ὑμῶν τὴν κλῆσιν... ποιεῖσθαι[115] illustrates the way in which 2 Peter, much like Jude, blends sovereignty and moral agency, divine grace and human cooperation. Both epistles preserve this necessary tension in the Christian ethos. Although God has called people to himself, the believer must respond to that call. While unmerited grace has been extended through the righteousness of Christ, the believer is to demonstrate gratitude by means of a virtuous life. That in 2 Peter the writer has lapsed Christians in view is plain, which raises particular questions regarding the nature of apostasy. However, the writer is not concerned to explore the psychology of apostasy, only to warn that a return to the old life has consequences of a cataclysmic nature. At the heart of moral exhortation in the letter is the balance between divine initiative and human response. On the one hand, great and precious promises have been provided the believer, indeed all the divine resources necessary for a life of godliness (1.3); on the other hand, the believer is to 'supply' to this a calculated response that is measured over time in terms of ethical quality (1.5-7). The burden clearly rests on the shoulders of the readers to hold up their side of the covenant agreement. If they are *willing*, they will never stumble.[116] The guarantee is not that they will not sin, only that they will not *fall*.

111. Cf. Jude 1.
112. Implied in 1 Cor. 9.27 and Col. 3.12. Cf. also Heb. 9.15 and 1 Pet. 2.21.
113. Green, *2 Peter, Jude*, p. 83.
114. J. Calvin, *Commentaries on the Catholic Epistles* (trans. J. Owen; Grand Rapids: Baker, rep. 1981), p. 377.
115. Note the middle voice, suggesting that the evidence is to oneself.
116. Cf. Jas 2.10; 3.2; Jude 24.

The final 'promise' extended by the gracious Lord and Savior is to 'lavishly provide' (once more, ἐπιχορηγέω)[117] entrance into his eternal kingdom. The reward, a full and exceedingly rich provision, awaits those who have 'confirmed their calling' by demonstrating a life 'worthy of the name'. Entrance is not *earned*, lest the Petrine ethic be misinterpreted. 2 Peter is not promoting a 'new law or 'new morality';[118] neither is it to be construed as advancing a sub-apostolic ethic of ascetic rigorism;[119] nor have we to do with a 'conventional bourgeois morality'.[120] Entrance is grace, all grace, lavishly provided at no (human) expense.

117. See the commentary on v. 5.
118. Contra Schulz, *Mitte*, p. 304.
119. Contra Käsemann, 'Apologia', p. 144.
120. Contra Fuller, *Introduction*, p. 167.

Chapter 7

CONCLUSION: THE FUNCTION OF THE CATALOG
OF VIRTUES IN 2 PETER 1.5-7

Our investigation began with a reconsideration of the 'early Catholic' thesis that by and large has governed interpretive approaches to 2 Peter. Given the tendency of an 'early Catholic' reading of 2 Peter to yield exegetical results that predetermine rather than issue out of literary, sociological and theological perspectives, the present study has been undertaken with the presumed need to interact with those fundamental assumptions whose trajectory has resulted in a highly derivative treatment of the epistle. That 2 Peter has suffered general neglect among exegetes and theologians can be understood to be a by-product of its perceived 'dubious' and 'problematic' character—a perception generated in the main by proponents of 'early Catholicism'.

The 'early Catholic' hypothesis posits an institutionalized post-apostolic church, in which the codification of creedal beliefs, the shifting of the Spirit from the laity to an episcopal office, the fading of the Parousia hope, and a legalistic endurance ethic have emerged in response to Gnostic intrusion. 2 Peter is said to mirror these sub-apostolic phenomena and thus fall within the category of pseudepigraphal 'testamental' literature.

Examining 2 Peter on the basis of the tenets of 'early Catholicism', however, raises obstacles which make it difficult to sustain the 'early Catholic' position. In 2 Peter, not eschatological 'disappointment' or 'mistakenness' but moral lapse was seen to lie at the root of the pastoral problem and thus constitute the focus of the writer's literary strategy. Not the timing of the Parousia but its *fact*, in response to the moral sceptic, was understood to be the prophetic-pastoral burden. The eschatological perspective in 2 Peter, upon closer examination, was observed to be consistent with that of Jesus and the writers of the New Testament. Furthermore, the institutionalization and codification of creedal beliefs normally adduced in 2 Peter were found to be strikingly absent, contrary to what proponents of 'early Catholicism' have contended. There is no evidence in the epistle of an emergent teaching office for the purposes of controlling doctrine. Rather, the readers themselves are exhorted toward obedience and discernment of what is genuinely prophetic and Spirit-induced.

Inasmuch as the 'early Catholic' view requires that doctrine—and specifically, false doctrine—be the center-point of the epistle, it follows that traditional exegesis has tended to give insufficient attention to the paraenetic character of 2 Peter. A closer and unified reading of the letter suggests that ethics and not doctrine per se constitutes the burden of the writer. This conclusion has far-reaching implications for the interpetation of 2 Peter, for it elucidates the social location of the audience, the theological perspective of the writer, and the corresponding literary strategy being mounted to address pastoral need.

It is in this vein that fresh attempts at analyzing 2 Peter are to be welcomed. One encouraging trend in New Testament scholarship is to view the epistle as an integral part of the New Testament paraenetic tradition, richly on display in the catholic epistles where ethics and 'pastoral theology' are accented. More recent attempts at understanding the social location of the readers in 2 Peter are particularly helpful, inasmuch as they underscore through comparative literary sources the apologetic function of the epistle as a response to a view of reality that denies personal moral accountability. Furthermore, these contributions present arguments for a *Sitz im Leben* which are consonant with apostolic preaching adapted to mid-to late-first-century Corinth, Athens or Asia Minor.

Because of the obvious literary relationship between Jude and 2 Peter that has sustained traditional 2 Peter commentary, it was noted that the literary markers distinguishing the two works have tended to receive short shrift. Comparison of Jude and 2 Peter reveals a notable contrast in the two audiences' social location. Whereas the distinctly Palestinian Jewish-Christian provenance of Jude accounts for the marshalling of literary tradition-material that is aimed at the Jewish matrix of the early church, in 2 Peter a markedly Gentile social environment calls for a literary strategy that reflects strongly pagan cultural influences. 2 Peter and Jude offer unique and eloquent testimony to the literary genius of their respective authors.

To the degree that ethics and virtuous living are central to literary strategy in 2 Peter, the virtuous life as a theme can be traced throughout the epistle. The logic of virtue permeates 2 Peter 1, underpinned by the abundant use of reminder terminology and Hellenistic ethical categories that together give 1.3-21 its didactic character. In the mind of the writer, the doctrinal foundation has already been previously laid for his readers; the present need is to remind them of what they already know. Hence, consistent with the paraenetic tradition in Jewish and Christian literature, moral paradigms are cited to concretize the moral lesson.

Of the paradigms that are listed in 2 Peter 2, the archetypes of Noah and Lot are set in contrast to the fallen angels, Noah's generation, Sodom and Gomorrah, and Balaam. Flood and fire typology, both of which are employed again in 3.5-7, 10, combine to create a point of identity with the readers. Both Noah and Lot were faced with incomparable social obstacles in seeking to live godly lives. Those obstacles notwithstanding, they illustrate that in the face of pending judgment God is able to rescue the righteous who persevere amidst moral corruption. The Balaam-typology is significant in that, not unlike the case of the angels, it illustrates the tragic fall of a man of God. Balaam's departure is a moral lesson, for it is a story of a prophet—one endowed with a divine trust—seduced by pagans for the ultimate purpose of leading Israel into apostasy. Thus, as a type Balaam poses considerable dangers.

Graphic depictions of the apostate follow the moral paradigms, climaxing in the use of several common but striking metaphors. Slave imagery and two secular proverbs underscore the absurdity of disavowing the ethical truth-claims of Christian faith. These pictures, while profoundly simple, are meant to shock the readers.

That moral skepticism has infiltrated the community is suggested by the material in 2 Peter 3, where a rhetorical response to moral autonomy is proffered. Although exegetes differ as to whether 2 Peter 3 mirrors specifically Epicurean or Stoic thought, what is clear is that the writer has incorporated aspects of contemporary Hellenistic cosmology in his rhetorical response. Mention of the Parousia in his argument is not to be interpreted as the advancement of a particular eschatological framework in response to a 'fading Parousia hope'; rather, at issue is the matter of ultimate moral accountability. Not the *timing* of the Parousia but its *fact* is being underscored. Any perplexity on the part of the readers as to a divine 'delay' is a question not of eschatology but of theodicy. What greater purpose does this divine forebearance serve? How does one interpret the seeming 'delay' of God's intervention? While not concerned to dissolve the theological tension inherent in the interplay of divine initiative and human moral freedom, the writer allows both elements to co-exist, even when he wishes chiefly to stress the human side of that equation. Notice is served, whether it is intended primarily for the apostate or the faithful: there *will* be a day of moral reckoning.

Following the identification of three redactive interests in 2 Peter 1—the repository of divine resources available for the ethical life, the surplus of reminder terminology characteristic of the paraenetic tradition, and the predisposition of the writer to assert his own moral authority—the moral grammar of this material was examined. The language being employed was viewed against the backdrop of contemporary Hellenistic moral philosophy, of which the Stoa were the chief propagandists. Stoic and Christian approaches to ethics were found to share some common philosophical ground. Both assume the individual to be rational and morally self-responsible. Both teach a doctrine of moral progress, even when the pagan understanding of this progress is void of grace. The language and logic of virtue in Stoic thinking come to expression in the ethical catalog as a teaching device. Lending themselves well to the popularizing of moral philosophy, vice and virtue lists are readily adaptable by Hellenistic Jewish and early Christian writers in the cause of furthering Christian ethics.

2 Pet. 1.5-7 represents perhaps the clearest echo in the New Testament of the pagan ethical list and manifests several features that are common to its Stoic counterpart. In contrast to pagan ethical catalogs, the catalog of virtues in 2 Peter 1 is no random listing, however. Verses 5-7 cohere in a foundation of faith that is a product of the righteousness of Christ, revealed graciously through the knowledge of God. An organic unity exists among the virtues, demonstrated not only by the catalog's syntactical arrangement but also by the virtues' interdependence as the necessary fruit of genuine faith.

This interconnection may be stated as follows. Faith produces virtue, which is moral excellence. Because there is a correlation between the character of God and our moral character, faith is a prerequisite. Virtue, if it is to increase in our lives, is affected by what we do with the knowledge of God that comes to us. Greater knowledge of the resources that God has graciously provided through Christ will yield self-control. That is to say, grace operative in our lives will curb the human passions within as well as enable us to withstand the forces of surrounding culture from without. An increase in self-control will strengthen our ability to endure, despite the overwhelming social forces that may come against us. Endurance, in turn, will reflect a godliness in our lives. This piety simultaneously pleases God while giving confirming evidence of our faith to those around us through our relationships. These relationships in turn will be characterized by brotherly affection, that is, a sense of kindred belonging that is not Pharisaical or sanctimonious, and they will ultimately be governed by and reflective of the highest virtue and goal of the Christian ethic, agape.[1] Love is the sign of the kingdom of God.

Whereas the acquisition of virtue in pagan ethics is an absolute good and the highest human goal, for the Christian it is the evidence of deeper theological realities. The significance of the Petrine catalog of virtues in vv. 5-7 becomes transparent. Because God through Christ has made provision for the ethical life—and this *abundantly*—does not mean that there is no cooperation in the ethical enterprise. To the contrary, the readers have a necessary part to play: 'For this reason make very effort to supply...' Arranged in pairs[2] and then distinguished for rhetorically stylized effect, the virtues build upon faith (πίστις) and culminate in love (ἀγάπη).[3] The purpose of the catalog is its demarcation of exemplary—and by implication, unacceptable—behavior. Ethical 'boundaries', however, are not intended in the present context to distinguish Christians from pagans; rather, they serve as a warning to the community itself. The writer may even be insinuating that ethical pagans are demonstrating greater moral fiber than some individuals in the community—a potential scandal in and of itself. At bottom, Christians are to live a life *worthy* of their calling.

While affirming certain ethical realities, 2 Peter confronts the reader with something of a theological tension. Both the sovereign work of

---

1.   The predominant role of ἀγάπη can be seen in the fact that it secures a place in the majority of New Testament virtue lists, for example, 2 Cor. 6.6; Gal. 5.22; Phil. 4.8; 1 Tim. 6.11; 2 Pet. 1.5-7; and Rev. 2.19.

2.   It should be said that the catalog in Wis. 6.17-19, frequently cited by commentators, bears limited resemblance to 2 Pet. 1.5-7.

3.   Thus Ignatius, in his letter to the Ephesians: 'Faith is the beginning, love the culmination' (14.1).

God and the necessity of the human response, both divine grace and human moral agency, are on exhibit in the epistle. Given this theological tension, we have sought to probe 2 Peter with the conviction of its distinctiveness over against Jude. One may justifiably assume that both letters mirror concrete pastoral situations—the one in a (most probably Palestinian) Jewish-Christian cultural context, the other in a pervasively Gentile social setting. While Jude consists largely of straightforward condemnations of the apostate in the form of a lament and woe-cry, 2 Peter, by contrast, contains significant didactic material and reminder terminology that are designed to exhort the faithful. The key words 'knowledge', 'savior', 'godliness', 'righteous' and 'righteousness' signal an unfolding literary strategy that has two prongs—judgment and salvation. It may well be that 2 Peter points to a pastoral situation in which apostasy has not fully ripened.

From the outset, the readers are exhorted in 2 Peter toward a life of piety. Ethical lapse—to the point of moral depravity and outright apostasy among some—is being spotlighted, with graphic imagery and moral paradigms serving to underscore the sobering lessons concerning ethical departure from the truth. The readers need not fall and be overwhelmed. Despite the strong eschatological argument in 2 Peter 3, in which the moral skeptic is caricatured and guaranteed a day of moral reckoning, the writer does not lose sight of grace and divine patience. Though impenetrable to human insight, the longsuffering of God has a redemptive aim: the human race. From a finite perspective, this divine forbearance manifests itself in a 'delay' that is most perplexing to the righteous. Why the agonizing 'slowness' of God's action? Why the seeming 'delay' in his response to evil? Yet, veiled in this 'slowness' is divine 'patience', the purpose of which is to lead people to repentance. Although the Parousia sets the limits of divine patience toward the world, which will one day be judged and reconstituted, God is willing that none would perish. To this end, he has left a record of having rescued those who were found persevering in the face of formidable cultural obstacles.

2 Peter, then, is an ethical call. It is a call to persevere.

Appendix

PREDESTINATION, PERSEVERANCE
AND THE PROBLEM OF APOSTASY

While the investigation of vice, virtue and moral exhortation in 2 Peter has not been constructed along the lines of a theological tract and while no particular theological model has been the basis for the investigation, questions of a profoundly theological nature are nevertheless raised. Is the author propounding a 'works righteousness', or, in the view of Ernst Käsemann and others, an ethic of legalism? In what relationship do virtue, the moral life and 'confirming one's calling' stand to divine grace? Does Petrine ethics stand in opposition to the Pauline formulation of justification by faith? Is human endeavor in 2 Peter emphasized to the negation or exclusion of grace? Is there a tension in 2 Peter between human responsibility and divine initiative? And if so, can these two poles indeed be reconciled?

Although any answers to these questions are eminently theological, their justification remains exegetical. Just as the exegetical enterprise for Luther necessarily informed responsible preaching, the theological enterprise can only proceed responsibly on the basis of exegetical conclusions. Any determinations we might make, given the knotty theological issues arising from the epistle, have their justification in the presence or absence of ethics and grace in the text of the letter.

The present investigation has proceeded under the guiding assumption that both poles—divine grace and human moral agency—undergird 2 Peter, with emphasis being given to the latter. The reason for this accent is the audience's social situation which necessitates a prophetic-paraenetic response. Justification for this reading of the epistle does not seem unreasonable: the bulk of the text of 2 Peter is devoted to the ethical question, as the structure of the letter strongly suggests:

1.1-2	introduction, greeting
.3-4	resources available for the ethical life
.5-7	catalog of virtues
.8-11	exhortation to confirm an ethical calling
.12-15	exhortation to recall
.16-18	assertion of the author's moral-prophetic authority
.19-21	nature of prophetic authority
2.1-3	prophetic denunciation of the morally reprobate
.4-10a	moral paradigms
.10b-18	portrait of the morally reprobate
.19-22	profile of apostasy

160 *Virtue amidst Vice*

3.1-2	exhortation to recall
.3-7	caricature of the moral sceptic
.8-13	promise of universal moral accountability
.14-18a	final exhortations
.18b	doxology

2 Peter 1: Introducing the Virtue Motif

Lest the recipients of 2 Peter misconstrue the letter as contradicting a Pauline understanding of justification by grace through faith, the author chooses to address them as 'those who have received a faith of equal standing through the righteousness of our God and Savior Jesus Christ' (1.1b). This address is calculated and appropriate for several reasons. First, some in the Christian community have already distorted Pauline teaching (3.15-16), and it is not implausible to conjecture that such teaching might have concerned the nature of an individual's justification. Secondly, in contrast to Christian truth-claims, a Jew may have asserted that ceremonial purity and keeping the law were sufficient for justification, while the Stoic Hellenist may have countered that the love of wisdom—philosophy—and ethical striving were ultimate in the human experience. Grace was indeed the scandal that set the Christian kerygma apart.

Thirdly, the tendency of human nature is to react in equal and opposite extremes. Because of the primacy of Christian grace in early Christian preaching, it is understandable that presumption and even ethical lapse might occur in the community over time. We are not being over-speculative in assuming that such lies behind the purpose of 2 Peter, insofar as the epistle is largely given to outlining the contours of the ethical life. Christian grace amidst pagan culture does not call for a jettisoning of the moral disciplines that undergird the virtuous life; rather, virtue issues naturally out of the life that has encountered divine grace. A virtuous life is the fruit of 'received' righteousness. 2 Peter not only mirrors a community surrounded by Hellenistic influence and in which grace has been taken for granted, it mirrors a social climate in which apostasy and outright moral rot have set in.

Nevertheless, it is ἡ δικαιοσύνη τοῦ θεοῦ ἡμῶν καί σωτῆρος, not human striving, that justifies one in the presence of God. Christ as σωτήρ (1.1, 11; 2.20; 3.2, 18) is an important subtheme in 2 Peter. Not only has Christ initially saved, he continues to 'rescue the godly from trial', even as he can 'keep the unrighteous under punishment until the day of judgment' (2.9). Moreover, grace and peace are multiplied to the individual who is rooted in the ἐπίγνωσις of God and Jesus Christ our Lord (1.2; 3.18a).

The knowledge of God has been identified as a primary motif in the letter. Within and immediately following the greeting, the author develops the contours of this knowledge. This is done by clothing distinctly Christian concepts in the language of contemporary pagan culture. The audience is reminded that Christian faith ultimately will express itself through a conspicuous piety (1.3). Two parallel features opening and concluding the epistle strike the reader's attention. The coupling of grace and knowledge in 1.2 and 3.18, in addition to opening and concluding exhortations to 'life and godliness' (1.3) and 'lives of holiness and godliness' (3.11), form something of a double inclusio for rhetorical effect.

Having stated his thesis, namely that virtue, holiness and piety should identify the Christian and 'confirm' or 'offer legal proof' of one's profession, the author marshalls supporting evidence constituting virtually the whole of the epistle—a catalog of virtues, paraenesis, moral paradigms, moral typology and caricatures. All of this admonition, however, hinges not merely on human will, important as this is, but on 'divine power' and 'precious and very great promises' that 'he has given us' (1.3). It is by means of this divine provision that the recipients achieve two things: (1) they escape the corruption that is in the world, and (2) they share in the divine nature (1.4) through union with Christ by the Holy Spirit.[1]

In these opening verses one encounters a theological tension. While the theme of the virtuous life—which preserves the literary unity of 2 Peter—is introduced (and developed with considerable rhetorical sophistication throughout all three chapters), it is understood to be predicated on received righteousness, grace and the knowledge of God—indeed, on boundless divine resources. On the one hand, the Christian life is sustained by the power and grace of God mediated through faith. On the other hand, the believer is expected to anticipate forces at work that would oppose spiritual progress. In theological terms, this persistence in faith is called perseverance. To fail to persevere is described both in 2 Peter and Jude in terms of 'stumbling'.[2] In 2 Peter, apostasy is suggested not only by moral typology (for example, the fallen angels, Balaam, the proverbial dog and pig), but also by the author's vocabulary. The occurrence of ἀπο-derivatives lends ample lexical evidence to support the contention that within the community there have been sown the seeds of apostasy, which, upon maturing, express themselves in a denial of Jesus Christ as Lord and moral authority in general (2.1-3).

The presence of two theological axes in the letter—divine grace and human moral agency—suggests that the possibility of apostasy is very real. The author is not concerned to eradicate or ease this theological tension; rather, both divine and human elements co-exist. Those being addressed have been recipients of grace and knowledge. They are nonetheless held accountable for their knowledge. The tone of 2 Peter, coupled with the use of moral typology and caricatures, indicates that the problem lies with the human factor. Being repudiated is a faith void of ethical fiber.

Into the resultant literary strategy the catalog of virtues is designed to fit. 'For this reason you must make every effort to supply. . . ' introduces a rhetorical device common among moral preachers of the day. Professing Christians, not pagans, are being admonished. To strive diligently in cultivating the virtues is to ensure against an ineffective and unfruitful ethical life (1.8). That apostasy, that is, a drifting away from Christian truth, is in the writer's view is already hinted at in 1.9: some in the

---

1. Contra Bauckham (*Jude, 2 Peter*, p. 182), 1.4 is not intended to reference a 'future prospect' and thus function eschatologically. It is, rather, the declaration of present realities and a parallel statement to 'escaping the pollution that is in the [present] world'. By fleeing (φεύγω), one participates experientially in union with Christ.

2. Jude 24; 2 Pet. 1.10.

community may have become 'forgetful of the cleansing of past sins'.[3] The possibility of apostasy surfaces again in the allusion to the fallen angels (2.4), the Balaam typology (2.15-16), the pagan proverb (2.22), as well as through the author's caricature of the moral skeptic (3.3-6). Christian discipleship, as it is to be properly grasped, does not take either divine or human factors lightly. Grace is not to be presumed upon, neither is the need to cultivate ethical and spiritual disciplines.

Grace received does not preclude the rigors of Christian discipleship, but neither does discipleship consist in perfectionist human striving divorced from divine resources. Both elements are necessarily at work; both constitute a unity. Because ethical lapse characterizes the community in the present situation, what demands immediate attention is a rhetorically sophisticated exhortation to the rigors of virtuous living; hence, the appropriateness of a catalog of virtues as a foundational element in the literary strategy of 2 Peter.

Yet even the catalog is far from a perfectionistic or legalistic work ethic. On the contrary, it is predicated on a foundation of faith ('to those who received a faith', 1.1; 'make every effort to add to your faith', 1.5) and is motivated by love (1.7). Even in the catalog, the divine and the human merge.

Nowhere in 2 Peter is the theological tension between divine sovereignty and human freedom more on display than in 1.10-11:

> Therefore, brothers and sisters, be all the more eager to confirm your calling and election, for if you do this you will never stumble. For in this way, entry into the eternal kingdom of our Lord and Savior Jesus Christ will be richly provided for you.

The person who approaches this text solely on the basis of a theological system may find it difficult—indeed, well nigh impossible—to reconcile the seeming contradictory strands of teaching in the letter. The tendency represented by one theological pole is to approach 1.10-11 with an accent on (a) the notion of divine calling and election that surface in v. 10, an echo of which is already found in v. 3 ('through him who called us'), (b) the provision of entry into the kingdom, and (c) the impossibility of falling away from the faith. A position representing the other theological pole, by contrast, will emphasize (a) the author's exhortation to eager striving, (b) the necessity of works and human cooperation, and (c) the possibility of falling, even to the point of apostasy. From a systematic-theological standpoint, each of these two positions will be inclined to negate biblical-textual evidence for the other position. In 2 Peter, however, the theological tension arising from the two seemingly opposite poles is preserved. Alongside the fact that the recipients of the letter are called and chosen by God stands the admonition to 'confirm' this calling, thereby providing insurance against stumbling in their faith.

How does one 'confirm' (βεβαιόω) one's calling and election? If the believer is called and chosen (cf. Jude 1), is an awareness of this reality, therefore, not sufficient? Rather than erect an insoluable theological tension that cannot be reconciled, 2 Peter presents two sides of one coin as it were to underscore the human need for cooperating with divine grace. In this regard, 2 Peter bears some resemblance to James,

---

3. Cf. similar language used by Paul in 1 Cor. 6.11.

a work that has endured its share of theological misunderstanding. Rather than exclude James from the heart of the biblical canon as Luther and his offspring were inclined to do, we may appreciate the epistle in light of the social situation that it would appear to address—that is, a setting where there are manifest the tendencies toward (a) divorcing hearing and doing the word of God (1.19-27), (b) neglecting genuine expressions of true religion (1.26-27), (c) repudiating the law as the disciple's abiding ethical standard (2.8-13), and (d) divorcing faith and works (2.14-26). As 2 Peter, James has an ethical and not doctrinal thrust per se. Behind both writings it is legitimate to presuppose a deficiency in the way professing believers were living. In James, faith and works cannot be divided, Abraham being the exemplar: 'You see that faith was operative alongside his works; indeed faith was fulfilled (τελειόω) by his works' (2.22). Given the indivisibility of faith and works, James can legitimately write that 'a person is justified by works and not by faith alone' (1.24).

The social situation behind 2 Peter in some respects suggests even greater urgency than that of James: some individuals are depicted as capable of denying Christ's lordship. Not only is a false dichotomy between faith and works being erected, faith is being negated by a scandalous lack of ethical evidence. In some cases it is being wholly obliterated by moral decay and hardened skepticism that have set in. In both 2 Peter and James, the call to 'confirm' or 'verify' one's election, one's convictions, indeed one's faith, is a clarion call. Thus, confirmation of calling is not so much a theological statement about divine activity as it is a moral exhortation to prove that one's profession is genuine in a disingenuous world.

By verifying one's calling and election, according to 2 Peter, one is prevented from falling: 'if you do this, you will never stumble' (1.10b). Parallel imagery is found in the conclusion of Jude, where the coupling of divine keeping (φυλάσσω)[4] and human effort ushers forth in doxological praise:

> Now to him who is able to keep you from stumbling and present you spotless in the presence of his glory with great joy, to the only God our Savior through Jesus Christ our Lord be glory, majesty, might and authority before all time and now and forever, amen.[5]

Because the stumbling motif is prominent in Jude, it bears some relation to 2 Peter and thus deserves some comment. Among the strong parallels between Jude and 2 Peter is the authors' use of triple moral paradigms. Whereas in 2 Peter the fallen angels, Noah's generation and Lot are highlighted (2.4-9), in Jude unbelieving Israel, the fallen angels and Sodom and Gomorrah are illustrative. Most significant is that each member of Jude's typological triplet is portrayed as having fallen and, consequently, having been disenfranchised.[6]

---

4.   In keeping with the language of foreknowledge and predestination throughout the epistle, 'to keep' is an important catchword in Jude (τηρέω: vv. 1, 6 [twice], 13, 21; φυλάσσω: v. 24). The verb τηρέω also occurs four times in 2 Peter: 2.4, 9, 17; 3.7.

5.   Jude 24-25.

6.   For a more detailed discussion of the typological triplet in Jude, see J.D. Charles, '"Those" and "These": The Use of the Old Testament in the Epistle of Jude', *JSNT* 38 (1990), pp. 113-18, and *idem, Literary Strategy*, pp. 103-25.

In Jude the prescription for preventing one's fall is fourfold: edifying oneself in the faith, praying in the Holy Spirit, remaining in the love of God, and anticipating the mercy of Christ (vv. 20-21). In 2 Peter the prescription calls for combining with one's faith virtue, knowledge, self-control, endurance, godliness, brotherly affection and love (2.5-7), in addition to growing in the grace and knowledge of the Lord (3.18). To be tempted is human, to stumble temporarily is even understandable; but to fall from the faith, from the perspective of 2 Peter and Jude, is to fail to respond to—indeed, to ignore—the grace of God. To confirm one's calling, by contrast, is to respond diligently to the grace that has been extended.

The tension between what the recipients of 2 Peter have received and what they must achieve also surfaces in the author's statement of purpose in 1.12-15. Being balanced in this paraenetic material are 'the truth that has already come to you' and multiple exhortations to recall 'these things'. While the community is said to be 'already established in the [received] truth', the emphasis is placed on what the community must henceforth do with the knowledge possessed:

> Therefore I intend to keep on reminding you of these things. . .
> . . . you know them already. . .
> I think it proper. . . to refresh your memory. . .
> . . . so that. . . you may be able to recall these things.

2 Peter 2: Illustrating the Virtue Motif

Having presented the case in 2 Peter for developing moral disciplines, the author—not unlike Jude—marshalls supporting evidence through historical-theological paradigms to buttress his argument. Lessons from the past find prophetic application in the social situation of the present. While 2.1ff might appear to be a somewhat abrupt transition, there is more than a mere lexical connection—'prophets'—between 1.19-21 and 2.1-3.[7] Not so much right doctrine per se, that is, orthodoxy, but orthopraxy and prophetic-moral authority (ὑπὸ πνεύματος ἁγίου φερόμενοι) is being asserted, given the moral decrepitude that has set in. (Prophetic authority is the chief reason for the author's credentials being inserted in 1.16-18.) Marks of this decay surface which point to a ripening in the future: licentiousness, the maligning of truth, greed and deception (vv. 2-3). From the prophetic standpoint, those instigating the moral malaise have already been condemned (v. 3b). On what basis, then, is this condemnation thought to be predicated?

Given the considerable parallel material in 2 Peter and Jude, traditional commentary in the main has focused its attention on literary dependence. A closer look, however, at the use of the moral paradigm in both epistles[8] brings about an awareness that they function slightly differently, due to the redactive interests of the authors. The

---

7.   H.C.C. Cavallin, 'The False Teachers of 2 Peter as Pseudo-Prophets', *NovT* 21 (1979), pp. 263-70, notes lexical links but stresses doctrine while missing the moral argument. Bauckham, *Jude, 2 Peter*, p. 243, catches the proper sense of prophetic inspiration and 'false prophets'.

8.   Cf. 2 Pet 2.4-10a and Jude 5-7.

shift away from straight condemnation in Jude to both condemnation *and* salvation in 2 Peter confronts the reader with the question of literary strategy. How do the paradigms in 2 Peter function in the context of the entire letter? What thematic link unites the fallen angels, Noah and his contemporaries, Lot and Balaam? What are the theological nuances absent in Jude?

Viewed together, the Petrine paradigms point to a state of moral decay and moral compromise that portend irrevocable judgment. Moreover, Noah's generation, Sodom and Gomorrah and Balaam all remind the audience of pagan socio-cultural forces— enormously pervasive forces—that inundated Noah, Lot, and in a more sinister way, Balaam. Nevertheless, while forces that opposed faith are depicted as intimidating, they are not overwhelming. To make this important distinction, the author employs the Savior-motif in three of these four cases: 'he saved Noah, a herald of righteousness, and seven others'; 'he rescued Lot, a righteous man'; 'a speechless ass spoke with a human voice and restrained the prophet's madness'. And lest the reader believe that Christian perseverance requires too much, the initial paradigm of the fallen angels serves an important function. It is a reminder of the utterly egregious nature of having access to divine glory and the knowledge of truth—an incomparable privilege—and yet renouncing that privilege. Such, incredibly, was the course of angels who rebelled. Veiled though it may be, the allusion to the disenfranchised angels should evoke a response of utter bewilderment on the part of the reader. Of all creatures it is the angels—exalted beings given the privilege of ministering in the presence of God— who are without excuse. For this reason they are, apocalyptically speaking, 'reserved in chains of deepest darkness' and 'held until the judgment' (2.4). With extraordinary privilege comes extraordinary accountability. In the end, the theological tension between divine keeping and the willingness to be 'kept', that is, moral agency, is preserved.

This tension is further retained in the examples of Noah and Lot. Both figures represent a beleaguered minority. Both faced daunting social and cultural resistance to their faith. Both constitute a reminder that divine judgment is temporal as well as eschatological. Yet, both also point to divine rescue—'if. . . he saved Noah. . . and seven others. . . and if he rescued Lot. . . then the Lord knows how to rescue the godly from trial' (2.5-9).

In some respects the portrait of Balaam (2.15-16) is even more disturbing. Consistent with the mixed review given to the Midianite prophet in the Old Testament, the biblical record is for the most part a negative memorial.[9] Traditional hostility toward Balaam in Jewish haggadic tradition would appear to be based on Num. 31.15-16. While being a paradigm of self-seeking and greed, Balaam more importantly led Israel into idolatry and immorality at Baal-Peor. Very much a subject of great fascination to the Jews, Balaam is described by Josephus in the following manner:

9. See, especially, Num. 22–24 and 31. In Num. 31.16, Deut. 23.4-5, Josh. 13.22, 24.9 and Neh. 13.2, Balaam is portrayed strictly as a negative memorial. As a prophet, he stands unique as one who hired himself out to curse and lead Israel astray.

> This was the man to whom Moses did the high honor of recording his prophecies. And though it was possible for him to claim credit for them himself. . . he has given Balaam his testimony and deigned to perpetuate his memory.[10]

In rabbinic literature Balaam is characterized as the antithesis to Abraham. The three qualities associated with the latter are a good eye, a lowly mind, and a humble soul. Balaam, by contrast, was the possessor of an evil eye, a haughty mind, and a proud soul.[11] The deception of Balaam is the deception of selfish profit.[12] The ἀπο-derivatives commonly employed throughout 2 Peter are perfectly embodied in Balaam as a type.

Balaam typology also surfaces in Jude, albeit without a nuanced description.[13] There the prophet is briefly listed as part of an apostate trio depicted in a standardization of type which more than likely had evolved as a result of Jewish haggadic tradition. Those being denounced by Jude 'abandon (ἐκχέω) themselves to Balaam's error (πλάνη)', a depiction that is highly suggestive of apostasy in the community. They do this, according to Jude, 'for the sake of gain'—a qualification that is amplified in 2 Peter: 'They have departed the straight road and have strayed (πλανάω), following the way of Balaam, son of Beor, who loved the wages of evil' (2.15).

The Balaam typology is incomplete, however, without taking into consideration antitypes of the present who are depicted in rather unsavory terms: 'They have eyes full of adultery and insatiable for sin, they seduce unstable souls, they have hearts that are exercised in greed. They are accursed children' (2.14). The unflattering parallels between Balaam and those infecting the community in many respects call to mind the depiction of Balaam in extrabiblical tradition. Of all the characters in the Old Testament and Jewish tradition, it is Balaam who epitomizes apostasy. Thus it is that in rabbinic literature Balaam is one of seven for whom there was reserved no place in paradise.[14]

Notwithstanding this excessive display of human depravity, the crowning touch of divine intervention is that a brute beast, a 'speechless ass', is supernaturally endowed with a human voice to bring a 'mad' prophet back to his moral senses. The rhetorical effect of this paradigm on the recipients of 2 Peter could not be any stronger. And lest anyone conclude that the epistle promotes a 'works righteousness' or an ethic of legalism, the intervention of God as 'savior' in Israel's history is here manifest in the extreme. The recipients doubtless identify Balak the pagan king with cultural forces that surround and would seduce them—forces that seem at times bewitching. Yet, viewed prophetically, the community—like Balaam—was endowed with a divine trust. This trust requires giving an account, and human moral depravity not withstanding, it is a trust under the jealous guard of God himself. Divine reproof through an ass should encourage the reader that God the Savior will go to virtually any length to rescue his own. In the end, Balaam is a sober reminder that apostasy, for whatever reason, is reprehensible.

---

10.   *Ant.* 4.6.13.
11.   *m. 'Abot* 5.19.
12.   Kelly, *Commentary*, p. 268.
13.   Jude 11.
14.   *m. Sanh.* 10.3.

To underscore the abomination of departing from the truth (whether among angels or humans), two metaphors are pressed into service. The slave image (denoting redemption from the marketplace and a subsequent return to bondage) and popular proverbial wisdom fortify the author's argument based on illustration. Apostasy is presented simultaneously as possible and unthinkable. Just as a slave, who discovers new-found freedom, would not rationally return to former bondage, so it is with the Christian disciple who renounces divine grace and the moral government of God. Equally revolting is the popular image of a dog returning to its vomit and a pig returning to the mud. But revolting as these images might be, they nevertheless constitute a warning:

> For if, having escaped the pollution that is in the world through the knowledge of our Lord and Savior Jesus Christ, they are again entangled therein and overcome, they are worse off in the end than they were at the beginning. For it would have been better for them never to have known the way of righteousness than to have known it and then turn their backs on the sacred commandment that was given to them (2.20-21).

While it may be argued that 2 Pet. 2.20-21 represents a hypothetical state and not an actual condition of some, the problem of apostasy is not hypothetical in 2 Peter. The paradigms are meant to illustrate; they are intended to warn. They remind the reader that it is precisely *because* the angels did in fact rebel and Balaam *was* in fact seduced for the purposes of leading Israel astray that apostasy is a real possibility. Thus, the warning that is proffered in 2 Peter cannot be construed as 'hypothetical'. Rather, the author is countering, through historical-theological types, a painfully real situation— a situation that constitutes the *Sitz im Leben* of paraenesis. Accordingly, the moral paradigms of 2 Peter 2 are adapted to the writer's literary strategy.

2 Peter 3: Defending the Virtue Motif

Following a return to paraenetic language—'I am trying to arouse your sincere intention by reminding you that you should recall the words spoken in the past' (3.1)— the author initiates a final shift in literary-rhetorical strategy. Insofar as the case for the ethical life has been presented (ch. 1) and its necessity through historical-theological paradigms has been graphically illustrated (ch. 2), it remains for the writer to expose and critique those individuals who by reason of moral license and moral skepticism are actually calling into question the very existence of a created moral order. We have already observed that traditional commentary on 2 Peter 3 normally proceeds along eschatological lines. That is, broadly assumed is a doctrinal-eschatological argument which is meant to address a purported 'Parousia delay'. Closer attention to literary strategy, however, suggests that the material of ch. 3 belongs to a foremost ethical argument and qualifies as a type of moral 'apologetic'.

Logically, apostasy breeds the necessity of returning to cosmological 'first things'. Carried to its end, apostasy manifests itself in wholesale denial of all authority—local or universal. It is the latter, the more fundamental denial, that would appear to lie behind the caricature of the moral skeptic in 3.3-6. The eventual fruit of 'indulging in one's lusts' (v. 3) is that moral accountability on the most basic level is called into

question (v. 4). This process entails an eventual—and calculated—denial of divine
intervention in history ('They deliberately ignore that by the word of God the heavens
existed long ago and the earth was formed out of water and with water. By water also
the world at that time was flooded and destroyed', vv. 5-6), a catastrophe that fore-
shadowed eschatological judgment (v. 7).

The effects of the moral skeptic on the believing community are by no means
benign. Given the chance, they undermine one's faith and expectation in the Lord,
one's ability to live righteously, and one's capacity to discern properly divine judgment: 'But do not ignore. . . this one fact, beloved, that with the Lord one day is as a
thousand years, and a thousand years are like a day' (v. 8). To be sure, it is humanly
natural that the faithful agonize over the presence—and pervasiveness—of evil, which
possibly causes some even to despair over why there is no imminent divine retribution:

> The Lord is not lax in keeping his promise, as some understand laxness; rather, he is for-
> bearing toward you, desirous that no one would perish but that all would come to a place
> of repentance (v. 9).

The faithful, consequently, are to be reassured that righteous and unrighteous deeds
will receive their due, whereby 'everything that is done [in the earth] will be disclosed'
(v. 10).

Divine intervention in the past is a foreshadow of a day of moral reckoning to come.
Divine judgment of the earth through the flood (2.5; 3.6) and the destruction of Sodom
and Gomorrah (2.6) portend a future day of universal judgment. Cosmic catastrophe
indicates that there are divine limits as to what God, morally speaking, will permit.
Skepticism among Noah's generation, for example, parallels the moral skepticism that
the community faces. Scoffers rationalize that God does not intervene in the world or
that there is a future judgment. Hence a reconstruction such as Neyrey has attempted,
in which pantheistic cosmology is countered with Judeo-Christian apocalyptic couched
in quasi-Stoic categories, is eminently plausible and fits well into the author's literary-
rhetorical strategy.[15] Bauckham's explanation of 3.5-7, furthermore, captures the
author's thrust:

> The final phrase reveals that although in this passage the author is certainly concerned
> with catastrophic upheavals in the physical world, which amount to the destruction and
> creation of worlds, he is not concerned with these for the sake of mere cosmology, but
> with their interpretation in a world-view which sees them as occurring by the sovereign
> decree of God as instruments of his judgment on humanity.[16]

In our wrestling with the theological tension between divine sovereignty and human
moral agency, it is the eschatological element that restores what might be perceived as
an imbalance in 2 Peter. One perseveres, one persists in the faith, precisely because
the sovereign Lord has predestined all humans to give account of themselves. This
awareness is not without its difficulties, however. It is the matter of timing that ever
remains a mystery for the believer. The cry of the righteous retains the same focus

---

15.   See Chapter 2.
16.   Bauckham, *Jude, 2 Peter*, p. 302.

from creation to consummation: 'Lord, how long? When will you intervene?'[17] Perseverance amidst periods of cultural apostasy is particularly difficult where the believer sees no evidence of divine intervention whatsoever. The human perspective is a limited perspective (3.8; cf. Ps. 90.4). The divine strategy in the short term calls for forbearance (μακροθυμία), both divine and human. Because the divine intention transcends human understanding, 'laxness' (βραδύτης) is a cause of human frustration. This divine delay, however, is not without its limits. The great day of moral reckoning *will* arrive. The readers are warned that it will come like a thief (3.10). Moreover, it will be accompanied by another—a final—cosmic catastrophe, at which time 'the earth and the works done on it will be manifest'.

The apocalyptic flavor of the material in 2 Pet. 3 serves a foremost apologetic rather than doctrinal purpose.[18] It serves to rebut the assumption of the moral skeptic that there is no judgment, no moral accountability in the temporal order. It is designed to counter the individual advancing a pagan life-view, that is, that we seek pleasure and happiness in the present life and tomorrow die, with no permanent consequences for our actions.[19] But the scandal of the Christian faith is that God 'has fixed a day on which he will judge the world in righteousness by a man whom he has appointed', a man whom he has raised from the dead (Acts 17.31).

In the end, the righteous in 2 Peter are simultaneously exhorted to allow for the forbearance of God and reminded that God indeed does judge the unrighteous. Holiness and godliness (3.11) are to be the confirmation of one's calling (1.10), while one awaits a day when 'righteousness is at home' (3.13).

The Problem of Apostasy

2 Peter presents us with a pastoral scenario in which the ideal of the Christian life is not being realized. Thus the author is moved to exhort his readers to persist in the faith with great effort, to endure. In theological terms, this persistence is normally described as perseverance. Howard Marshall expresses the corresponding theological dilemma in the following manner:

> The question then arises whether the Christian can be infallibly certain of final victory in his battle against temptation or is in danger of defeat. We must ask whether Christians are predestined to emerge victoriously from the conflict and whether the nature of the life which is bestowed upon them by God is such that it cannot possibly be lost. On the other hand, if the Christian may possibly suffer defeat, we must ask whether such defeat is permanent in its effects, so that it is impossible to regain faith in Jesus Christ . . . or merely temporary with the possibility of restoration of the former relationship with God. If the evidence suggests that a believer is infallibly certain to persevere, an

---

17. This can be heard, for example, of Abraham in Gen. 18; in innumerable Psalms; in the frequent cries of Isaiah and Jeremiah; in the perplexity of the disciples in Acts 1.6; in 2 Pet. 3.8-9; and in the cry of the righteous who are martyred in Revelation.

18. Thus Bauckham, *Jude, 2 Peter*, pp. 321-22.

19. Cf. 1 Cor. 15.32b-33.

explanation must be found for the various apparent cases of falling away and apostasy which take place in the Church and are described in the New Testament.[20]

2 Peter presents the reader with a pastoral dilemma of crisis proportions that cannot simply be explained away as hypothetical. From the standpoint of the writer, the danger is very real.

In the Old Testament, the possibility of apostasy was not only acknowledged, it was *the* ongoing burden of the prophets. Not infrequently, Yahweh's prophetic messengers stood at a crucial juncture in Israel's history. At the core of their message was the call to repent, turn from wickedness, and return to the Lord. Israel is continually called to give account of itself amidst covenant-breaking, transgressing the law, immorality, idol-worship, and spiritual adultery. This adultery, moreover, is not confined merely to certain individuals; it typifies Israel as a nation. Pronouncements of judgment are not mere idle threats; they are designed to bring the chosen to a place of repentance and turning. Ultimately, national judgment in the form of exile accomplishes this purpose. Yet even when judgment is meted out, it is redemptive in its trajectory. Contained within is an element of mercy, for it is the mercy of God that breaks the cycle of hard-heartedness affecting generations to come. God in his faithfulness initiates with a view to restore those who are his own. Whether or not the decision is made to return rests with Israel.

In the post-exilic period, the divine call to repentance reaches its apex in the ministry of John the Baptist. It is by no means welcome news that not every child of Abraham is deemed fit for the kingdom of God. By John's account, every tree not bearing good fruit is liable for judgment (Mt. 3.10; Lk. 3.9). Significantly, John's ministry is after the model of Elijah, the mighty prophet called upon to counter spiritual corruption among his contemporaries, many of whom in some respects are as pagan as the surrounding nations. Inasmuch as the Baptist is to prepare the way for the one bringing the kingdom, he is commissioned to call a nation to return—a nation that once more stands before catastrophic judgment.

The potential for falling away constitutes an undeniable part of Jesus' message. His teaching on discipleship, for example, stresses a variety of types of 'hearers'—and responses. Some seed of the evangel falls on good ground and brings forth a harvest. But some falls by the wayside, on rocky soil, or among thorns (Mt. 13.1-23). The seed sown on rocky ground is likened to the person who hears the word, responds in faith, but perseveres only for a while; when trouble or persecution arises, 'that person falls away' (Mt. 13.21). It is in the context of discipleship that the message of cross-bearing and self-denial emerges, both of which represent the very heart of what it means to be a disciple (for example, Mt. 16.24-26; Mk 8.34-38; Lk. 9.23-26). The implication is that some are unwilling to take up their cross and deny themselves. Cross-bearing, self-denial and following the Master require commitments of the will—conscious and ongoing decisions that are costly. One does not automatically persevere. Along with suffering and hardship, temptations abound for the disciple. The possibility of deception surfaces as well in Jesus' teaching. For this reason, the disciples

---

20. I.H. Marshall, *Kept by the Power of God* (Minneapolis: Bethany Fellowship, 1969), p. 23.

are admonished to heed Jesus' warnings to be watchful and alert (Mk 13). With the emergence of false messiahs and false prophets, it is even possible that the elect could be led astray (Mk 13.22). Since in Jesus' teaching this is not theoretical but considered rather to be a distinct possibility, the disciple is consequently admonished to 'be alert' (13.23). Perseverance lies at the heart of discipleship: 'the one who endures to the end will be saved' (13.13). Ultimately, both the promise of divine provision and the requirement of steadfast faith and endurance stand alongside one another.

One of Jesus' more perplexing teachings concerns the 'unforgivable sin'. The context in which this appears in Mark and Luke differs somewhat. In Mark 3, it follows Jesus' teaching on binding the strong man; in Luke 10, the lesson is confessing or denying the Son of Man before others. For all its difficulty, what may be said about this teaching is that it is possible to turn away from the gift of divine forgiveness as a result of a calculated decision.

Judas and Peter illustrate two contrasting responses to Christian discipleship and 'falling', as one considers the knotty issue of departing the faith. Both men were 'called' to be disciples; both were amply confirmed in the frailty of their 'humanity'. Yet this calling to be a disciple of the Lord, this 'predestination', did not serve as a *guarantee* that each would persevere. Consider Jesus' sobering warning to Peter, which is illuminating: 'Simon, Simon, listen! Satan has earnestly desired to sift you like wheat, but I have prayed for you that your faith might not fail. And when you have returned, be a support to your brethren' (Lk. 22.31-32). Peter was permitted to reap the consequences of moral agency. Jesus' admonition, rather than stressing the assurance of Peter's predestination, contains the staggering concession of Jesus' intercessory prayer for Peter that the disciple's faith might not 'come to an end' (ἐκλείπω). Discipleship, then, entails a conscious attempt to move forward by faith, despite trial, persecution and the cloak of mystery that veils the purposes of God.

Reflecting on the theological tension inherent in divine calling and human cooperation, Howard Marshall writes:

> To assert that God gives some individuals such [persevering] grace and refuses it to others would be to attribute an intolerable arbitrariness to the mercy of God. In any case, it is difficult to see how this doctrine would help the individual believer, since there is no way in which he can know for certain what is the secret will of God concerning himself; he can only know that he is one of the 'elect' only by the evidence of his own faith and 'fruitfulness', and the condition of final salvation is precisely that he goes on showing this evidence.[21]

As far as the teaching of Jesus is concerned, the perplexing question of why some disciples persevere and others do not remains an enigma. No explanation is offered. One can only view it for what it is—a divine mystery, impenetrable to human understanding. Nevertheless, what biblical revelation does indicate concerning discipleship, namely that divine grace and human cooperation must merge, is confirmed in the pages of the New Testament. And nowhere is this mysterious tension between sovereignty and moral agency more on display than in the letters of 2 Peter and Jude.

---

21. Marshall, *Kept*, p. 90.

In the life of the early church as recorded in Acts, there is no explicit account of apostasy, although two occasions faintly suggest the possibility of falling away through 'tempting' or grieving the Holy Spirit. Admittedly, the accounts of Annas and Sapphira (Acts 5.1-11) and Simon Magus (Acts 8.9-24) raise more questions than they perhaps answer. What is the precise meaning of the death penalty? How real was the faith of these individuals? Were they excluded from the kingdom of God? At the very least, we may conclude that at issue is a question of serious sin which requires discipline. The prior possibility of repentance and restoration may not be ruled out, even when the text is strangely silent on such matters.

While much is made in Pauline theology of the element of predestination (for example, Rom. 8.28-30; 9.1-11.36; Eph. 1.3-12; 3.9-12), the apostle indicates in his letters that some individuals were shipwrecked in their faith—among these, for example, Hymenaeus and Alexander (1 Tim. 1.18-20). For this reason, Timothy is exhorted to 'fight the good fight (of faith)' (1.18), the implication being that some have rejected conscience, and consequently, lost their faith. Two other persons, Phygelus and Hermogenes, are said to have deserted Paul in Asia (2 Tim. 1.15; cf. 4.16), along with Demas, who was 'in love with this present world' (4.9). These instances, coupled with the hymn of endurance in 2 Tim. 2.8-13, allow Howard Marshall to speak of a Pauline 'theology of perseverance'.[22]

> If we have died with him, we shall also live with him.
> If we endure, we shall also reign with him.
> If we deny him, he also will deny us.
> If we are faithless, he remains faithful,
> For he cannot deny himself.

The well-known warning passages in the epistle to the Hebrews constitute another reminder that a lapse in faith is a very real possibility for those who were 'once enlightened'. The defining characteristics of certain individuals, said to be incapable of restoration to a place of repentance, are a tasting of the heavenly gift, a sharing in the life of the Holy Spirit, and a tasting of the goodness of the word of God and the powers of the age to come (Heb. 6.4-6). Having fallen away (παραπίπτω), these are said to re-crucify the Son of God and hold him in contempt (4.6). Significantly, these rather strong depictions are followed by the metaphor of ground that produces thorns and thistles rather than a crop for harvest (6.7-8). While those who deny that the New Testament teaches the possibility of apostasy view these verses as addressing a merely hypothetical situation, the danger that the writer is confronting does not seem to be theoretical or imaginary. Confronting these warnings head-on at the very least acknowledges a potential danger. And that danger is incurred by the possibility of apostasy.

It is in this light that the exhortation to hold fast one's confession (10.23) in Hebrews is to be understood. The writer sheds further light on the pastoral problem: 'If we persist in sin after having received knowledge of the truth, there is no longer a sacrifice for sins; rather, a fearful prospect of judgment' (10.26-27). It is, hence,

---

22. Marshall, *Kept*, p. 132.

logical that the catalog of faithful in Hebrews 11 and the admonition in 12.1 to 'run with perseverance the race that is set before us' follows. The readers are not confronted merely with a hypothetical case; they are, on the contrary, to know with certitude that there are boundaries to sin that *may not be ignored.*

In the epistle of Jude, unbelieving Israel (v. 5) is listed as the first in a triad of examples of hard-heartedness and unfaithfulness. These paradigms together resemble extrabiblical catalogs of unfaithfulness, in which Sodom and Gomorrah, the fallen angels (the 'Watchers'), giants, the Flood and unbelieving Israel most frequently appear.[23] In Jude 5-7 the triplet functions as part of a prophetic denunciation of those who have apostatized and who are influencing the community. Along with the fallen angels, the allusion to Israel in Jude is telling, particularly because of the ἅπαξ. . . δεύτερον construction. Jude writes:

> Now I wish to remind you, though you already know all things, namely that the Lord, having once and for all (ἅπαξ) delivered a people from Egypt, the second time (δεύτερον) destroyed those who did not believe.

This example has particular relevance for the church. By implication, Jude is saying that because of the perpetual validity of Christ's redemptive work, just as Yahweh's deliverance of his people from Egypt once and for all, those who deny the Lord (Jude 4) and fall away, like Israel in the wilderness, stand under divine judgment. The allusion to Israel as a type suggests that the apostate are former 'orthodox', that is, those who had formerly experienced divine redemption.

Reconciling a Theological Tension

The New Testament possesses more than adequate evidence to show that alongside the faithfulness and grace of God stands the need for humans to persevere. In the end, we must confess our limited perspective which is incapable of penetrating the mysteries of God. Exegetically, we are prevented from ignoring the witness of the Scriptures as a result of promoting systematic-theological constructs that fail to confront with hermeneutical integrity the biblical evidence.

The call to virtuous living, consistent with the Christian paraenetic tradition, is what makes 2 Peter an invaluable contribution to the New Testament canon. The epistle mirrors a community in which individuals are not only lapsed in their faith, but some are openly—and vigorously—denying the faith as a result of moral depravity. The teaching of 2 Peter, as already argued, does not approximate a works-righteousness, neither does it negate the grace of God. Rather, the epistle teaches that perseverance must accompany the knowledge and grace of God. Persevering, one need not stumble and be led astray. One perseveres, moreover, with the knowledge that God is Savior.

Although the Parousia establishes a limit as to divine forbearance with the world, this forbearance nonetheless provides time and opportunity for people to repent. In

---

23. For example, Sir. 16.5-15; *Jub.* 20.2-7; *3 Macc.* 2.3-7; *T. Naph.* 2.8-4.3; CD 2.14-3.12.; *m. Sanh.* 10.3.

the meantime, the believers are to rouse themselves and add to their faith every kind of virtue, thereby confirming their calling and election as those who have received a faith through the righteousness of Christ.

Bibliography

Aall, A., *Geschichte der Logosidee in der griechischen Philosophie* (Leipzig: Reisland, 1896).

Aland, K., 'The Problem of Anonymity and Pseudonymity in Christian Literature of the First Two Centuries', in K. Aland (ed.), *The Authorship and Integrity of the New Testament* (London: SPCK, 1965), pp. 1-13.

Alexander, T.D., 'Lot's Hospitality: A Clue to his Righteousness', *JBL* 104.2 (1985), pp. 289-91.

Aune, D.E., *The New Testament in its Literary Environment* (Philadelphia: Westminster Press, 1987).

Bahr, G.J., 'Paul and Letter Writing in the First Century', *CBQ* 28 (1966), pp. 465-77.

Balz, H.R., 'Anonymität und Pseudonymität im Urchristentum', *ZTK* 66 (1969), pp. 403-36.

Balz, H., and W. Schrage, *Die katholischen Briefe: Die Briefe des Jakobus, Petrus, Johannes und Judas* (NTD, 10; Göttingen: Vandenhoek & Ruprecht, 1973).

Bauckham, R.J., 'James, 1 and 2 Peter, Jude', in D.A. Carson and H.G.M. Williamson (eds.), *It Is Written: Scripture Citing Scripture. Essays in Honour of B. Lindars* (Cambridge: Cambridge University Press, 1988), pp. 303-17.

—*Jude, 2 Peter* (WBC, 50; Waco, TX: Word Books, 1983).

—'Pseudo-Apostolic Letters', *JBL* 107 (1988), pp. 469-94.

Beckwith, R., *The Old Testament Canon of the New Testament Church* (Grand Rapids: Eerdmans, 1985).

Berger, K., 'Hellenistische Gattungen im Neuen Testament', in W. Haase (ed.), *Aufstieg und Niedergang der römischen Welt: Geschichte und Kultur Roms im Spiegel der neueren Forschung* (Berlin: de Gruyter, 1984), II.25.2, pp. 1075-77.

—'Streit um Gottes Versehung. Zur Position der Gegner im 2. Petrusbrief', in J.W. van Henton *et al.* (eds.), *Tradition and Re-Interpretation in Jewish and Early Christian Literature* (Leiden: Brill, 1986), pp. 121-35.

Bigg, C., *A Critical and Exegetical Commentary on the Epistles of St Peter and St Jude* (ICC; New York: Scribner, 1922).

Böckle, F., *Die Idee der Fruchtbarkeit in den Paulusbriefen* (Fribourg: Fribourg Universität, 1953).

Bommer, J., *Die Idee der Fruchtbarkeit in den Evangelien* (Pfullingen: Mohn, 1950).

Boring, M.E. *et al.* (eds.), *Hellenistic Commentary to the New Testament* (Nashville: Abingdon Press, 1995).

Bradley, D.J.M., 'The Transformation of the Stoic Ethic in Clement of Alexandria', in E. Ferguson (ed.), *Christian Life: Ethics, Morality, and Discipline in the Early Church* (New York: Garland, 1993), pp. 41-66.

Brox, N., *Falsche Verfasserangaben: Zur Erklärung der frühchristlichen Pseudepigraphie* (Stuttgart: KBW, 1975).

—*Pseudepigraphie in der heidnischen und jüdisch-christlichen Antike* (Darmstadt: WBG, 1977).

Bruce, F.F., 'Tradition and the Canon of Scripture', in D.K. McKim (ed.), *The Authoritative Word: Essays on the Nature of Scripture* (Grand Rapids: Eerdmans, 1983), pp. 59-84.

Bultmann, R., 'γινώσκω. . . . ἐπίγνωσις', *TDNT*, I, pp. 689-719.

—'New Testament and Mythology', in H.W. Bartsch (ed.), *Kerygma and Myth*. I (London: Methuen, 1954), pp. 1-12.

Calvin, J., *Commentaries on the Catholic Epistles* (trans. J. Owen; Grand Rapids: Baker, rep. 1981).

Campbell, K., *A Stoic Philosophy of Life* (Lanham: University Press of America, 1986).

Candlish, J.S., 'On the Moral Character of Pseudonymous Books', *Expos* 4.4 (1891), pp. 91-107, 262-79.

Cavallin, H.C.C., 'The False Teachers of 2 Peter as Pseudo- prophets', *NovT* 21 (1979), pp. 263-70.

Chaine, J., 'Cosmogonie aquatique et conflagration finale d'après la Secunda Petri', *RB* 46 (1937), pp. 207-16.

—*Les épîtres catholiques: La seconde épître de saint Pierre, les épîtres de saint Jean, l'épître de saint Jude* (EBib; Paris: Gabalda, 2nd edn, 1939).

Charles, J.D., 'Engaging the (Neo)Pagan Mind: Paul's Encounter with Athenian Culture as a Model of Cultural Apologetics', *TJ* 16 NS (1995), pp. 47-62.

—*Jude and 2 Peter* (BCBC; Scottdale: Herald Press, forthcoming).

—'Jude's Use of Pseudepigraphal Source-Material as Part of a Literary Strategy', *NTS* 37 (1991), pp. 130-45.

—'Literary Artifice in the Epistle of Jude', *ZNW* 82.1 (1991), pp. 106-24.

—*Literary Strategy in the Epistle of Jude* (Scranton: University of Scranton; London: Associated University Presses, 1993).

—'The Old Testament in the General Epistles', in R.P. Martin and P.H. Davids (eds.), *Dictionary of the Later New Testament* (Downers Grove: InterVarsity Press, 1997).

—'"Those" and "These": The Use of the Old Testament in the Epistle of Jude', *JSNT* 38 (1990), pp. 109-24.

Charles, R.H., *Apocrypha and Pseudepigrapha of the Old Testament*, I (Oxford: Clarendon, 2 vols, 1913).

Chester, A., and R.P. Martin, *The Theology of the Letters of James, Peter, and Jude* (Cambridge: Cambridge University Press, 1994).

Crehan, J., 'New Light on 2 Peter from the Bodmer Papyrus', in E.A. Livingstone (ed.), *Studia Evangelica. Vol. VII* (Berlin: Akademie, 1982), pp. 145-49.

Cullmann, O., 'Parousieverzögerung und Urchristentum', *TLZ* 83 (1958), pp. 1-12.

Curran, J.T., 'The Teaching of 2 Peter i.20', *TS* 4 (1943), pp. 364- 67.

Danker, F.W., '2 Peter 1: A Solemn Decree', *CBQ* 40 (1978), pp. 64-82.

—'II Peter 3.10 and Psalm of Solomon 17.10', *ZNW* 53 (1962), pp. 82-86.

Deissmann, A., *Bible Studies: Contributions Chiefly from Papyri and Inscriptions to the History of the Language, the Literature, and the Religion of Hellenistic Judaism and Primitive Christianity* (trans. A. Grieve; Edinburgh: T. & T. Clark, 1901).

—*Light from the Ancient East* (trans. L.R.M. Strachan; New York: G.H. Doran, 1927).

Desjardins, M. 'The Portrayal of the Dissidents in 2 Peter and Jude: Does it Tell Us More about the "Ungodly" than the "Godly"?' *JSNT* 30 (1987), pp. 89-102.

Dibelius, M., *Die Pastoralbriefe* (Tübingen: Mohr, 2nd edn, 1931).

Dittenberger, F. (ed.), *Orientis Graeci Inscriptiones Selectae: Supplementum Sylloges Inscriptionum Graecarum* (Hildesheim: Georg Olms, 1970).

Dodds, E.R., *Pagan and Christian in an Age of Anxiety* (Cambridge: Cambridge University Press, 1965).

Donelson, L.R., *Pseudepigraphy and Ethical Argument in the Pastoral Epistles* (HUT, 22; Tübingen: Mohr [Siebeck], 1986).

Drane, J.W., 'Eschatology, Ecclesiology and Catholicity in the New Testament', *ExpTim* 83 (1971–72), pp. 180-84.

Dunn, J.D.G., *Unity and Diversity in the New Testament: An Inquiry into the Character of Earliest Christianity* (Philadelphia: Westminster Press, 1977).

Dupont, J., *Gnosis: La connaissance religieuse dans les épîtres de saint Paul* (Louvain: E. Nauwelaerts; Paris: J. Gabalda, 1949).

Dyroff, A., *Ethik der alten Stoa* (Berlin: S. Calvary & Co., 1897).

Easton, B.S., 'New Testament Ethical Lists', *JBL* 51 (1932), pp. 1- 12.

Edelstein, L., *The Meaning of Stoicism* (Cambridge, MA: Harvard University Press, 1966).

Elliott, J.H., 'A Catholic Gospel: Reflections on "Early Catholicism" in the New Testament', *CBQ* 31 (1969), pp. 213-23.

Ellis, E.E., *Prophecy and Hermeneutic in Early Christianity* (WUNT, 18; Tübingen: Mohr, 1978).

—'Pseudonymity and Canonicity of New Testament Documents', in W.J. Wilkins and T. Paige (eds.), *Worship, Theology and Ministry in the Early Church* (JSNTSup, 87; Sheffield: JSOT Press, 1992), pp. 212-24.

Eltester, W., 'Gott und die Natur in der Areopagrede', in *Neutestamentliche Studien für R. Bultmann* (Berlin: Töpelmann, 1954), pp. 202-27.

Engberg-Pedersen, T., *The Stoic Theory of Oikeiōsis: Moral Development and Social Inter-action in Early Stoic Philosophy* (SHC, 2; Aarhus: Aarhus University Press, 1990).

Falconer, R.A., 'Is 2 Peter a Genuine Epistle to the Christians of Samaria?', *Expos* 6.5 (1902), pp. 459-69.

Fischel, H.A., 'The Uses of Sorites (Climax, Gradiatio) in the Tannaitic Period', *HUCA* 44 (1973), pp. 119-51.

Fischer, K.M., 'Anmerkungen zur Pseudepigraphie im Neuen Testament', *NTS* 23 (1976) 76-81.

Foerster, W., 'εὐσέβεια', *TDNT*, VII, pp. 175-85.

G. Forkman, *The Limits of the Religious Community* (ConBNT, 5; Lund: Gleerup, 1972).

Fornberg, T. *An Early Church in a Pluralistic Society: A Study of 2 Peter* (ConBNT, 9; Lund: Gleerup, 1977).

Fox, R.L., *Pagans and Christians* (New York: A.A. Knopf, 1987).

Fuller, R.H., *A Critical Introduction to the New Testament* (London: Gerald Duckworth, 1966).

Gaffin, R.B., Jr, 'The New Testament as Canon', in H.M. Conn (ed.), *Inerrancy and Hermeneutic: A Tradition, A Challenge, A Debate* (Grand Rapids: Baker, 1988), pp. 165-83.

Gaertner, B., *The Areopagus Speech and Natural Revelation* (ASNU, 21; Uppsala: Almquist, 1955).

Glasson, T.F., *Greek Influence in Jewish Eschatology* (London: SPCK, 1961).

Goppelt, L., 'The Nature of the Early Church', in W. Klassen and G. Snyder (eds.), *Current Issues in New Testament Interpretation* (Grand Rapids: Eerdmans, 1962), pp. 193-209.

—*TYPOS: The Typological Interpretation of the Old Testament in the New* (trans. D.H. Madvig; Grand Rapids: Eerdmans, 1982).

Grässer, E., *Die Naherwartung Jesus* (SB, 61; Stuttgart: KBW, 1973).

Green M. (E.M.B.), *2 Peter and Jude* (TNTC, 18; Leicester: InterVarsity Press; Grand Rapids: Eerdmans, 3rd edn, 1989).

—*2 Peter Reconsidered* (London: Tyndale Press, 1961).

Grundmann, W., *Der Brief des Judas und der zweite Brief des Petrus* (THKNT, 15; Berlin: Evangelische Verlagsanstalt, 1974).

—'ἐγκράτεια', *TDNT*, II, pp. 339-42.

Gudeman, A., 'Literary Fraud among the Greeks', in *Classical Studies in Honour of H. Drisler* (New York: Macmillan, 1894), pp. 52-74.

Guthrie, D., 'Acts and Epistles in Apocryphal Writings', in W.W. Gasque and R.P. Martin (eds.), *Apostolic History and the Gospel* (Grand Rapids: Eerdmans, 1970), pp. 328-45.

—'The Development of the Idea of Canonical Pseudepigrapha in New Testament Criticism', in R.P. Martin (ed.), *Vox Evangelica I* (London: Tyndale Press, 1962), pp. 43-59.

—*New Testament Introduction* (Leicester: InterVarsity Press, 4th edn, 1990).

—*The Pastoral Epistles* (TNTC, 14; London: Tyndale Press, 1957).

Hadas, M., *The Stoic Philosophy of Seneca* (Garden City: Doubleday, 1958).

Hahm, D.E., *The Origins of Stoic Cosmology* (Columbus: Ohio State University Press, 1977).

Hahn, F., 'Randbemerkungen zum Judasbrief', *TZ* 37 (1981), pp. 209-18.

Hauck, F., 'ὑπομονή', *TDNT*, IV, pp. 581-88.

Hengel, M., *Judaism and Hellenism: Studies in their Encounter in Palestine during the Early Hellenistic Period* (2 vols.; trans. J. Bowden; Philadelphia: Fortress Press, 1974).

Hermann, A., *Untersuchungen zu Platons Auffassung von der Hēdonē: Ein Beitrag zum Verständnis des platonischen Tugendbegriffes* (Hypomnemata, 35; Göttingen: Vandenhoek & Ruprecht, 1972).

Hillyer, N., *1 and 2 Peter, Jude* (NIBC, 16; Peabody: Hendrickson, 1992).

Inwood, B., *Ethics and Human Action in Early Stoicism* (Oxford: Clarendon Press, 1985).

James, M.R., *The Apocryphal New Testament* (Oxford: Clarendon Press, 1924).

—*The Second Epistle General of St Peter and the General Epistle of Jude* (Cambridge: Cambridge University Press, 1912).

Johnson, S.E., 'Asia Minor and Early Christianity', in J. Neusner (ed.), *Christianity, Judaism and Other Greco-Roman Cults*, II (Leiden: Brill, 1975), pp. 77-145.

Kamlah, E., *Die Form der katalogischen Paränese im Neuen Testament* (Tübingen: Mohr, 1964).

Käsemann, E., 'An Apologia for Primitive Christian Eschatology', in *Essays on New Testament Themes* (London: SCM Press, 1964), pp. 135-57.

—'The Beginnings of Christian Theology', in *New Testament Questions for Today* (Philadelphia: Fortress Press, 1969), pp. 82-107.

—'The Canon of the New Testament and the Unity of the Church', in *Essays on New Testament Themes* (London: SCM, 1964), pp. 215-23.

—'Paul and Early Catholicism', in *New Testament Questions of Today* (Philadelphia: Fortress Press, 1969), pp. 236-59.

Kelly, J.N.D., *A Commentary on the Epistles of Peter and Jude* (BNTC; London: A. & C. Black, 1969).

Kidd, G., 'Moral Actions and Rules in Stoic Ethics', in J.M. Rist (ed.), *The Stoics* (Berkeley: University of California Press, 1978), pp. 247-58.

Kiley M., *Colossians as Pseudepigraphy* (Sheffield: JSOT Press, 1986).

Klein, G., 'Der zweite Petrusbrief und der neutestamentliche Kanon', in *Ärgernisse: Konfrontationen mit dem Neuen Testament* (Munich: Chr. Kaiser Verlag, 1970), pp. 109-14.

Klinger, J., 'The Second Epistle of Peter: An Essay in Understanding', *SVTQ* (1973), pp. 152-69.

Knoch, O., *Die 'Testamente' des Petrus und Paulus: Die Sicherung der apostolischen Überlieferung in der spätapostolischen Zeit* (SBB, 62; Stuttgart: KBW, 1973).

—'Das Vermächtnis des Petrus: Der 2. Petrusbrief', in H. Feld and J. Nolte (eds.), *Wort Gottes in der Zeit: Festschrift K.H. Schelkle* (Düsseldorf: Patmos, 1973), pp. 149-65.

Köster, H., 'φύσις', *TDNT*, IX, pp. 251-77.

Kolenkow, A.B., 'The Genre Testament and Forecasts of the Future in the Hellenistic Jewish Milieu', *JSJ* 6 (1975), pp. 57-71.

Küng, H., 'Frühkatholizismus im Neuen Testament als kontroverztheologishes Problem', *TQ* 143 (1962), pp. 385-424.

Kurz, W.S., *Farewell Addresses in the New Testament* (Collegeville, MN: Liturgical Press, 1990).

Lea, T.D., 'The Early Christian View of Pseudepigraphic Writings', *JETS* 27 (1984), pp. 65-75.

—'Pseudepigraphy and the New Testament', in D.A. Black and D.S. Dockery (eds.), *New Testament Criticism and Interpretation* (Grand Rapids: Zondervan, 1991), pp. 535-59.

Leconte, R., *Les épîtres catholiques de saint Jacques, saint Jude, et saint Pierre* (Paris: Cerf, 1953).

Lefrance, Y., *La théorie platonicienne de la Doxa* (Montréal: Bellarmin; Paris: Les Belles Lettres, 1981).

Legrand, L., 'The Areopagus Speech: Its Theological Kerygma and its Missionary Significance', in J. Coppens (ed.), *La notion de Dieu* (Louvain: Gembloux, 1974), pp. 338-41.

Lenhard, H., 'Ein Beitrag zur Übersetzung von II Ptr 3.10d', *ZNW* 52 (1961), pp. 128-29.

Lewis, J.P., *A Study of the Interpretation of Noah and the Flood in Jewish and Christian Literature* (Leiden: Brill, 1968).

Lövestam, E., 'Eschatologie und Tradition im 2. Petrusbrief', in W.C. Weinrich (ed.), *The New Testament Age. Essays in Honor of B. Reicke* (2 vols.; Macon, GA: Mercer University Press, 1984), II, pp. 287-300.

Lowe, J., *St Peter* (London: SPCK, 1962).

Luck, U., 'φιλανθρωπία', *TDNT*, IX, pp. 107-12.

Luz, U., 'Erwägungen zur Entstehung des "Frühkatholizismus"', *ZNW* 65 (1974), pp. 88-111.

Malherbe, A., *Moral Exhortation: A Greco-Roman Sourcebook* (Philadelphia: Westminster Press, 1986).

Marshall, I.H., 'Is Apocalyptic the Mother of Christian Theology?', in G.F. Hawthorne and O. Betz (eds.), *Tradition and Interpretation in the New Testament* (Grand Rapids: Eerdmans; Tübingen Mohr [Siebeck], 1987), pp. 33-42.

—*Kept by the Power of God* (Minneapolis: Bethany Fellowship, 1969).

Martin, T., *Metaphor and Composition in 1 Peter* (Atlanta: Scholars Press, 1994).

Marxsen, W., *Der 'Frühkatholizismus' im Neuen Testament* (BibS, 21; Neukirchen: Neukirchener Verlag, 1958).

—*Introduction to the New Testament: An Approach to its Problem* (trans. G. Buswell; Philadelphia: Fortress Press, 1970).

—*New Testament Foundations for Christian Ethics* (trans. O.C. Dean, Jr; Minneapolis: Fortress Press, 1993).

Mayor, J.B., *The Epistle of St Jude and the Second Epistle of St Peter* (New York: Macmillan, 1907).

McEleney, N.J., 'The Vice Lists of the Pastoral Epistles', *CBQ* 36 (1974), pp. 203-19

McNamara, M., 'The Unity of 2 Peter: A Reconsideration', *Scr* 12 (1960), pp. 13-19.

Meade, D.G., *Pseudonymity and Canon: An Investigation into the Relationship of Authorship and Authority in Jewish and Earliest Christian Tradition* (WUNT, 39; Tübingen: Mohr, 1986).

Meeks, W.A., *The Moral World of the First Christians* (Philadelphia: Westminster Press, 1986).

Merklein, H. (ed.), *Neues Testament und Ethik* (Stuttgart: KBW, 1989).

Metzger, B.M., 'Literary Forgeries and Canonical Pseudepigrapha', in *New Testament Studies—Philological, Versional and Patristic* (Leiden: Brill, 1980), pp. 1-22 (= *JBL* 91 [1972], pp. 3-24).

Meyer, A., 'Religiöse Pseudepigraphie als ethisch-psychologisches Problem', *ZNW* 35 (1936), pp. 262-79.

Michaelis, W., *Einleitung in das Neue Testament* (Bern: Buchhandlung der Evangelischen Gesellschaft, 3rd edn, 1961).

Moffatt, J., *An Introduction to the Literature of the New Testament* (New York: Charles Scribner's Sons, 1915).

Moore, A.L., *The Parousia in the New Testament* (Leiden: Brill, 1966).

Munck, J., 'Discours d'adieu dans le Nouveau Testament et dans la littérature biblique', in *Aux sources de la tradition chrétienne* (Festschrift M. Goguel; Paris: Neuchâtel, 1950).

Mussner, F., 'Die Ablösung des Apostolischen durch das nachapostolische Zeitalter und ihre Konsequenzen', in *Wort Gottes in der Zeit* (Festschrift K.H. Schelkle; Düsseldorf: Patmos, 1972), pp. 166-77.

—'Anknüpfung und Kerygma in der Areopagrede (Apg 17, 22b-31)', in *Praesentia Salutis: Gesammelte Studien zu Fragen und Themen des Neuen Testaments* (Düsseldorf: Patmos, 1967), pp. 235-43.

—'Frühkatholizismus', *TTZ* 68 (1959), pp. 237-45.

—'Spätapostolische Briefe als frühkatholisches Zeugnis', in J. Blinzer *et al.* (eds.), *Neutestamentliche Aufsätze für J. Schmid* (Regensburg: F. Pustet, 1963), pp. 225-32.

Neufeld, K.H., 'Frühkatholizismus—Idee und Begriff', *ZKT* 94 (1972), pp. 1-28.

Neyrey, J.H., 'The Apologetic Use of the Transfiguration in 2 Peter 1.16-21', *CBQ* 42 (1980), pp. 504-19.

—'The Form and Background of the Polemic in 2 Peter', *JBL* 99.3 (1980), pp. 407-31.

—*2 Peter, Jude: A New Translation with Introduction and Commentary* (AB, 37c; Garden City, NY: Doubleday, 1993).

O'Hagan, A.P., *Material Recreation in the Apostolic Fathers* (TU, 100; Berlin: Akademie Verlag, 1968).

Osborn, E.F., *Ethical Patterns in Early Christian Thought* (Cambridge: Cambridge University Press, 1976).

Osborne, G.R., *The Hermeneutical Spiral: A Comprehensive Introduction to Biblical Interpretation* (Downers Grove: InterVarsity Press, 1991).

Pearson, B., 'A Reminiscence of Classical Myth at II Peter 2.4', *GRBS* 10 (1969), pp. 75-78.

Pelikan, J., *The Christian Tradition. I. The Emergence of the Catholic Tradition (100-600)* (Chicago: University of Chicago Press, 1971).

Perkins, P., *First and Second Peter, James, and Jude* (IBC; Louisville: John Knox Press, 1995).

Picirelli, R.E., 'The Meaning of "Epignosis"', *EvQ* 47.2 (1975) 85- 93.

Pohlenz, M., 'Paulus und die Stoa', *ZNW* 42 (1949), pp. 69-104.

—*Die Stoa* (2 vols.; Göttingen: Vandenhoeck & Ruprecht, 4th edn, 1972), II, pp. 277-99.

Porter, S.E., 'Did Jesus Ever Teach in Greek?', *TynBul* 44.2 (1993), pp. 229-35.

—'Pauline Authorship and the Pastoral Epistles: Implications for Canon', *BBR* 5 (1995), pp. 105-24.

Preisker, H., *Das Ethos des Urchristentums* (Darmstadt: Wissenschaftliche Buchgesellschaft, 1968).

Reicke, B., *The Epistles of James, Peter, and Jude* (AB; New York: Doubleday, 1964).

Richardson, T.W.B., *An Introduction to the Theology of the New Testament* (London: SPCK, 1958).

Riesner, R., 'Der zweite Petrus-Brief und die Eschatologie', in G. Maier (ed.), *Zukünftserwartung in biblischer Sicht: Beiträge zur Eschatologie* (Wuppertal: Brockhaus, 1984), pp. 124-43.

Rist, J.M., *Stoic Philosophy* (Cambridge: Cambridge University Press, 1969).

Rist, M., 'Pseudepigraphy and the Early Christians', in D.E. Aune (ed.), *Studies in New Testament and Early Christian Literature: Essays in Honor of A.P. Wikgren* (NovTSup, 33, Leiden: Brill, 1972), pp. 75-91.

Robinson, J.A.T., *Redating the New Testament* (Philadelphia: Westminster Press, 1976).

Robson, E.I., 'Composition and Dictation in New Testament Books', *JTS* 18 (1917), pp. 288-301.

Rydbeck, L., *Fachprosa: Vermeintliche Volkssprache und Neues Testament* (SGU, 5; Uppsala: Uppsala University Press, 1967).

Sandbach, F.H., *Aristotle and the Stoics* (Cambridge: Cambridge Philological Society, 1985).

Sanders J.T., *Ethics in the New Testament* (Philadelphia: Fortress Press, 1975).

Schelkle, K.H., *Die Petrusbriefe. Der Judasbrief* (HTKNT, 13.2; Freiburg: Herder, 1961).

—'Spätapostolische Briefe und Frühkatholizismus', in *Wort und Schrift: Beiträge zur Auslegung und Auslegungsgeschichte des Neuen Testaments* (Düsseldorf: Patmos, 1966), pp. 117-25.

Schlosser, J., 'Les jours de Noé et de Lot: A propos de Luc xvii, 26-30', *RB* 80 (1973), pp. 13-36.

Schmid, J., 'Petrus der "Fels" und die Petrusgestalt in der Urgemeinde', in J.B. Baur (ed.), *Evangelienforschungen* (Graz: Verlag Styria, 1968), pp. 170-75.

Schnackenburg, R., *The Moral Teaching of the New Testament* (trans. J. Holland-Smith and W.J. O'Hara; 2 vols.; Freiburg: Herder, 1965).

Schneider, G., 'Anknüpfung, Kontinuität und Widerspruch in der Areopagrede. Apg. 17,22-31', in P.G. Müller and W. Stenger (eds.), *Kontinuität und Einheit* (Freiburg: Herder, 1981), pp. 173-78.

Schrage, W., *The Ethics of the New Testament* (trans. D.E. Green; Philadelphia: Fortress Press, 1988).

Schulz, S., *Die Mitte der Zeit: Frühkatholizismus im Neün Testament als Herausforderung an den Protestantismus* (Stuttgart: Kreuz Verlag, 1976).

—(ed.), *Neutestamentliche Ethik* (Zürich: Theologischer Verlag, 1987).

Schweizer, A., *The Mystery of the Kingdom of God* (London: Macmillan, 1925).

Sevenster, J.N., 'Education or Conversion: Epictetus and the Gospels', *NovT* 8 (1966), pp. 247-62.

Shaw, R.D., 'Pseudonymity and Interpretation', in *The Pauline Epistles: Introduction and Expository Outlines* (Edinburgh: T. & T. Clark, 1903), pp. 477-86.

Sint, J.A., *Pseudonymität im Altertum: Ihre Formen und ihre Gründe* (Innsbruck: Universitätsverlag, 1960).

Smalley, S.S., 'The Delay of the Parousia', *JBL* 83 (1964), pp. 41- 54.

Smith, M., 'Pseudepigraphy in Israelite Literary Tradition', in K. von Fritz (ed.), *Pseudepigrapha I* (Geneva: Revedin, 1972), pp. 191-215.

Speyer, W., *Die literarische Fälschung im heidnischen und christlichen Altertum: Ein Versuch ihrer Deutung* (HAW, 1.2; Munich: Beck, 1971).

—'Religiöse Pseudonymität und literarische Fälschung im Altertum', *JAC* 8.9 (1965–66), pp. 88-125.

Spicq, C., *Théologie morale du Nouveau Testament* (2 vols.; Paris: Gabalda, 1970).

Stählin, G., 'ἴσος', *TDNT*, III, pp. 343-55.

—'φιλέω.... φιλία', *TDNT*, IX, pp. 113-71.

Stelzenberger, J., *Die Beziehungen der frühchristlichen Sittenlehre zur Ethik der Stoa* (Munich: Beck, 1933).

—*Lehrbuch der Moraltheologie* (Paderborn: Schöningh, 1965).

Stowers, S.K., 'The Diatribe', in D.E. Aune (ed.), *Greco-Roman Literature and the New Testament* (Atlanta: Scholars Press, 1988), pp. 71-83.

—*Letter Writing in Greco-Roman Antiquity* (Philadelphia: Westminster Press, 1986).

Streeter, B.H., 'Synoptic Criticism and the Eschatological Problem', in W. Sanday (ed.), *Studies in the Synoptic Problem* (Oxford: Clarendon Press, 1909), pp. 425-36.

Talbert, C.H., 'II Peter and the Delay of the Parousia', *VC* 20 (1966), pp. 137-45.

Thiede, C.P., 'A Pagan Reader of 2 Peter: Cosmic Conflagration in 2 Peter 3 and the OCTAVIUS of Minucius Felix', *JSNT* 26 (1986), pp. 79-96.

Todd, R.B., 'Stoics and their Cosmology in the First and Second Centuries A.D.', in W. Haase (ed.), *Aufstieg und Niedergang der römischen Welt: Geschichte und Kultur Roms im Spiegel der neueren Forschung* (Berlin: W. de Gruyter, 1989), II.36.3, pp. 1365-78.

Törm, F., *Die Psychologie der Pseudonymität im Hinblick auf die Literatur des Urchristentums* (Gütersloh: Bertelsmann, 1932).

Tröger, K.-W., 'Zum gegenwärtigen Stand der Gnosis- und Nag- Hammadi-Forschung', in K.-W. Tröger (ed.), *Altes Testament—Frühjudentum—Gnosis: Neue Studien zu 'Gnosis und Bibel'* (Gütersloh: Mohn, 1980), pp. 11-33.

Trüb, H., *Kataloge in der griechischen Dichtung* (Zürich: Buchdruckerei Winterthur, 1952).

Turner, N., 'The Literary Character of New Testament Greek', *NTS* 20 (1974), pp. 107-14.

VanderKam, J.C., 'The Righteousness of Noah', in J.J. Collins and G.W.E. Nickelsburg (eds.), *Ideal Figures in Ancient Judaism: Profiles and Paradigms* (Chico: Scholars Press, 1980), pp. 13- 32.

Vermes, G., 'The Story of Balaam', in *Scripture and Tradition in Judaism: Haggadic Studies* (SPB, 4; Leiden: Brill, 1973), pp. 127-77.

Vögtle, A., 'Kirche und Schriftprinzip nach dem Neuen Testament', *BuL* 12 (1971), pp. 153-62, 260-81.

—'Die Schriftwerdung der apostolischen Paradosis nach 2. Petr 1,12-15', in H. Baltenswerter and B. Reicke (eds.), *Neues Testament und Geschichte: O. Cullman zum 70. Geburtstag* (Zürich: Theologischer Verlag; Tübingen: Mohr, 1972), pp. 297- 306.

—*Die Tugend- und Lasterkataloge im Neuen Testament* (NTAbh, 16/4-5; Münster: Aschendorff, 1936).

von Arnim, H. (ed.), *Stoicorum Veterum Fragmenta* (3 vols.; Leipzig: F. Pustet, 1903–1905).

von Campenhausen, H., *The Formation of the Christian Bible* (trans. J.A. Baker; Philadelphia: Fortress Press, 1972).

Wall, R.W., 'James as Apocalyptic Paraenesis', *RestQ* 32 (1990), pp. 11-22.

Watson, D.F., *Invention, Arrangement, and Style: Rhetorical Criticism of Jude and 2 Peter* (SBLDS, 104; Atlanta: Scholars Press, 1988).

Wendland, P., *Die hellenistisch-römische Kultur in ihren Beziehungen zu Judentum und Christentum* (HNT, 1.2; Tübingen: Mohr, 1907).

Werner, W., *The Formation of Christian Dogma* (London: A. & C. Black, 1957).

Wibbing, S., *Die Tugend- und Lasterkataloge im Neuen Testament und ihre Traditionsgeschichte unter besonderer Berücksichtigung der Qumrantexte* (BZNW, 25; Berlin: Töpelmann, 1959).

Wilken, R.L., 'Serving the One True God', in C.E. Braaten and R.W. Jensen (eds.), *Either/Or: The Gospel or Neopaganism* (Grand Rapids: Eerdmans, 1995), pp. 61-74.

Windisch, H., *Die katholischen Briefe* (HNT, 4.2; Tübingen: Mohr, 2nd edn, 1930).

Zeller, D., *Charis bei Philon und Paulus* (SBS, 142; Stuttgart: KBW, 1990).

Zöckler, O., *Die Tugendlehre des Christentums* (Gütersloh: Bertelsmann, 1904).

INDEXES

INDEX OF REFERENCES

OLD TESTAMENT

Genesis
6.1-4	79
18	169
18.16-33	88
19	88
19.16	88

Exodus
20	112
22–23	112
33	112

Leviticus
10.1-5	74
18	112
19	112

Numbers
22–24	165
31.15-16	165
31.16	165
35.30	76

Deuteronomy
17.6	76
19.15	76
23.4-5	165
34.1-4	54

Joshua
13.22	165
24.9	165

Nehemiah
13.2	165

Psalms
90.4	169

Proverbs
26.11	91

Isaiah
14.5-23	78
24.21-22	78
43.21 LXX	141

Ezekiel
16.49	89
22.29	89
28.1-19	78

Daniel
10.5-12	55

Joel
2.31	79

Wisdom of Solomon
4.11	121
6.17-19	157
8.4	120
8.7	120
10.4	88
10.6	88
12.10	121
14.22	120
14.25-26	120
19.17	88

Ecclesiasticus
16.5-15	173
16.7-11	89
44.17-18	88

Matthew
3.10	170
5	125
5.16	145
12.36	149
13.1-23	170
13.21	170
13.22	149
15.13	127
15.14	149
15.19	122
16.13-20	59
16.16-17	59
16.18	59
16.24-26	170
18.16	76
23.165	149
24	31
24.36-51	28
24.37-39	87
24.43	28
28.16-20	30

Mark
3	171
4.19	149
7.1-13	72
7.21-22	122, 123
8.34-38	170
13	31, 171

13.13	171	17.28-29	82	6.20	87
13.22	171	17.28	103	7.21-23	87
13.23	171	17.29	137	8.1-3	141
13.32	28	17.30-31	103, 109	8.7-13	141
		17.31	169	9	97
Luke		17.32	109	9.27	151
3.9	170	20	57	10.11	28
9.23-26	170	20.17-37	57	12	82
10	171	24.25	142	13.1-13	111
10.18	78	27.15	35	13.2	141
11.49-51	71			13.7	143
12.35-40	28	*Romans*		13.13	126
12.39	28	1	114, 124	15	95
17.26-28	87	1.18-19	150	15.1-11	85
21	31	1.28	114	15.3-8	97
22.14-38	57	1.29-31	114, 122-24	15.3-7	59
22.24-30	54	1.32	114	15.32-33	169
22.28-32	54	5.1-5	146	15.33	82
22.31-32	171	6	32	16.21	61
24.49	30	6.1-14	150		
		7	32	*2 Corinthians*	
John		7.4	127, 145	5.2	28
5.31-33	76	8.9	34	6.6	122, 125,
8.17-18	76	8.19	28		146, 157
9.40-41	149	8.23	28	6.9-10	122
12.31	78	8.28-30	172	7.11	64
13–17	54, 57	9.1–11.36	172	8.23	59
15	145	12.9-10	145	9.8	104
15.1-7	127	13.10	127	9.10	148
21.18-19	53	13.13	122-24	12.20-21	122
21.18	58, 133	16.22	61	13.1	76
				13.8	65
Acts		*1 Corinthians*			
1.1-5	30	1–11	95	*Galatians*	
1.6	31, 169	1.2	151	3.5	148
1.8	31	1.5-7	34	3.28-29	87
2.39	34	1.30-31	126	5	145
5.1-11	172	2.1-16	35	5.13	151
8.9-24	172	3.5-9	145	5.14	127
14.8-18	137	3.9	127	5.19-24	127
14.12	136	3.10-15	66	5.19-23	125
14.18	137	3.11	59	5.19-21	122, 123
15.14	96, 129, 130	4	97	5.22-23	122, 125
17	106-108	5.8	64	5.22	125, 157
17.16-34	104, 106,	5.10-11	122	5.23	142, 143
	107	6.9-10	122, 123	6.11	61
17.18	109	6.9	123		
17.23	140	6.11	123, 162		

Ephesians

1.3-12	172
2.20	51, 65, 66
3.5	65
3.9-12	172
4.1-3	145
4.1	151
4.2-5	126
4.3	150
4.15	65
4.22	124
4.23	122
4.25	65
4.31	122, 124
4.32	122
5.3-5	122
5.5	123
5.9	65, 122
14.1	127

Philippians

1.15	65
1.18	65
1.20	28
1.25	85
4.2	145
4.5	145
4.8	122, 125, 135, 141, 157
4.11	104

Colossians

1.4-5	126
1.10	127, 145, 149
2.19	148
3.5	122, 123
3.8	122, 124
3.9	65
3.12-15	145
3.12-14	126
3.12	122, 151
4.16	36
4.18	61

1 Thessalonians

1.3	126
1.12	82
4.3-7	122
4.9	145
4.13-18	27
5.2	28
5.8	126

2 Thessalonians

1	26
2	26
2.1-12	27
2.1-2	65
2.2	68, 71, 75
2.5	27
2.15	27
3.17	62, 75

1 Timothy

1.5	127
1.9-10	122, 125
1.18-20	172
1.18	172
2.7	65
3	125
3.2-3	125
3.2	123
3.15	65
3.16	127
4.12	122
4.15	85
5.19	76
6.3-5	125
6.6	104
6.11	122, 125, 157
6.12	151
6.20	66

2 Timothy

1.15	172
2.8-13	172
2.11-13	127
2.22	122
3	124
3.2-5	122, 124, 125
3.10	122
4.6	172

4.9	172
4.11	62
4.16	172
6.7-8	172

Titus

1.1	66
1.7-8	125
1.8	143
2	117
2.4-5	117
3.1-7	125
3.1-2	125
3.3-5	91
3.3	91, 122, 123

Philemon

| 19 | 62 |

Hebrews

1.3	150
4.11	150
6	32
6.4-6	172
9.15	151
10	32
10.23	172
10.26-27	172
10.28	76
10.36-39	27
10.36-37	27
11	173
11.7	88
12.2	144
13	32
13.1	145
13.22	27

James

1.12	143
1.21	124
1.22-25	82
2.10	151
2.20	149
3.2	151
3.7	101
3.13-18	125
3.15	122

3.17	111, 122, 126	1.3-15	107	1.11	84, 88, 130, 144, 147, 148, 160
4.1-2	91	1.3-11	50, 63, 96, 128		
5.7-8	27	1.3-7	98, 146	1.12-15	16, 41, 48, 51, 53, 55, 84, 96, 159, 164
5.8	27	1.3-4	84, 95, 133-35, 137, 139, 147, 159		
1 Peter				1.12	85, 86, 133, 134, 138
1.14	142				
1.18-19	87	1.3	42, 85, 113, 132, 134-36, 138, 141, 144, 147, 151, 161, 162	1.13-15	75
1.22	145			1.13-14	57, 58, 74
2.1	122, 124			1.13	85, 88, 130, 163
2.9	135, 141				
2.20	144			1.14	54, 58, 133, 138
2.21	151				
3.8	122	1.4	86, 101, 130, 135, 136, 142, 147, 161	1.15	85, 86, 139
3.15	104			1.16-21	53
3.19	89			1.16-18	35, 55, 56, 68, 74, 84, 85, 96, 159, 164
3.20-21	89				
3.20	89	1.5-7	38, 42, 44, 84, 85, 121, 122, 125, 126, 128, 134, 138-41, 145, 146, 151, 153, 156, 157, 159		
4.3	122, 123			1.16	55, 58, 84, 85, 132, 138
4.7	27				
4.15	122			1.18	58, 85
5.1	55			1.19-27	163
5.9	32			1.19-21	47, 55, 68, 159, 164
5.12	62				
2 Peter		1.5	33, 85, 127, 132, 133, 135, 137-41, 147, 148, 162	1.19	35, 54, 55
1	42, 48, 84, 85, 96, 98, 106, 126, 134, 136-39, 141, 146, 148, 155, 156, 160, 167			1.20-21	35, 74, 164
				1.20	35, 138
				1.21	35, 163
		1.6	134, 138, 144, 163	1.24	163
		1.7	134, 144, 147, 162	1.26-27	163
1.1-11	148			2	37, 48, 49, 86, 87, 155, 164, 167
1.1-4	96, 128, 129, 148	1.8-15	41	2.1-3	51, 81, 86, 87, 159, 161, 164
		1.8-11	128, 148, 159		
1.1-2	159				
1.1	43, 74, 88, 101, 129-31, 135, 149, 160, 162, 163	1.8	85, 134, 138, 149, 161	2.1-2	48, 86
				2.1	38, 42, 47-49, 58, 74, 86, 87, 93, 95, 150, 164
		1.9	85, 86, 149, 150, 161		
1.2	132, 134, 135, 138, 141, 160	1.10-11	162	2.2-3	164
		1.10	54, 85, 86, 139, 161, 163, 169	2.2	48, 66, 93
				2.3	150, 151
1.3-21	155			2.4-10	42, 47, 49,

	87, 88, 93,	2.22	91, 149,		139
	159, 164		162, 163	3.15-16	36, 37, 44,
2.4-9	49, 89, 163	3	27, 37, 39,		160
2.4	47, 79, 80,		42, 46-49,	3.15	58, 74, 94,
	89, 162,		91-94, 107,		144
	163, 165		108, 121,	3.16	36
2.5-9	150, 165		155, 158,	3.17	41, 44, 48,
2.5-8	94		167, 169		94, 138, 142
2.5-7	164	3.1-13	91	3.18	88, 130,
2.5	87, 88, 130,	3.1-4	51		132, 138,
	150, 168	3.1-2	41, 48, 160		160, 164
2.6	87, 168	3.1	48, 58, 95		
2.7	87, 88, 94,	3.2-6	48	*1 John*	
	130, 142	3.2	88, 130, 160	1.1-3	97
2.8	88, 94, 130,	3.3-7	49, 84, 160	2.21	66
	142	3.3-6	48, 162, 167	4.14	97
2.9-13	163	3.3-5	44, 86, 93	5.1	145
2.9	87, 141,	3.3-4	46, 48		
	160, 163	3.3	138, 142	*Jude*	
2.10-21	90	3.4	15, 48, 55,	1	151, 162
2.10-18	47, 87, 159		93, 168	4	86, 87
2.10-12	143	3.5-7	47, 155, 168	5–7	164, 173
2.10-11	47	3.5-6	93, 168	5	131, 173
2.10	142, 150	3.5	46	6	78, 79
2.11	90	3.6	168	7	89
2.12	94, 101,	3.7	46, 93, 163,	11	166
	103, 142		168	13	82
2.13	87, 91, 93	3.8-13	26, 36, 94,	20–21	126
2.14-26	163		160	24–25	163
2.14	90, 150, 166	3.8-10	46, 55	24	151, 161
2.15-16	44, 47, 90,	3.8-9	46, 169		
	150, 162,	3.8	46, 93, 168,	*Revelation*	
	165		169	2.19	127, 157
2.15	90, 93, 166	3.9	26, 46, 168	2.20-22	90
2.17	163	3.10-13	92	3.3	28
2.18	91, 93, 130,	3.10-12	47	3.17	149
	142, 150	3.10	28, 47, 93,	5.9	87
2.19-22	39, 159		155, 168	6.17	79
2.19	39, 44, 45,	3.11-13	107	9.21	122
	87, 91, 93,	3.11	41, 48, 84,	12.4	78
	94, 142,		92, 94, 134,	12.7	78
	143, 149		161, 169	12.9	78
2.20-22	44, 91, 108	3.12	47, 94	12.10	78
2.20-21	133, 150,	3.13	88, 93, 101,	16.14	79
	167		108, 130,	18.2	78
2.20	88, 130,		169	20.3	78
	138, 160	3.14-18	160	20.7	78
2.21	88, 130	3.14	48, 92, 93,	21.8	122, 123

| 22.15 | 122, 123 | 22.18-19 | 66 | 22.20 | 27 |

PSEUDEPIGRAPHA

1 En.		84.4	79	*Jos. Asen.*	
6–11	78	88.1	78	10	88
10.4	78, 79	88.3	78		
10.6	79	90.23	78	*Jub.*	
10.12-14	78	90.24	78	5.10	78, 79
10.12	79	90.26	78	5.19	88
12.4	79	94.9	79	20.2-7	173
13.1	78	98.10	79		
15.3	79	99.15	79	*Ps.-Phoc.*	
18.11	78	104.5	79	103-104	137
18.14-16	78	106–107	88		
21.3	78			*T. Abr.*	
21.6	78	*2 Bar.*		1.1-5	57, 129
21.7	78	56.13	78		
21.10	78			*T. Job*	
22.1-2	78	*3 Macc.*		1.1-4	56, 129
22.4	79	2.3-7	87, 173		
22.11	79			*T. Naph.*	
54.4	78	*4 Ezra*		2.8–4.3	173
54.6	79	8-36	50		
56.3	78			*T. Reub.*	
67.4	78	*Did.*		1.1-5	56, 129
69.8	78	10.6	27		

OTHER ANCIENT SOURCES

Qumran		*Conf. Ling.*		*Leg. All.*	
CD 2.14–3.12	173	154	136, 137	1.38	109, 136, 137
Mishnah		*De prov.*		2.14	136
Ab.		126-28	46	3.18	142
5.19	166			3.78	110
		Dec.		1.19.56	120
Sanh.		1.4	137	2.23.24	120
10.3	166, 173	104	136		
				Plant.	
Midrash		*Deus Imm.*		23	109
Gen. R.		45–50	109		
30.7	88			*Praem. Poen.*	
		Ebr.		419	119
Philo		19	120		
Abr.					
107	137	*Exsecr.*			
		159-60	120		

Sacr.			*Virt.*			17.5.6	136
20–45	118		51	144		2.6.9	150
20–21	119		95	144		20.204	147
22	119					4.6.13	166
27	119		*Vit. Mos.*			4.8.44	150
32	116		2.58	88			
3.63	120					*Apion*	
			Josephus			26	136
Spec. Leg.			*Ant.*				
4.97	144		1.3.1	88			

CHRISTIAN AUTHORS

Barn.			7.46.55	138		Hesiod	
4.3	27		7.7.44	85		*Theog.*	
2.2	127					77-79	113
2.2.3	140		Eusebius				
			Hist. eccl.			Ignatius	
1 Clem.			2.23	69		*Eph.*	
23.5	27		3.3	69		14.1	157
62.2	127		3.3.2	70			
62.2.43	140		3.3.25	72		Jerome	
64	127		6.12	69, 70		*Ep.Hed.*	
			6.14	69		120.9	62
2 Clem.			6.25	69			
12.1	27					Origen	
12.6	27		Hermas, *Man.*			*De prin.*	
			8.9	127		8	69
Clement							
Strom.			Hermas, *Vis.*			*Hom.in Josh.*	
1.13.1	141		3.8	27, 127		7.1	69
2.19.102	111		3.9	27			
6.9.78	111		3.8.1	140		Tertullian	
7.46	142					*Ad mart.*	
						3	143

CLASSICAL

Aelius Aristedes			*Frogs*			1103	100
1.40-48	103		5.145	113		1104-1105	100
						1115-1145	115
Aeschylus			Aristotle			1115-1117	143
Sept.			*Apol.*			1129	131
610	114		7.1.2	136		1145-1154	142
Aristophanes			*Eth. Nic.*			*Part. Anim.*	
Brev. vit.			1100	148		4.10	136
10.4	113		1102	100			

Pol.

1253 100

Rhetorik

1366 115

Chrysippus
Gal.

437 105

Cicero
Ad Att.

13.9.25 61
14.21 61
16.15 61
2.23 61
7.13 61
8.12 61

Ad Quint. frat.

3.3 61

De nat. deo

2.71 138

Ep.

39 138

Fam.

3.6 61

Leg.

1.12.33 138

Cleanthes

75 105

Diogenes Laertius

10.97 103, 136

Epictetus
Diss.

1.20.5 102
1.29.1 103
1.8.16 103
2.10.25 103
2.20.21 102

31.1 138

Horace
Ep.

1.1.33-40 117

Philodemus
Pap. Herc.

1005.4.19 46

Plato
Phaed.

230 136

Rep.

366 136

Theaet.

117 143
176 100, 136

Pliny
Letter to Maximus

8.24 40

Plutarch
Arist.

6.3 136

De Is. et Os.

358 137

De vit. Pud

535 136

Mor.

13 148

Polybius
Hist.

21.29.12 147
3.78.8 148

Quintilian
Inst.

3.6.47 40
9.2.103 40

Seneca
Ep. Mor.

15 138
67.10 143
92.30 136
94.45 38
95.47 138

Fr.

123 138

Socrates
Charmides

159b2-3 99
160e3-5 99

Laches

190e4-6 99

Protagoras

333d 99

Stobaeus
Diog. Lart.

7.92 142

Ecl.

2.60.20 142
2.61.11 142

Strabo

11.14.16 148

Vergil
Aen.

6.732 117

Xenophon
Hist. Graec.

7.1.1 131

Mem.

1.2.19 114
1.5.4 142
3.4.3 148

Zeno

148 105

INDEX OF AUTHORS

Aall, A. 102
Achtemeier, P. 12, 13
Aland, K. 71
Alexander, T.D. 88
Aune, D.E. 52, 122

Bahr, G.J. 61, 63
Balz, H. 20, 66
Bauckham, R.J. 16, 25, 26, 33, 37,
    47, 50-54, 62, 63, 81, 145, 146,
    150, 161, 164, 168, 169
Baur, F.C. 16
Beckwith, R. 67, 70-72
Berger, K. 41, 45, 118
Betz, O. 29
Bigg, C. 58
Black, D.A. 71
Blinzer, J. 17
Böckle, F. 127
Bommer, J. 127
Boring, M.E. 92
Bradley, D.J.M. 110
Brox, N. 52
Bruce, F.F. 12
Bultmann, R. 18, 133
Calvin, J. 68, 74, 151
Campbell, K. 105
Campenhausen, H. von 60
Candlish, J.S. 65
Carson, D.A. 37
Cavallin, H.C.C. 38, 164
Chaine, J. 27, 49, 81, 92
Charles, J.D. 33, 37, 38, 74, 76, 77,
    90, 106, 108, 136, 163
Chester, A. 73, 75, 83
Collins, J.J. 88
Conn, H.M. 24

Coppens, J. 135
Crehan, J. 36
Cullmann, O. 28, 30

Danker, F.W. 93, 148
Davids, P.H. 38, 41
Deissmann, A. 135, 139, 148
Desjardins, M. 87
Dibelius, M. 125
Dockery, D.S. 71
Dodds, E.R. 104
Donelson, L.R. 69
Drane, J.W. 19, 26
Dunn, J.D.G. 11, 22, 33
Dupont, J. 140
Dyroff, A. 115

Easton, B.S. 121, 123-25
Edelstein, L. 102
Elliott, J.H. 17
Ellis, E.E. 37, 52, 58-60, 75
Eltester, W. 106
Engberg-Pedersen, T. 102, 103

Falconer, R.A. 35
Feld, H. 17, 49
Fischel, H.A. 146
Fischer, K.M. 68
Foerster, W. 144
Forkham, G. 90
Fornberg, T. 21, 25, 26, 37, 41, 42,
    44, 48, 54, 55, 57, 80, 82, 84, 85,
    94, 138, 140, 144, 150
Fox, R.L. 99
Fritz, K. von 52
Fuller, R.H. 20, 152
Furnish, V.P. 39

Gaffin, R.B. Jr 24, 25, 59, 60
Gärtner, B. 106, 135
Gasque, W.W. 41, 69
Glasson, T.F. 79
Goppelt, L. 26, 27
Grässer, E. 29
Green, M. 26, 37, 47, 50, 52, 62, 64, 74, 75, 97, 131, 150, 151
Grundmann, W. 34, 49, 142
Gudeman, A. 67
Guthrie, D. 14, 26, 37, 52, 57, 58, 62, 64, 66, 68, 74, 91, 93, 130

Hadas, M. 101
Hahm, D.E. 92, 102
Hahn, F. 17
Hanson, P.D. 78
Hauck, F. 143
Hawthorne, G.F. 29
Hengel, M. 79
Henten, J.W. van 45
Hermann, A. 135
Hillyer, N. 55, 85, 88, 89, 130, 140, 150
Hitchcock, F.R.M. 61

Inwood, B. 103
Irwin, T. 100

James, M.R. 68, 96, 130
Johnson, S.E. 29

Kamlah, E. 38
Käsemann, E. 15-19, 23-26, 28-30, 33-35, 43-45, 48, 92, 93, 97, 152, 159
Kelly, J.N.D. 49, 69, 86, 94, 96, 98, 129, 131, 136, 137, 141, 142, 144, 150, 166
Kidd, G. 105
Kiley, M. 60
Klassen, W. 26
Klein, G. 19, 20
Klinger, J. 46, 84, 138
Knoch, O. 49, 51, 53
Kolenkow, A.B. 50
Küng, H. 17
Kurz, W.S. 54, 57

LaSor, W.S. 41
Lea, T.D. 71, 74
Leconte, R. 49
Lefrance, Y. 135
Legrand, L. 135
Lenhard, H. 93
Lewis, J.P. 87
Loevestam, E. 47
Lowe, J. 97
Luck, U. 144
Luther, M. 11, 22, 159
Luz, U. 18

Maier, G. 46
Malherbe, A. 40, 41, 117, 119
Marshall, I.H. 29, 30, 37, 169-72
Marshall, R.H. 40
Martin, R.P. 38, 52, 69, 73, 75, 83
Martin, T. 41
Marxsen, W. 14, 15, 17, 39
Mayor, J.B. 69, 70, 76, 81, 92, 136, 146, 149
McEleney, N.J. 121-23
McKim, D.K. 12
McNamara, M. 53
Meade, D.G. 52, 53, 63, 64, 74
Meeks, W.A. 40, 109
Merklein, H. 39
Metzger, B. 52, 53, 71
Meyer, A. 52, 66
Micheälis, W. 47
Moffatt, J. 66, 96, 136
Moore, A.L. 18, 27, 31
Müller, P.G. 106
Munck, J. 51
Mussner, F. 17, 18, 31, 136

Neufeld, K.H. 15
Neusner, J. 29
Neyrey, J.H. 45, 46, 49, 53, 92, 93, 106, 108, 168
Nickelsburg, G.W.E. 88
Nolte, J. 17, 49

O'Hagan, A.P. 101
Osborn, E.F. 109
Osborne, G.R. 23, 24

Paige, T. 52
Pearson, B. 80
Pelikan, J. 29
Perdue, L.G. 41
Perkins, P. 94
Picirelli, R.E. 69, 132
Pohlenz, M. 135
Porter, S.E. 59, 71
Preisker, H. 111

Reicke, B. 49
Richardson, T.W.B. 32
Riesner, R. 46, 47, 49, 92, 108
Rist, J.M. 60, 103, 105
Robinson, J.A.T. 35, 68
Robson, E.I. 60, 61
Rydbeck, L. 81

Sanday, W. 18
Sandbach, F.H. 115
Sanders, J.T. 39
Schelkle, K.H. 16, 17, 140
Schlosser, J. 88
Schmid, J. 96
Schnackenburg, R. 40
Schneider, G. 106
Schrage, W. 20, 39
Schulz, S. 16, 18, 21, 39, 43, 152
Schweizer, A. 18
Sevenster, J.N. 121
Shaw, R.D. 65
Sint, J.A. 52
Smalley, S.S. 93
Smith, M. 52
Snyder, G. 26
Speyer, W. 52, 74

Spicq, C. 39, 145, 149
Stählin, G. 131
Stelzenberger, J. 102, 111, 145
Stenger, W. 106
Stowers, S.K. 41, 117
Streeter, B.H. 18

Talbert, C.H. 49
Thiede, C.P. 47, 92, 93, 108
Todd, R.B. 107
Törm, F. 52
Trobisch, D. 36
Tröger, K.-W. 139
Trüb, H. 113
Turner, N. 81

Vanderkam, J.C. 88
Vermes, G. 90
Vögtle, A. 16, 18, 38, 113, 116, 118,
    119, 122, 126, 127, 140, 141, 144

Wall, R.W. 38, 43
Watson, D.F. 50, 81
Weinrich, W.C. 47
Wendland, P. 101, 118
Werner, M. 18
Wesley, J. 11
Wibbing, S. 38, 116, 121, 122
Wilken, R.L. 139
Wilkins, M.J. 52
Williamson, H.G.M. 37
Windisch, H. 16, 145

Zeller, D. 109, 110
Zöckler, O. 38, 134

JOURNAL FOR THE STUDY OF THE NEW TESTAMENT
SUPPLEMENT SERIES

1   W.R. Telford, *The Barren Temple and the Withered Tree: A Redaction-Critical Analysis of the Cursing of the Fig-Tree Pericope in Mark's Gospel and its Relation to the Cleansing of the Temple Tradition*

2   E.A. Livingstone (ed.), *Studia Biblica 1978, II: Papers on the Gospels (Sixth International Congress on Biblical Studies, Oxford, 1978)*

3   E.A. Livingstone (ed.), *Studia Biblica 1978, III: Papers on Paul and Other New Testament Authors (Sixth International Congress on Biblical Studies, Oxford, 1978)*

4   E. Best, *Following Jesus: Discipleship in the Gospel of Mark*

5   M. Barth, *The People of God*

6   J.S. Pobee, *Persecution and Martyrdom in the Theology of Paul*

7   C.M. Tuckett (ed.), *Synoptic Studies: The Ampleforth Conferences of 1982 and 1983*

8   T.L. Donaldson, *Jesus on the Mountain: A Study in Matthean Theology*

9   S. Farris, *The Hymns of Luke's Infancy Narratives: Their Origin, Meaning and Significance*

10 R. Badenas, *Christ the End of the Law: Romans 10.4 in Pauline Perspective*

11 C.J. Hemer, *The Letters to the Seven Churches of Asia in their Local Setting*

12 D.L. Bock, *Proclamation from Prophecy and Pattern: Lucan Old Testament Christology*

13 R.P. Booth, *Jesus and the Laws of Purity: Tradition History and Legal History in Mark 7*

14 M.L. Soards, *The Passion according to Luke: The Special Material of Luke 22*

15 T.E. Schmidt, *Hostility to Wealth in the Synoptic Gospels*

16 S.H. Brooks, *Matthew's Community: The Evidence of his Special Sayings Material*

17 A.T. Hanson, *The Paradox of the Cross in the Thought of St Paul*

18 C. Deutsch, *Hidden Wisdom and the Easy Yoke: Wisdom, Torah and Discipleship in Matthew 11.25-30*

19 L.J. Kreitzer, *Jesus and God in Paul's Eschatology*

20 M.D. Goulder, *Luke: A New Paradigm*

21 M.C. Parsons, *The Departure of Jesus in Luke–Acts: The Ascension Narratives in Context*

22 M.C. de Boer, *The Defeat of Death: Apocalyptic Eschatology in 1 Corinthians 15 and Romans 5*

23 M. Prior, *Paul the Letter-Writer and the Second Letter to Timothy*

24 J. Marcus & M.L. Soards (eds.), *Apocalyptic and the New Testament: Essays in Honor of J. Louis Martyn*

25 D.E. Orton, *The Understanding Scribe: Matthew and the Apocalyptic Ideal*

26 T.J. Geddert, *Watchwords: Mark 13 in Markan Eschatology*

27   C.C. Black, *The Disciples according to Mark: Markan Redaction in Current Debate*

28   D. Seeley, *The Noble Death: Graeco-Roman Martyrology and Paul's Concept of Salvation*

29   G.W. Hansen, *Abraham in Galatians: Epistolary and Rhetorical Contexts*

30   F.W. Hughes, *Early Christian Rhetoric and 2 Thessalonians*

31   D.R. Bauer, *The Structure of Matthew's Gospel: A Study in Literary Design*

32   K. Quast, *Peter and the Beloved Disciple: Figures for a Community in Crisis*

33   M.A. Beavis, *Mark's Audience: The Literary and Social Setting of Mark 4.11-12*

34   P.H. Towner, *The Goal of our Instruction: The Structure of Theology and Ethics in the Pastoral Epistles*

35   A.P. Winton, *The Proverbs of Jesus: Issues of History and Rhetoric*

36   S.E. Fowl, *The Story of Christ in the Ethics of Paul: An Analysis of the Function of the Hymnic Material in the Pauline Corpus*

37   A.J.M. Wedderburn (ed.), *Paul and Jesus: Collected Essays*

38   D.J. Weaver, *Matthew's Missionary Discourse: A Literary Critical Analysis*

39   G.N. Davies, *Faith and Obedience in Romans: A Study in Romans 1–4*

40   J.L. Sumney, *Identifying Paul's Opponents: The Question of Method in 2 Corinthians*

41   M.E. Mills, *Human Agents of Cosmic Power in Hellenistic Judaism and the Synoptic Tradition*

42   D.B. Howell, *Matthew's Inclusive Story: A Study in the Narrative Rhetoric of the First Gospel*

43   H. Räisänen, *Jesus, Paul and Torah: Collected Essays* (trans. D.E. Orton)

44   S. Lehne, *The New Covenant in Hebrews*

45   N. Elliott, *The Rhetoric of Romans: Argumentative Constraint and Strategy and Paul's Dialogue with Judaism*

46   J.O. York, *The Last Shall Be First: The Rhetoric of Reversal in Luke*

47   P.J. Hartin, *James and the Q Sayings of Jesus*

48   W. Horbury (ed.), *Templum Amicitiae: Essays on the Second Temple Presented to Ernst Bammel*

49   J.M. Scholer, *Proleptic Priests: Priesthood in the Epistle to the Hebrews*

50   D.F. Watson (ed.), *Persuasive Artistry: Studies in New Testament Rhetoric in Honor of George A. Kennedy*

51   J.A. Crafton, *The Agency of the Apostle: A Dramatistic Analysis of Paul's Responses to Conflict in 2 Corinthians*

52   L.L. Belleville, *Reflections of Glory: Paul's Polemical Use of the Moses–Doxa Tradition in 2 Corinthians 3.1-18*

53   T.J. Sappington, *Revelation and Redemption at Colossae*

54   R.P. Menzies, *The Development of Early Christian Pneumatology, with Special Reference to Luke–Acts*

55   L.A. Jervis, *The Purpose of Romans: A Comparative Letter Structure Investigation*

56   D. Burkett, *The Son of the Man in the Gospel of John*

57   B.W. Longenecker, *Eschatology and the Covenant: A Comparison of 4 Ezra and Romans 1–11*

58   D.A. Neale, *None but the Sinners: Religious Categories in the Gospel of Luke*

59   M. Thompson, *Clothed with Christ: The Example and Teaching of Jesus in Romans 12.1–15.13*

60   S.E. Porter (ed.), *The Language of the New Testament: Classic Essays*

61   J.C. Thomas, *Footwashing in John 13 and the Johannine Community*

62   R.L. Webb, *John the Baptizer and Prophet: A Socio-Historical Study*

63   J.S. McLaren, *Power and Politics in Palestine: The Jews and the Governing of their Land, 100 BC–AD 70*

64   H. Wansbrough (ed.), *Jesus and the Oral Gospel Tradition*

65   D.A. Campbell, *The Rhetoric of Righteousness in Romans 3.21-26*

66   N. Taylor, *Paul, Antioch and Jerusalem: A Study in Relationships and Authority in Earliest Christianity*

67   F.S. Spencer, *The Portrait of Philip in Acts: A Study of Roles and Relations*

68   M. Knowles, *Jeremiah in Matthew's Gospel: The Rejected-Prophet Motif in Matthaean Redaction*

69   M. Davies, *Rhetoric and Reference in the Fourth Gospel*

70   J.W. Mealy, *After the Thousand Years: Resurrection and Judgment in Revelation 20*

71   M. Scott, *Sophia and the Johannine Jesus*

72   S.M. Sheeley, *Narrative Asides in Luke–Acts*

73   M.E. Isaacs, *Sacred Space: An Approach to the Theology of the Epistle to the Hebrews*

74   E.K. Broadhead, *Teaching with Authority: Miracles and Christology in the Gospel of Mark*

75   J. Kin-Man Chow, *Patronage and Power: A Study of Social Networks in Corinth*

76   R.W. Wall & E.E. Lemcio, *The New Testament as Canon: A Reader in Canonical Criticism*

77   R. Garrison, *Redemptive Almsgiving in Early Christianity*

78   L.G. Bloomquist, *The Function of Suffering in Philippians*

79   B. Charette, *The Theme of Recompense in Matthew's Gospel*

80   S.E. Porter & D.A. Carson (eds.), *Biblical Greek Language and Linguistics: Open Questions in Current Research*

81   In-Gyu Hong, *The Law in Galatians*

82   B.W. Henaut, *Oral Tradition and the Gospels: The Problem of Mark 4*

83   C.A. Evans & J.A. Sanders (eds.), *Paul and the Scriptures of Israel*

84   M.C. de Boer (ed.), *From Jesus to John: Essays on Jesus and New Testament Christology in Honour of Marinus de Jonge*

85   W.J. Webb, *Returning Home: New Covenant and Second Exodus as the Context for 2 Corinthians 6.14–7.1*

86   B.H. McLean (ed.), *Origins of Method: Towards a New Understanding of Judaism and Christianity—Essays in Honour of John C. Hurd*

87   M.J. Wilkins & T. Paige (eds.), *Worship, Theology and Ministry in the Early Church: Essays in Honour of Ralph P. Martin*

88   M. Coleridge, *The Birth of the Lukan Narrative: Narrative as Christology in Luke 1–2*

89   C.A. Evans, *Word and Glory: On the Exegetical and Theological Background of John's Prologue*

90   S.E. Porter & T.H. Olbricht (eds.), *Rhetoric and the New Testament: Essays from the 1992 Heidelberg Conference*

91   J.C. Anderson, *Matthew's Narrative Web: Over, and Over, and Over Again*

92   E. Franklin, *Luke: Interpreter of Paul, Critic of Matthew*

93   J. Fekkes, *Isaiah and Prophetic Traditions in the Book of Revelation: Visionary Antecedents and their Development*

94   C.A. Kimball, *Jesus' Exposition of the Old Testament in Luke's Gospel*

95   D.A. Lee, *The Symbolic Narratives of the Fourth Gospel: The Interplay of Form and Meaning*

96   R.E. DeMaris, *The Colossian Controversy: Wisdom in Dispute at Colossae*

97   E.K. Broadhead, *Prophet, Son, Messiah: Narrative Form and Function in Mark 14–16*

98   C.J. Schlueter, *Filling up the Measure: Polemical Hyperbole in 1 Thessalonians 2.14-16*

99   N. Richardson, *Paul's Language about God*

100   T.E. Schmidt & M. Silva (eds.), *To Tell the Mystery: Essays on New Testament Eschatology in Honor of Robert H. Gundry*

101   J.A.D. Weima, *Neglected Endings: The Significance of the Pauline Letter Closings*

102   J.F. Williams, *Other Followers of Jesus: Minor Characters as Major Figures in Mark's Gospel*

103   W. Carter, *Households and Discipleship: A Study of Matthew 19–20*

104   C.A. Evans & W.R. Stegner (eds.), *The Gospels and the Scriptures of Israel*

105   W.P. Stephens (ed.), *The Bible, the Reformation and the Church: Essays in Honour of James Atkinson*

106   J.A. Weatherly, *Jewish Responsibility for the Death of Jesus in Luke–Acts*

107   E. Harris, *Prologue and Gospel: The Theology of the Fourth Evangelist*

108   L.A. Jervis & P. Richardson (eds.), *Gospel in Paul: Studies on Corinthians, Galatians and Romans for R.N. Longenecker*

109   E.S. Malbon & E.V. McKnight (eds.), *The New Literary Criticism and the New Testament*

110   M.L. Strauss, *The Davidic Messiah in Luke–Acts: The Promise and its Fulfillment in Lukan Christology*

111   I.H. Thomson, *Chiasmus in the Pauline Letters*

112   J.B. Gibson, *The Temptations of Jesus in Early Christianity*

113   S.E. Porter & D.A. Carson (eds.), *Discourse Analysis and Other Topics in Biblical Greek*

114   L. Thurén, *Argument and Theology in 1 Peter: The Origins of Christian Paraenesis*

115   S. Moyise, *The Old Testament in the Book of Revelation*

116   C.M. Tuckett (ed.), *Luke's Literary Achievement: Collected Essays*

117   K.G.C. Newport, *The Sources and Sitz im Leben of Matthew 23*

118   T.W. Martin, *By Philosophy and Empty Deceit: Colossians as Response to a Cynic Critique*

119   D. Ravens, *Luke and the Restoration of Israel*

120   S.E. Porter & D. Tombs (eds.), *Approaches to New Testament Study*

121   T.C. Penner, *The Epistle of James and Eschatology: Re-reading an Ancient Christian Letter*

122   A.D.A. Moses, *Matthew's Transfiguration Story in Jewish-Christian Controversy*

123   D.L. Matson, *Household Conversion Narratives in Acts: Pattern and Interpretation*

124   D.M. Ball, *'I Am' in John's Gospel: Literary Function, Background and Theological Implications*

125   R.G. Maccini, *Her Testimony is True: Women as Witnesses according to John*

126   B.H. Mclean, *The Cursed Christ: Mediterranean Expulsion Rituals and Pauline Soteriology*

127   R.B. Matlock, *Unveiling the Apocalyptic Paul: Paul's Interpreters and the Rhetoric of Criticism*

128   T. Dwyer, *The Motif of Wonder in the Gospel of Mark*

129   C.J. Davis, *The Names and Way of the Lord: Old Testament Themes, New Testament Christology*

130   C.S. Wansink, *Chained in Christ: The Experience and Rhetoric of Paul's Imprisonments*

131   S.E. Porter & T.H. Olbricht (eds.), *Rhetoric, Scripture and Theology: Essays from the 1994 Pretoria Conference*

132   J.N. Kraybill, *Imperial Cult and Commerce in John's Apocalypse*

133   M.S. Goodacre, *Goulder and the Gospels: An Examination of a New Paradigm*

134   L.J. Kreitzer, *Striking New Images: Roman Imperial Coinage and the New Testament World*

135   C. Landon, *A Text-Critical Study of the Epistle of Jude*

136   J.T. Reed, *A Discourse Analysis of Philippians: Method and Rhetoric in the Debate over Lierary Integrity*

137   R. Garrison, *The Graeco-Roman Contexts of Early Christian Literature*

138   K. Clarke, *Textual Optimism: The United Bible Societies' Greek New Testament and its Evaluation of Evidence Letter-Ratings*

139   Y.-E. Yang, *Jesus and the Sabbath in Matthew's Gospel*

140   T.R. Yoder Neufeld, *Put on the Armour of God: The Divine Warrior from Isaiah to Ephesians*

141   R.I. Denova, *The Things Accomplished Among Us: Prophetic Tradition in the Structural Pattern of Luke–Acts*

142   S. Cunningham, *'Through Many Tribulations': The Theology of Persecution in Luke–Acts*

143   R. Pickett, *The Cross in Corinth: The Social Significance of the Death of Jesus*

144   S.J. Roth, *The Blind, the Lame and the Poor: Character Types in Luke–Acts*

145   L.P. Jones, *The Symbol of Water in the Gospel of John*

146   S.E. Porter & T.H. Olbricht (eds.), *The Rhetorical Analysis of Scripture: Essays from the 1995 London Conference*

147   K. Paffenroth, *The Story of Jesus according to L*

148   C.A. Evans and J.A. Sanders (eds.), *Early Christian Interpretation of the Scriptures of Israel: Investigations and Proposals*

149   J.D. Gordon, *Sister or Wife?: 1 Corinthians 7 and Cultural Anthropology*

151   D. Tovey, *Narrative Art and Act in the Fourth Gospel*

152   E.-J. Vledder, *Conflict in the Miracle Stories: A Socio-Exegetical Study of Matthew 8 and 9*